FORMATIVE JUDAISM V

Program in Judaic Studies
Brown University
BROWN JUDAIC STUDIES
Edited by
Jacob Neusner,
Wendell S. Dietrich, Ernest S. Frerichs,
Calvin Goldscheider, Alan Zuckerman

Project Editors (Project)

David Blumenthal, Emory University (Approaches to Medieval Judaism)
William Brinner (Studies in Judaism and Islam)
Ernest S. Frerichs, Brown University (Dissertations and Monographs)
Lenn Evan Goodman, University of Hawaii (Studies in Medieval Judaism) (Studies in Judaism and Islam)
William Scott Green, University of Rochester (Approaches to Ancient Judaism)
Ivan Marcus, Jewish Theological Seminary of America
(Texts and Studies in Medieval Judaism)
Marc L. Raphael, Ohio State University (Approaches to Judaism in Modern Times)
Norbert Samuelson, Temple University (Jewish Philosophy)
Jonathan Z. Smith, University of Chicago (Studia Philonica)

Number 91
FORMATIVE JUDAISM:
RELIGIOUS, HISTORICAL, AND LITERARY STUDIES
Fifth Series
Revisioning the Written Records of a Nascent Religion

by
Jacob Neusner

Formative Judaism: Religious, Historical, and Literary Studies
Fifth Series

Revisioning the Written Records of a Nascent Religion

by
Jacob Neusner

Scholars Press
Chico, California

FORMATIVE JUDAISM:
RELIGIOUS, HISTORICAL, AND LITERARY STUDIES
Fifth Series

Revisioning the Written Records of a Nascent Religion

by
Jacob Neusner

© 1985
Brown University

Library of Congress Cataloging in Publication Data

Neusner, Jacob, 1932–
  Formative Judaism.

  (Brown Judaic studies ; no. 91,   )
  Includes index.
  1. Judaism—History—Talmudic period, 10–425—
Addresses, essays, lectures. 2. Rabbinical literature—
History and Criticism—Addresses, essays, lectures.
I. Title. II. Series.
BM177.N4725 1985   296'.09'015   85-2189
ISBN 0-89130-850-4 (alk. paper)
ISBN 0-89130-851-2 (pbk. : alk. paper)

Printed in the United States of America
on acid-free paper

For

A. THOMAS KRAABEL

Friend and co-worker on diverse projects for several decades.

Important scholar on the archaeology of ancient Judaism and Christianity.

A token of thanks for Chicago, December 10, 1984.

Psalm 23:5

CONTENTS

Introduction   1

   i. Studying Judaism as a Religion   1
  ii. Revisioning the Written Records, One Document at a Time   4

I
THE RELIGIOUS STUDY OF FORMATIVE JUDAISM

   I. Early Rabbinic Judaism: The Evidence of the Mishnah in Particular   13

  II. Judaism in Babylonia: The Evidence of the Babylonian Talmud   31

II
THE HISTORICAL STUDY OF FORMATIVE JUDAISM

 III. Three Pictures of the Pharisees: A Reprise   51

  IV. The History of a Biography: Yohanan ben Zakkai in the Canonical Literature of Formative Judaism   79

   V. When Tales Travel. The Interpretation of Multiple Appearances of a Single Saying in Talmudic Literature   87

  VI. Contemporary Scholarship on Ancient Judaism. Three Schools. Urbach, Himmelfarb, Bokser   105

 VII. The Judaic Side of New Testament Studies. Chilton and McNamara   113

III
THE LITERARY STUDY OF FORMATIVE JUDAISM

VIII. Form-Analysis and Exegesis: The Case of Mishnah Tohorot 2:1-2   119

  IX. Redaction and Formulation: The Talmud of the Land of Israel   135

   X. Studying Synoptic Texts Synoptically: The Case of Leviticus Rabbah   163

IV
THE BAVLI AS THE ONE WHOLE TORAH

  XI. The Bavli in Particular. Defining a Document in the Canon of Judaism   207

Index   221

INTRODUCTION

i. Studying Judaism as a Religion

When we seek to understand religion, two tasks demand immediate attention. We have, first, to specify what we wish to know about religion. We must, second, explain how we shall know when we are right and how we can tell when we are wrong in conclusions we propose about religion. Without a clear statement on both of these matters, we shall continue that endless exercise of hunting and gathering, selecting and arranging, that now serves many as theory of, and method for, the study of religion. That is to say, the generality of researches scarcely reaches that level of self-awareness that requires a statement of what, exactly, we wish to know. The larger number of books rarely contains an explanation of how we may claim to know right from wrong. The result is an endless gathering of information, the hunting and gathering stage of learning, and the aimless presentation of information that falls into the capacious space of show-and-tell we dignify as ethnography. Purposeful inquiry and rigorous reasoning transform what is now hunting and gathering into the quest for understanding, on the one side, and turn what is now the childhood pastime of show and tell into reasoned presentation of significant theories and theses, on the other. So, in a word, what we have constantly to explain about our work is precisely what we wish to know and exactly how we shall know when we have found it out.

These rather pragmatic and down-to-earth criteria for scholarly worth leave ample place for the theorizing about religion and for abstract discussion of methods for the study of religion. But from my perspective they also do define that part of the larger realm of theory that makes its impact upon the actual practice of the study of religion. For if I can tell you what I want to know and why, then I may also know how to design concrete and attainable projects of research. And if I can explain to myself how to tell right from wrong in the this-worldly quest for accurate information and defensible explanation, then I can carry out projects of research in full confidence of reaching results (whether positive or negative, things proved, things shown wrong or beyond proof) to share with others.

These same criteria -- clear statements of what we want to know and how we shall know when we know it -- also permit us to learn from others, not only from our own researches. For when I have a clear grasp of what another scholar wishes to tell me and why, and how that other scholar knows right from wrong, I can draw the necessary connections. I can build the required bridges, from here to there, even produce the illuminating analogies and metaphors, so I can grasp the work of that other scholar in all of its detail and complexity. The alternative -- I mean the failure to make an explicit statement of the scholarly program and method, the theory and the mode of inquiry -- I just now claimed produces at least the labor of hunting and gathering, the exercise of selecting and arranging for the purposes of show-and-tell. Why is that not enough?

Because without metaphors and relationships none of us learn from the work of scholars who hunt and gather in some field other than our own. Why not? Because it is exceedingly difficult to read ethnography, including ethnography of religion, without discovering early on that we are learning a good bit more than we wish to know about the subject at hand. Too much is a mark of not enough, specifically, of insufficient explanation. Scholars who play show-and-tell end up talking mainly to a small in-group, and whether it is a group made of co-religionists or one composed of co-conspirators of an academic politics makes no difference. For information without purpose, inquiry without public and communicable results -- these mark the parochial scholar, the ones who speak only to their own kind at first, and in the end, talk only to themselves. Self-absorption and narcissism may mark neurosis in the world at large, but they characterize the generality of scholarship in the academic realm. Theory and method present the indicated therapy.

What then do I wish to know, and how do I go about learning it? What I want to know is what from my youth I have always wanted to know, which is how religion relates to the social life of communities, and how the ideas that people hold relate to the world in which they live, or which they propose to create for themselves. These questions concern one aspect of religion, religion as a social force and a critical power in the formation of culture and imagination. They obviously do not exhaust what all of us wish to know about religion. But they do define one cogent program of learning. I need hardly point to the scholars, dead and alive, who have taught me the urgency of posing just these questions and modes of finding answers to them. They are not only represented by the names of Weber and Durkheim, Leach, Turner, Fernandez, Perry, and Douglas. They also are invoked by the names of Isaiah, Jeremiah, Ezekiel, not the mention the astounding framers of the pentateuchal traditions into what became, in Ezra's time, the Torah, or the founders of Judaism in the Talmudic canon. Nor would the founders and framers of the Christian Church who thought deeply about the city of God and the city of man regard as alien this central inquiry. We human beings are political animals. Religion has nearly always defined the political perimeters of the polis; of the nation and the community; of the holy people, Israel, and the Church, the body of Christ. So let us know what religion is as a social fact and a cultural force. That collective and social dimension does not measure all that religion is, but it surely defines one critical dimension.

If that is what I wish to know, in the modest realm of Judaism, then how do I find out? The answer derives from the character of the data at hand. I work on the formative period of Judaism. I ask why the form of Judaism that took shape in late antiquity (the Talmudic or rabbinic form, to use the adjectives supplied by the principal document and the honorific title of the principal hero of the faith) served when it did and flourished when it did. Why, also, and how did that same form of Judaism cease to serve where and whom and when it did and so in specific times and places now did it lose that quality of self-evidence that had long sustained Israel, the Jewish people.

What data I have in hand for late antiquity derive from the founders and the framers, and the data consists of a sizable and essentially cogent set of writings. I study not a religion but a library. This set of books I propose to transform into the data of a religion. That is to say, I want to know whether the library at hand forms a mere collection of books, or constitutes a cogent canon, the literary expression of the world-view and way of life we know as the religious system, Judaism.

So I know about not the social life of an entire nation but the imaginative and intellectual life of a small group. I want to know how that vision -- the fantasy of a handful of intellectuals -- came to shape the perceptions of people everywhere, I mean nearly the whole of the Jewish nation, where ever they lived. I can describe, analyze, and interpret a single form of Judaism. I want to know how that Judaism succeeded while other Judaisms did not. I seek a theory of interpretation, one framed in relationship to the deepest and most dense layers of social meaning to which Jews responded -- if in superficial detail, yet always cogently. What I wish to interpret is why his particular set of ideas turned out to serve the social group that held them and accepted the leadership of those who expounded them, and why other sets of ideas did not. I ask why a set of ideas of the type or character of the set at hand, I mean, the Judaism that served so long and well, proved self-evident to a group of the type or character of the group under study. Clearly, I therefore take a keen interest in the comparison of one construction of ideas, in one social setting, to another such construction, in a different social setting. And these societies self-evidently permit comparison and contrast in the two dimensions of our inquiry, the synchronic but also the diachronic. It is, therefore, a formidable program.

How I shall know whether I am right and where I am wrong? Obviously, where work is underway and a theory is as yet in progress, we may postpone answering the question of falsification and verification. But where work is done or nearly so, we have to confront that painful question. I will allege that I have finished some things. I do have clear ideas. I do make concrete claims to describe, analyze, and interpret phases in the history of the formation of the Judaism under study and important components of the larger evidence, the larger literary canon that constitutes the data, for that Judaism. But if I have said what I think a document is and why I think it exhibits the traits that it exhibits and not some other traits, I have yet to frame that theory that ultimately will become susceptible to the test of falsification and verification. Why not? Because the ultimate test cannot derive from one system, or to state matters in a language different from the one we ordinarily use, no theory of explanation can posit that $N = 1.0$. So I shall know right from wrong, in the description, analysis, and interpretation of the formation of Judaism, only when I can compare what I think is so with what others think is so in the description, analysis, and interpretation of a Judaism different from the one at hand. All the more so, I must compare what I say about this kind of Judaism with what is to be said to interpret a religious formation or a religious tradition other than one that bears the adjective Judaic or falls into the classification of Judaisms. Until we gain that level of comparison, we work with mysteries. We describe with no perspective of depth and dimension. We analyze with no insight into what sustains a cogent structure. We interpret with no guidance other than plausible guesses. So the generation to follow will have an interesting task for itself.

ii. Revisioning the Written Records, One Document at a Time

In this book I work my way through a number of the principal documents of formative Judaism, in particular, the Mishnah (Chapters One, Six, and Seven), the Bavli or Talmud of Babylonia (Chapters Two and Eleven), the Yerushalmi or Talmud of the Land of Israel (Chapter Seven), and Leviticus Rabbah (Chapter Eight). Not only so, but in two other chapters, I address the question of how one document, seen by itself, intersects with and relates to another document, also seen as an autonomous text. In Chapter Five I ask what conclusions we should draw when we see a given story or saying traveling from one document to the next. I wonder, in particular, about the meaning of changes in a story as the story moves from one text to the next. Do editors of documents impose their aesthetic or theological views on received stories? In Chapter Eight I ask about what conclusions we should draw when we find that a given document intersects, in a segment of its sayings and stories, with those found in another document. Finally, in Chapter Four I point to the importance, in assessing the meaning of a saying or story, of sizing up a given document and the interests and points of emphasis of its authors. I point to the particular interests, with reference to the biography of Yohanan ben Zakkai, not only of circles of story-tellers but also circles of editors or framers of documents. This too approaches the canonical writings of formative Judaism in the same way.

So I do regard it as critical to read these writings text by text, each whole and by itself, and not only as a set of connected writings, let alone solely as a unitary and harmonious, continuous whole. Since I find myself criticized for this approach, standard in so many other fields in ancient studies, I think it important to explain why I regard as urgent the revisioning the written records, one document at a time, and only then as connected and ultimately continuous. Recently someone made the curious claim that "synoptic texts must always be studied synoptically." That statement justifies my view that procedures deemed self-evidently correct elsewhere in the field at hand, the study of ancient Judaism, have here to be carefully spelled out and explained. Let me now do so. In this way I place into the correct methodological context most of the chapters of this book.

When we take up a single book or document in the canon of Judaism and propose to describe, analyze, and interpret that book in particular, we violate the lines of order and system that have characterized earlier studies of these same documents. Until now, people have tended to treat all of the canonical texts as testimonies to a single system and structure, that is, to Judaism. What sort of testimonies texts provide varies according to the interest of the scholars, students, and saints who study them. Scholars look for meanings of words and phrases, better versions of a text. For them all canonical documents equally serve as a treasury of philological facts and variant readings. Students also look for the sense of words and phrases and follow a given phrase hither and yon, as their teachers direct them on their treasure hunt. Saints study all texts equally, looking for God's will and finding testimonies to God in each component of the Torah of Moses our Rabbi.

Among none of these circles will the discrete description, analysis, and interpretation of a single text make sense. Why not? Because all texts ordinarily are taken to form a common statement, "Torah" in the mythic setting, "Judaism" in the theological one. Since I spent the first half of my scholarly life trying to use all of the texts in the canon, more or less without differentiation and equally, to answer historical questions, I participated in the approach now rejected. I thought that what was definitive, what laid forth lines of structure and order, was not the text at hand but the problem I had defined. So I did not tease out of the texts the threads of context, looking for the fabric's coherence in its small details in the interstices of warp and woof. I set up my own loom. I pulled the texts apart and made them into mere threads, then rewove them my way. On that, as is clear, I have changed my mind, and, I would claim, my field.

Let me spell out the change at hand. To begin with, however, I emphasize that nothing I say will surprise scholars in the biblical fields of Old and New Testament, Israel in ancient times and earliest Christianity. They understand that the work of the hour does not demand more harmonies of the Gospels. They rigorously debate issues of orthodoxy and heterodoxy in earliest Christianity and whether and where, among the diverse Christianities, they may find patterns of Christian truth. In the nineteenth century they abandoned any notion of using all of the (canonical) texts equally and for a single purpose. In the twentieth, such giants as H.E.W. Turner and Walter Bauer ended for all time the simple notions that you can open a book, thumb the pages and pull out a Christianity. When my mind changed, under the influence of the examples of my colleagues in other areas of history, the history and comparison of religion, and, obviously, in the biblical areas and those of earliest Christianity, I had to relive two hundred years of scholarship in twenty years. Permit me, then, to report in my field what are methodological commonplaces of other fields.

We begin with theology and move to texts. For the hermeneutical issue defines the result of description, analysis, and interpretation. From today's perspective the entire canon of Judaism -- "the one whole Torah of Moses, our rabbi" -- equally and at every point testifies to the entirety of Judaism. Why so? Because all documents in the end form components of a single system. Each makes its contribution to the whole. If, therefore, we wish to know what "Judaism" or, more accurately, "the Torah," teaches on any subject, we are able to draw freely on sayings relevant to that subject wherever they occur in the entire canon of Judaism. Guided only by the taste and judgment of the great sages of the Torah, as they have addressed the question at hand, we thereby describe "Judaism."

Composites of sayings drawn from diverse books in no way violate the frontiers and boundaries that distinguish one part of the canon from some other part of the same canon. Why not? It is a theological conviction that defines the hermeneutic. Viewed as serving the Torah, which is a single and continuous revelation, all frontiers, all boundaries stand only at the outer limits of the whole. Within, as the saying has it, "There is neither earlier nor later," that is to say, temporal considerations do not apply. But if temporal distinctions make no difference, no others do either.

Accordingly, as Judaism comes to informed expression in the Judaic pulpit, in the Judaic classroom, above all in the lives and hearts and minds of Jews loyal to Judaism, all parts of the canon of Judaism speak equally authoritatively. All parts, all together, present us with one harmonious world-view and homogenous way of life, one Torah ("Judaism") for all Israel. That view of "the Torah," that is to say, of the canon of Judaism, characterizes every organized movement within Judaism as we now know it, whether Reform or Orthodox, whether Reconstructionist or Conservative, whether in the "Exile" (diaspora) or in the State of Israel. How so? Among circles of Judaism indifferent to considerations of time and place, anachronism and context, every document, whenever brought to closure, testifies equally to that single system. For those circles Judaism emerges at a single moment ("Sinai"), but comes to expression in diverse times and places, so that any composition that falls into the category of Torah serves, without further differentiation, to tell us about the substance of Judaism, its theology and law.

An important qualification, however, has now to make its mark. Among those circles of Judaism to whom historical facts do make a difference, for example, Orthodoxy in the West, Reconstructionist, Conservative and Reform Judaism and the like, considerations of what was completed earlier as against what came to closure only later on, for instance, in the second century as against the eighteenth century, do make some difference. Earlier documents provide more compelling and authoritative evidence than later ones. But even in the view of this other sector of Judaism, all documents, if not everywhere equally authoritative, still form part of a continuous whole, Judaism. The distinction between the two positions makes no material difference. Why not? Because both circles hold as self-evident that the numerous components of the canon of Judaism form a continuity, beginning, middle, and end. That is why considerations of priority and of closure, should these considerations find their way into discourse at all, change little and affect nothing. Torah is Torah, early, middle, and late. And so it is -- except from the perspective of one outside the magic circle of the faith. Here we ask exactly _how_ various documents became "Torah," _what_ each document added to the whole, in _which_ ways do the several documents relate to one another and to the larger system, and so, in all, reverting to mythic language, what makes Torah Torah.

For a person engaged in such an inquiry into the formation of Judaism studied through the analysis of the literary evidence of the canon, documents stand in three relationships to one another and to the system of which they form part, that is, to Judaism, as a whole. The specification of these relationships constitutes the principal premise of my work. It is a premise since, to begin with, the relationships I perceive derive not inductively, from the documents at hand, but from the mind of the one who turns to analyze the documents. So at this point I cannot claim to approach matters inductively.

Each document, as a matter of theory, is to be seen all by itself, that is, as autonomous of all others.

Each document, again as a matter of theory, is to be examined for its relationships with other documents universally regarded as falling into the same classification, as Torah.

And, finally, each document is to be allowed to take its place as part of the undifferentiated aggregation of documents that, all together, constitute the canon of Judaism, that is to say, "Torah."

Simple logic makes self-evident the proposition that, if a document comes down to us within its own framework, as a complete book with a beginning, middle, and end, in preserving that book, the canon presents us with a document on its own and not solely as part of a larger composition or construct. So we too see the document as it reaches us, that is, as autonomous.

If, second, a document contains materials shared verbatim or in substantial content with other documents of its classification, or if one document refers to the contents of other documents, then the several documents that clearly wish to engage in conversation with one another have to address one another. That is to say, we have to seek for the marks of connectedness, asking for the meaning of those connections.

Finally, since, as I said at the outset, the community of the faithful of Judaism, in all of the contemporary expressions of Judaism, concur that documents held to be authoritative constitute one whole, seamless "Torah," that is, a complete and exhaustive statement of God's will for Israel and humanity, we take as our further task the description of the whole out of the undifferentiated testimony of all of its parts. These components in the theological context are viewed, as is clear, as equally authoritative for the composition of the whole: one, continuous system. In taking up such a question, we address a problem not of theology alone, though it is a correct theological conviction, but one of description, analysis, and interpretation of an entirely historical order.

In this way we may hope to trace the literary evidence -- which is the only evidence we have -- for the formation of Judaism, what it is, how it works. By seeing the several components of the canon of Judaism in sequence, first, one by one, then, one after the other, and finally, all together all at once, we may trace the literary side of the history of Judaism. We may see how a document came into being on its own, in its context (so far as we may posit the character of that context). We interpret the document at its site. As a matter of fact, moreover, all documents of the rabbinic canon except for the Hebrew Scriptures relate to prior ones, on the one side, and all, especially the Scriptures, stand before those to follow, on the other. The Mishnah normally is understood to rest upon the written Torah, and, later in its history in Judaism, came to be called the oral Torah. So even the Mishnah stands not distinct and autonomous, but contingent and dependent. The two Talmuds rest upon the Mishnah, and the several compilations of exegeses of Scripture, called "midrashim", rest upon Scripture. So, in all, like the bones of the body, each book is connected to others (with Scripture and the Mishnah the backbone). All together they form a whole, a frame that transcends the parts and imparts proportion, meaning, and harmony to them.

The bones of the body develop more or less in shared stages, however, while the documents of the Torah, the canon of Judaism, developed in a sequence. The order, if not so linear as it seems on the surface, is mostly clear. First came Scripture, then the Mishnah, then the Talmud of the Land of Israel and earlier compilations of biblical exegeses, then the Talmud of Babylonia and the later compilations of biblical exegeses. In that sequence of the important texts we shall find whatever evidence of growth, development, and change, as we shall ever have available to tell us the history of

Judaism. To complete the matter, what do we hope to learn as we relate growth, development, and change in the history of Judaism, traced through the formation and character of its canon, to the growth, development, and change in the history of the Jewish people? It is not only to describe and analyze, but also to explain, the history of the formation of Judaism. That is to say, we may frame theories not only on the formative history of the world-view and way of life we call Judaism, but on the reasons that the history went the route it took, rather than some other route. How so? We may ask why people thought what they thought and did what they did, rather than thinking other thoughts and doing other things. When we can relate the ideas people held and the way they lived their life to the context in which they found themselves, we shall have reached that level of interpretation at which present and past come together in the setting of shared human existence: the meeting of text and context. But we stand at a distance from that elusive goal.

What I have said in general makes sense in particular of <u>Judaism: The Evidence of the Mishnah</u> and <u>Judaism in Society: The Evidence of the Yerushalmi</u>. I mention two other titles, <u>Judaism and Scripture: The Evidence of Leviticus Rabbah</u> and <u>Judaism in Conclusion: The Evidence of the Bavli</u>. These four works yield yet a final one of this series, <u>The Oral Torah: An Introduction</u>. What each item proposes is two exercises which are one. First, I wish to describe a single document. Second, I also want to address to a given document one important question. These two exercises really complement one another. My premise is that a document ordinarily is <u>about</u> something. Except for anthologies of information, people write books to make points, to answer questions, to say something important. In the ancient world people copied and preserved books at great expense, so books had to matter. The premise, then, that a given document tells us something important to those who wrote it and their successors, seems to me self-evident.

It follows that we have to find out what polemic, what point of insistence, what aspect of self-evidence a given text reveals. As I have stressed in every work of mine, we begin the search with the smallest details, we then ask what the details of the text repeatedly stress. This commonly emerges not from what the text says, but from how it says what it says. In the main beams of rhetoric, in the repeated details, ubiquitous, implicit, self-evident, and therefore definitive, I claim to find that principal message that speaks for the work as a whole. The deepest structures of syntax may convey the principles of order. The techniques of rhetoric, broadly construed, properly understood, may speak also to us. They accordingly may deliver a text's substantive message through the forms of proportion and of intelligible, therefore logical, speech.

About what main point do the texts at hand then speak? I see the Mishnah as a complete statement of an entire system. I see the documents of succession, typified by the Yerushalmi, as large-scale efforts to translate the Mishnah's philosophical system into social order. I see counterpart documents of Scripture-exegesis, which treat Scripture as the two Talmuds treat the Mishnah, as exercises in the construction of dialogue between Scripture and the Mishnah. And I see the final document of the canon, the Bavli, as a synthetic work of restatement and completion. The Bavli joins the two main lines of order and systemic structure, the Mishnah and Scripture, and makes them the basis for its proportions and the foundations of its social order.

In my view the various documents of the canon of Judaism produced in late antiquity demand a different hermeneutic altogether from the one of homogenization and harmonization, the ahistorical and anti-contextual one I have outlined. It is one that does not harmonize but that differentiates. It is a hermeneutic shaped to teach us how to read the texts at hand one by one and in a particular context, exactly in the way in which we read any other text bearing cultural and social insight. The texts stand not as self-evidently important but only as examples, sources of insight for a quite neutral inquiry. Let me spell out what I think is at issue between the established hermeneutic and the one I propose.

The three key-words of the inherited hermeneutic are <u>continuity</u>, <u>uniqueness</u>, and <u>survival</u>. Scholars who view the texts as continuous with one another seek what is unique in the system formed by the texts as a whole. With the answer to what is unique, they propose to explain the survival of Israel, the Jewish people. Hence: continuity, uniqueness, survival.

The words to encapsulate the hermeneutic I espouse are these: <u>description</u>, <u>analysis</u>, and <u>interpretation</u>. I am trying to learn how to <u>describe</u> the constituents of the canon, viewed individually, each in its distinctive context. I wish to discover appropriate <u>analytical</u> tools, questions to lead me from description of one text to comparison and contrast between two or more texts of the canon. Only at the end do I address the question of <u>interpretation</u>: how do all of the texts of the canon at hand flow together into a single continuous statement, a "Judaism."

Within the inherited hermeneutic of continuity, survival, and uniqueness, the existence of the group defines the principal concern, an inner-facing one, hence the emphasis on uniqueness in quest, in continuities, for the explanation of survival. Within the proposed hermeneutic of description, analysis, and interpretation, by contrast, the continued survival of a "unique" group does not frame the issue. For my purposes, it is taken for granted, for the group is not the main thing at all. The problematic emerges from without. What I want to know is not how and why the group survived so as to help it survive some more. It is how to describe the society and culture contained within, taken as a given, how to interpret an enduring world-view and way of life, expressed by the artifacts in hand. How did, and does, the group work?

So I claimed that the results of the literary inquiry will prove illuminating for the study of society and culture. I have now to explain why I think so. The answer lies in our will and capacity to generalize, out of details, a judgment on a broad issue of culture, as it is exemplified in the small problem at hand. The issue here is secular. True, I too ask how the components of the canon as a whole form a continuity. I wonder why this document in particular survived to speak for the whole. But for me the answers to these questions generate theories, promise insight for the study of other canonical religions. So far as I shall succeed, it will be because I can learn from these other canonical religions. I have tried to learn from, and also to teach something to, those who study the history, the thought, the social reality, of religions that, like Judaism, form enduring monuments to the power of humanity to endure and to prevail so far.

I suppose that, in the end, we who do this work this way also want to see things whole. True, God alone is the one who really sees things whole, complete, in context and appropriate perspective. But to be like God to us can then mean to try, ourselves, to see that entire context. Alas, our vision is only in and through detail. Being mortal, that is what we are given to see: Torah ("Judaism") in a single document the world in a grain of sand, and God in the detailed likeness, in the detailed image, of humanity, seen one by one and all at once.

PART ONE

THE RELIGIOUS STUDY OF FORMATIVE JUDAISM

I
EARLY RABBINIC JUDAISM
THE EVIDENCE OF THE MISHNAH IN PARTICULAR

Rabbinic Judaism is that Judaic system -- way of life, world-view, addressed to the Jewish people or nation -- that uniquely affirms the revelation, by God to Moses at Mount Sinai, of the dual Torah, one in writing, the other oral. The dual Torah is handed on from generation to generation by sages, honored with the title of rabbi. Sages, through mastering the Torah-teachings and serving and imitating the ways of their masters, become themselves authentic representatives of the Torah, that "one whole Torah of Moses, our rabbi," that God reveals. No other system of Judaism then or now speaks of the dual Torah, appeals to the authority of the rabbi, and lays stress upon the holy way of life and world view, encompassing both sanctification in the here and how and salvation at the end of time, that is defined by the faith of the dual Torah.

The canon of Judaism of the sort under discussion begins, beyond Scripture itself, with the Mishnah, ca. A.D. 200, and concludes its formative age with the Talmud of Babylonia, ca. A.D. 600. In between the canonical literature in the formative age consists of two types of books, one that provides systematic expansion and exegesis of the Mishnah, the other that does the same for Scripture. In the former category fall the two Talmuds, the one of the Land of Israel, the other of Babylonia, and some related writings. In the latter category are several compilations of scriptural exegesis, in particular of pentateuchal books. Some of these lay stress on how the Mishnah, a document that does not systematically join to its several statements scriptural proof-texts, in fact rests upon Scripture. Others provide verse by verse explanations of various biblical books. Still others develop ideas or themes by whole bursts of proof texts, selected without relationship to their position in various biblical compositions.

The earliest stage in the formation of rabbinic Judaism, hence "early rabbinic Judaism," is represented, in literary form, by the Mishnah. When, therefore, we wish to describe the foundations of the now-dominant and normative kind of Judaism, we look to the Mishnah for its evidence about its own formation. While other compositions in the canon of Judaism probably contain sayings framed in the period before the closure of the Mishnah, and while no one can doubt that ideas that surface only later on can have been held in an earlier period, the Mishnah is the sole evidence that indubitably testifies to the state of ideas held in those circles that laid the foundations for Judaism as it would come to fruition in the literature ending with the Talmud of Babylonia. Hence when we seek to describe early rabbinic Judaism, that is to say, that stage in the formation of Judaism in its rabbinic formulation prior to the turn of the third century, we best start with the Mishnah in particular. What we seek to discover is those layers of the Mishnah's ideas that attest to the state of belief and behavior prior to the closure of the Mishnah itself.

To the degree that we can find out, within the Mishnah, about ideas held in the later first and through the second centuries, we have a picture of the important fundamental traits of rabbinic Judaism, if, to be sure, not a complete picture of all of the traits characteristic of that earliest period.

The Mishnah takes shape in four distinct periods of development. These are marked off by groups of names, commonly found in juxtaposition with one another but not found in juxtaposition with any other names, e.g., Rabbis A, B, C, D intersect very often with one another, but never with Rabbis W, X, Y, and Z, who, for their part, come together in completed units of tradition only with themselves. There are four such groups. Ideas held in sayings attributed to one such group may be shown, on the basis of fact or logic, to be presupposed in sayings attributed to another such group. On that basis, the first of the two groups may be regarded as prior in logic and possibly also in time to the second of the two groups. Stories told about the first of the four groups indeed place that group in the period before 70; these would be sayings that correspond to rabbinic traditions about the Pharisees, since the names are the same as those on the chain of tradition of M. Avot 1:1-18. Stories told about the second of the four groups place that group in the period after the destruction of the Temple. Stories told about the third of the four groups take for granted that authorities of that group survived the Bar Kokhba War, 132-135. Stories told about the fourth of the four put the members of that group in the period of the closure of the Mishnah itself, that is, toward c.a. A.D. 200. An account of the earliest phase in the formation of the ideas now fully exposed in the Mishnah, therefore, places us in the first century, in the period just before and just after the destruction of the Temple. To state matters simply, earliest rabbinic Judaism is that system of Judaism, surviving and developing in later rabbinic writings, that got under way in the aftermath of the destruction of the Second Temple in A.D. 70.

The only extant documents originating in the decades immediately after the destruction of the Temple in A.D. 70 are 2 Baruch and 4 Ezra. If we ask how the character of the Mishnah's system, its "Judaism," differs from that of the writings of other Jewish thinkers of the same general period, the first and second centuries after the destruction of the Temple, we have only 2 Baruch and 4 Ezra for comparison. Those writings give some perspective on the work of the framers of Mishnah, even though they have absolutely nothing in common with Mishnah. Still, it is in precisely the same period and under essentially common conditions that the authors of Baruch and Ezra choose one set of topics, which they treat in a particular way, and the earliest framers of Mishnah choose another set of topics, to be treated in a quite different way. If we wish to know what Mishnah does not discuss, all we need to do is to list the issues and concerns we have seen in writings in the names of Baruch and Ezra -- and vice versa.

The crisis precipitated by the destruction of the Second Temple affected both the nation and the individual, since, in the nature of things, what happened in the metropolis of the country inevitably touched affairs of home and family. What made that continuity natural was the long-established Israelite conviction that the fate of the individual and the destiny of the Jewish nation depended upon the moral character both of the one and of the other. Disaster came about because of the people's sin, so went the message of biblical history and prophecy. The sins of individuals and of nation alike ran against the revealed will of God, the Torah. So reflection upon the meaning of the recent catastrophe inexorably followed paths laid out long ago, trod from one generation to the next. But there were two factors which at just this time made reflection on the question of sin and history, atonement and salvation, particularly urgent.

First, with the deep conviction of having sinned and the profound sense of guilt affecting community and individual alike, the established mode of expiation and guilt and of atonement for sin proved not inadequate but simply unavailable. The sacrificial system, which the priestly Torah describes as the means by which the sinner attains forgiveness for sin, lay in ruins. So when sacrifice turned out to be acutely needed for the restoration of psychological stability in the community at large, sacrifice no longer was possible -- a crisis indeed.

Second, in August, A.D. 70, minds naturally turned to August, 586 B.C. From the biblical histories and prophecies emerged the vivid expectation that, through the suffering of the day, sin would be atoned, expiation attained. So, people supposed, just as before, in three generations whatever guilt had weighed down the current generation and led to the catastrophe would be worked out through the sacrifice consisting of the anguish of a troubled time. It must follow that somewhere down the road lay renewal. The ruined Temple would yet be rebuilt, the lapsed cult restored, the silent Levites' song sung once more.

Now these several interrelated themes -- suffering, sin, atonement, salvation -- from of old had been paramount in the frame of the Israelite consciousness. A famous, widely known ancient literature of apocalyptic prophecy for a long time had explored them. The convictions that events carry preponderant weight, that Israelites could control what happened through their keeping, or not keeping, the Torah, that in the course of time matters will come to a resolution -- these commonplaces were given concrete mythic reality in the apocalyptic literature. Over many centuries in that vast sweep of apocalyptic-prophetic writings all of the changes had been rung for every possible variation on the theme of redemption in history. So it is hardly surprising that, in the aftermath of the burning of the Temple and cessation of the cult, people reflected in established modes of thought upon familiar themes. They had no choice, given the history of the country's consciousness and it Scriptural frame of reference, but to think of the beginning, middle, and coming end of time as it was known.

The second stage in the formation of the earlier phases of rabbinic Judaism coincided with the flowering, in the second century, of that rather general movement, both within Christianity and also outside of its framework, called Gnosticism. It is as important as the apocalyptic movement in establishing a base for comparison and interpretation of earlier rabbinic Judaism. How so? One principal theme of the Mishnah, and of the Judaism beyond it, involved the affirmation of God's beneficence in creating the world and in revealing the Torah. A principal motif of diverse Gnostic systems was God's malevolence in creating the world, or the malicious character of the creator-god, and the rejection of the Torah. In these two critical aspects of the Judaism of the sages represented in the Mishnah and later writings, we see a direct confrontation on paramount issues of the day between rabbinic Judaism and the family of systems we call, for convenience' sake, Gnosticism.

The second-century Church Fathers refer to Christian heretics called Gnostics, people who believed, among other things, that salvation came from insightful knowledge of a god beyond the creator-god, and of a fundamental flaw in creation revealed in the revealed Scriptures of Moses. Insight into the true condition of the believer derives not from revelation but from self-knowledge, which is knowledge of God. Now in introducing the viewpoint of second-century Gnostics and juxtaposing their principal emphases with those of the Mishnah, I must emphasize that we know no writings of Gnostics who were Jews. We cannot claim that the viewpoint of Gnostic thinkers on two questions of fundamental importance to the Mishnah -- creation, revelation -- derives from Israelites of the Land of Israel. The only certainty is that the Mishnah takes up a position both specifically and totally at variance with the position framed, on identical issues, by people writing in exactly the same period. No one can claim that Gnostic and Mishnaic thinkers addressed, or even knew about, one another. But they did confront precisely the same issues, and when placed into juxtaposition with one another, they present a striking and suggestive contrast. It is that contrast which we now shall briefly contemplate.

If the apocalyptic prophets focused upon historical events and their meaning, the Gnostic writers of the second century sought to escape from the framework of history altogether. For Israel, Jerusalem had become a forbidden city. The Temple had long stood as the pinnacle of creation and now was destroyed. The Gnostic thinkers deemed creation, celebrated in the cult, to be a cosmic error. The destruction of the Temple had evoked the prophetic explanations of the earlier destruction and turned attention in the search for meaning in the destruction to the revealed Torah of God to Moses at Mount Sinai. The Gnostic thinkers declared the Torah to be a deceit, handed down by an evil creator. It is as if the cosmic issues vital to the first-century apocalyptic prophets were taken up one by one and declared closed, and closed in a negative decision, by the second-century Gnostics.

The thinkers of the Mishnah for their part addressed two principal issues also important to Gnostic thought, the worth of creation and the value of the Torah. They took a quite opposite position on both matters. The Mishnah's profoundly priestly celebration of creation and its slavishly literal repetition of what clearly is said in Scripture gain significance specifically in that very context in which, to others, these are subjected to a different, deeply negative, valuation. True, as I said, we have no evidence that Gnostics were in the Land of Israel and formed part of the people of Israel in the period in which the Mishnah reaches full expression and final closure. So we speak of a synchronic debate at best. In fact what we know in Gnostic writings is a frame of mind and a style of though characteristic of others than Israelites, living in lands other than the Land of Israel. What justifies our invoking two ubiquitous and fundamental facts about Gnostic doctrine in the description of the context in which the Mishnah took shape is the simple fact that, at the critical points in its structure, the Mishnaic system counters what are in fact two fundamental and generative assertions of all Gnostic systems. Whether or not there were Gnostics known to Mishnah's philosophers, who, specifically in response to the destruction and permanent prohibition of the Temple, declared to be lies and deceit the creation celebrated in the Temple and the Torah governing there, we do not know. But these would be appropriate conclusions to draw from the undisputed facts of the hour in any case. The Temple designed by the Torah for celebrating the center and heart of creation was no more. Would this not have meant that the creator of the known creation and revealer of the Torah, the allegedly one God behind both, is either weak or evil? And should the elect not aspire to escape from the realm of creation and the power of the demiurge? And who will pay heed to what is written in the revelation of creation, Temple, and Torah? These seem to me conclusions distinctively suitable to be drawn from the ultimate end of the thousand-year-old-cult: the final and total discrediting of the long-pursued, eternally fraudulent hope for messianic deliverance in this time, in this world, and in this life. So it would have been deemed wise for those who know to seek and celebrate a different salvation, coming from a god unknown in this world, unrevealed in this world's revelation, not responsible for the infelicitous condition of creation.

In so far as Gnosticism incorporated a cosmic solution to the problem of evil, the Gnostic mode of thought had the power to confront the disaster of Israel's two wars against Rome and their metaphysical consequences. The Gnostic solution, if we may posit what someone might have been intelligent to conclude, is not difficult to discern. These events proved beyond doubt the flaw in creation, for the Temple had been the archetype of creation. The catastrophes demonstrated the evil character of the creator of this world. The catastrophes required the conclusion that there is another mode of being, another world beyond this one of creation and cult. So, whatever positive doctrines may or may not have found adherents among disappointed Israelites of the later first and second centuries, there are these two negative conclusions which anyone moving out of the framework of the cult, priesthood, and Temple, with its Torah, celebration of creation and the creator, and affirmation of this world and its creations, would have had to reach. First, the creator is not good. Second, the Torah, the record of creator and the will of the creator, is false.

In the same time as the Mishnah's formation and promulgation, Christian communities from France to Egypt encompassed groups which took a position sharply at variance with that of the Hebrew Scriptures affirmed in the Church in general on precisely the questions of creation and revelation and redemption confronting the Israelite world of the second century. Among the many and diverse positions taken up in the systems reported by Christian writers or now documented through Christian-Gnostic writings found at Nag Hammadi there are three which, as I have emphasized, are remarkably pertinent. First, the creator-god is evil, because, second, creation is deeply flawed. Third, revelation as Torah is a lie. These conclusions yield, for one Gnostic-Christian thinker after another, the simple proposition that redemption is gained in escape; the world is to be abandoned, not constructed, affirmed, and faithfully tended in painstaking detail. It is in the context of this widespread negative judgment on the very matters on which, for their part, Mishnah's sages register a highly affirmative opinion, that the choices made by the framers of the Mishnah become fully accessible.

Characterizing the Mishnah's ultimate system as a whole, we may call it both locative and utopian, in that it focuses upon Temple but is serviceable anywhere. In comparison to the Gnostic systems, it is, similarly, profoundly Scriptural; but it also is deeply indifferent to Scripture, drawing heavily upon the information supplied by Scripture for the construction and expression of its own systemic construction, which in form and language is wholly independent of any earlier Israelite document. It is, finally, a statement of affirmation of this world, of the realm of society, state, and commerce, and at the same time a vigorous denial that how things are is how things should be, or will be. For the Mishnaic system speaks of the building of a state, government, and civil and criminal system, of the conduct of transactions of property, commerce, trade, of forming the economic unit of a family through transfer of women and property and the ending of such a family-economic unit, and similar matters, touching all manner of dull details of ordinary and everyday life.

So the Mishnah's framers deemed the conduct of ordinary life in this world to be the critical focus and central point of tension of all being. At the same time, their account of these matters drew more heavily upon Scripture than upon any more contemporary and practical source. The philosophers designed a government and a state utterly out of phase with the political realities of the day, speaking, as we shall see, of king and high priest, but never of sage, patriarch, and Roman official. They addressed a lost world of Temple cult as described by the Torah, of cleanness, support of priesthood, offerings on ordinary days and on appointed times in accord with Torah law, and so mapped out vast tracts of a territory whose only reality lay in people's imagination, shaped by Scripture. Mishnah's map is not territory.

Accordingly, for all its intense practicality and methodical application of the power of practical reason and logic to concrete and material things, the Mishnah presents a made-up system which, in its way, is no more practical or applicable in all ways to ordinary life than are the diverse systems of philosophy and myth, produced in its day in other parts of the world, which fall under the name, Gnostic.

What the framers of Mishnah have in common with the framers of the diverse world constructions of the Gnostic sort thus is, first, a system building, and second, confrontation with two issues addressed in the diverse Gnostic systems of antiquity, the nature of creation and the creator and the character of the revelation of the creator-god. If I may state in a few simple words the position of the Mishnah on these two burning issues of the day, it is that creation is good and worthy of man's best consideration, and that the creator of the world is good and worthy of man's deepest devotion. So out of creation and revelation will come redemption. The Torah is not only not false but the principal source of truth. A system which intersects with the rules of the Torah therefore will patiently and carefully restate, and, so, blatantly reaffirm, precisely what Scripture has to say about those same points in common. A structure coming in the aftermath of the Temple's destruction which doggedly restated rules governing the Temple so reaffirmed, in the most obvious possible way, the cult and the created world celebrated therein. For as soon as we speak of sacrifice and Temple, we address the questions of creation and the value of the created world and of redemption. When, therefore, a document emerges rich in discourse on these matters and doggedly repetitive of precisely what Scripture says about exactly the same things, the meaning in context is clear.

From these comparative remarks on the context of the system, let us turn directly to the earliest phases of the Mishnaic system, that is, those ideas that appear to have circulated in the period before A.D. 70.

Those strata of Mishnaic law which appear to go back to the period before the wars, prior to A.D. 70, deal specifically with the special laws of marriage (in Yebamot), distinctive rules on when sexual relations may and may not take place (in Niddah), and the laws covering the definition of sources of uncleanness and the attainment of cleanness, with specific reference to domestic meals (in certain parts of Chalot, Zabim, Kelim, and Miqvaot). For the conduct of the cult and the sacrificial system, about which the group may have had its own doctrines but over which it neither exercised control nor even aspired to exercise control, there appears to be no systemic content or development whatsoever.

How do we account for these points of interest? Once a group takes shape around some distinctive, public issue or doctrine, as in odd taboos about eating, it also must take up the modes of social differentiation which will ensure the group's continued existence. For the group, once it comes into being, has to aspire to define and shape the ordinary lives of its adherents and to form a community expressive of its larger world view. The foundations of an enduring community will then be laid down through rules governing what food may be eaten, under what circumstances, and with what sort of people; whom one may marry and what families may be joined in marriage; and how sexual relationships are timed. Indeed, to the measure that these rules not only differ from those observed by others but in some aspect or other render the people who keep them unacceptable to those who do not, as much as, to the sect, those who do not keep them are unacceptable to those who do, the lines of difference and distinctive structure will be all the more inviolable.

The Mishnah before the wars begins its life among a group of people who are joined together by a common conviction about the eating of food under ordinary circumstances in accord with cultic rules to begin with applicable, in the mind of the priestly lawyers of Leviticus and Numbers, to the Temple alone. This group of lay people pretending to be priests, moreover, had other rules which affected who might join and who might not. These laws formed a protective boundary, keeping in those who were in, keeping out those who were not. If we wish to identify the social group in which the Mishnah originated, it is at this point that discourse must come to a conclusion. The reason is that the Mishnah does not tell us the name of the group represented by the names of Shammai and Hillel and their Houses, Gamaliel, Simeon b. Gamaliel, his son, and others who appear in the Mishnah and who clearly form the earliest stratum of its named authorities. More important: the convictions of the named authorities deal with details. The vast territories of agreement have not been surveyed and marked out by them in particular. So, for all we know, the concrete matters subject to dispute represent the points at issue for no more than a tiny sector of a much larger group, which, in other ways, will have had still other points of discourse and contention. What I say elsewhere on the pharisees will give body to this proposal.

We come now to the second stage in the formation of the earliest expression of rabbinic Judaism, the period beyond the destruction in 70. The principal initiatives and propositions of the law after 70 and before 135, prove to be either predictable on the basis of what had just now happened or wholly continuous with what had gone before. The point of interest in the catastrophe of the First War against Rome, for the people whose ideas came down to the framers of the Mishnah, therefore lies in the stunning facts that, first, the Temple building had been destroyed, and, second, the cult had come to a halt. To them these points of total disorientation and socio-cultic disorganization formed the problematic of the age. At issue were not salavation, tragedy and catastrophic history, but sanctification, the shaking of the foundations of orderly life extending out of the Temple and heaven that governed the cult. Needed was not poetry but order. To the founders of the Mishnah the aftermath of the first defeat brought to an end the orderly life of the villages and the Land, the reliable relationship of calendar and crop with cult, all joined at the movement of moon, sun, and fixed stars. The problematic of the age therefore was located in that middle range of life between the personal tragedy of individuals, who live and die, and the national catastrophe of the history of Israel. The pivot had wobbled; everything organized around it and in relationship to it had quaked. Left out were those two things at the extremes of this middle world: private suffering, and national catastrophe in the context of history, the encompassing history of Israel and of the world alike. That is why, when we contemplate how others of the same time framed the issues of the day, we are struck by the contrast.

The obvious and accessible dilemmas of Israel's suffering at the hand of gentiles, the deeper meaning of the age in which the Temple had been ruined and Israel defeated, the resort for expressing public sorrow to evocative symbols of private suffering and its mystery, the discourse on the meaning of human history in the light of this awful outcome for Israel -- none of these to us accessible and sympathetic themes and modes of thought comes to the surface in those themes and topics which the precursors of the Mishnaic system deem the appropriate focus of discourse. It is as if before us in the Mishnah are bystanders. These are people taken up with the result of the catastrophe and determined to make a quite distinctive statement about what was important in it. But the miserable world of the participants -- the people who had fought, lost, and suffered -- seems remote. It would stand to reason that before us is the framing of the issue of 70 by the priests, alongside people who, before the wars, had pretended to be priests and imitated their cultic routines. To such people as these, the paramount issues of 70 were issues of cult. The consequences demanding sustained attention, as I said, therefore were the effects of the wobbling of the pivot for the continued life of the cult in those vast stretches of the Israelite Land which remained holy, among those sizable Israelite populations of the country which remained vital. Israel had originally become Israel and sustained its perpetual vocation through its living on the holy Land and organizing all aspects of its holy life in relationship to the conduct of the holy Temple, eating like priests and farming in accord with the cultic taboos and obsessions with order and form, dividing up time between profane and holy in relationship to the cult's calendar and temporal division of its own rites. Now Israel remained Israel, loyal to its calling, through continuing to live in the mirror and under the aspect of that same cult. Let us now survey those laws which appear to have emerged in the age between the wars.

The sole fact to be adduced as definitive for the interpretation of materials attributed to authorities in the aftermath of the destruction of the Temple is that the Temple was destroyed. That fact by definition affected all else. But it also is general. There is no way to move from the self-evident facts that the Temple building was destroyed, the cult was no longer carried on, and the priesthood and Levites were now unemployed, to the specificities of the laws on these topics reliably assigned to the period under discussion. But there is no need to do so. For the main point of interest in an account of Judaism's unfolding is the expansion of the topics subject to discussion among precursors of the Mishnah's ultimate form, frame, and system. And the two new themes brought under systematic discourse directly relate to the destruction of the Temple, namely, laws affecting the taxes paid to the class of the poor and the caste of the priests, on the one side, and laws governing the conduct of the cult itself, on the other side. Since, moreover, the production of crops in accord with certain taboos was intimately related to the life of the cult, the sustained interest in the application of at least one significant taboo, that concerning mixed seeds, formed part of a larger statement about the way in which the country would respond to the loss of the Temple. Matters were to go forward as if the Temple still stood, because the Land retained its holiness, and God, his title to and ownership of the Land. Therefore the class of the poor, for its part, retained a right to a portion of crops prior to the completion of their harvest, and the priesthood, its claim to a part of them afterward. Sustained interest in the conduct of the cult, of course, represented a similar act of hope, an expression of the certainty that, just as God retained ownership of the Land, so too Israel remained responsible to maintain knowledge of the proper conduct of the sacrificial cult which returned to God part of what belonged to God out of the herds and crops of the hold Land and which so secured Israel's right to the rest. So far from the viewpoint of the Mishnah's precursors, what required sustained reflection in the aftermath of the destruction was the disorientation of the country's cultic life, both in its conduct of the agricultural -- that is, the economic -- affairs, governed as they were by laws emanating from the cult and meant to place economic life into relationship with the cult, and in its performance of the cult itself. The profound disorientation of defeat and destruction, the disorder brought about by the collapse of basic institutions of government, culture, and faith -- these form the crisis defined in this particular way by these people.

Alongside these two fresh points of interest, the established one in the conduct of a meal in conditions of cleanness enjoyed continued interest. In addition to a close continuation of thinking already evidenced prior to the war, moreover, a number of new topics came up.

First, systematic attention was paid to sources of uncleanness which, prior to the war, seem in legal thought to have been neglected. That is, sources of uncleanness on which no work had been done in organizing and amplifying laws now received sustained attention. Important here is significant and rigorous work on the unclean persons and objects (houses, clothing) discussed at Lev. 13 and 14. These now join the unclean persons and objects of Lev. 11, 12, and 15, to which ample attention already had been paid.

Second, there was a quite original essay attempted on the one rite of the cult which was performed outside of the Temple building itself, namely, burning the red cow and mixing its ashes with spring water to make purification water for persons affected by corpse uncleanness (Num. 19:1ff.). What is said in this essay, as it is worked out between the wars, is that a place of true cleanness can be formed outside of the Temple. (Whether or not the rite itself was carried on is not information provided by the Mishnah; in fact, we do not know.) What had to be done was situating the conduct of the rite outside the Temple in an appropriate relationship to the Temple itself. That is, determining whether or not the rite should be done precisely as rites were done in the Temple, or, in a mirror image, precisely the opposite of the way rites were done in the Temple, was the principal focus. This fundamental inquiry into the governing analogies generated ongoing exegesis. Through imposing on participants in the rite perfect attentiveness and perpetual concern for what they were doing while they were engaged in the rite, the law would make possible that state of cleanness appropriate to the conduct of a sacred rite in the otherwise unclean secular world. It would follow that a state of cleanness still higher than that of the Temple would be contemplated. The rules would demand remarkable attentiveness. Why all of this should come under discussion at just this time is obvious. For the underlying notion is continuous with that of the laws of Purities prior to 70, that is to say, cleanness outside of the Temple building *is* possible. A state of cleanness outside of the conduct of the Temple cult therefore may be required for certain purposes. What now is added thus is predictable, given what had been said before 70. Just as a meal can and should be eaten in a state of cultic cleanness by people not engaged in the eating of bread and meat originating as priestly gifts in the Temple, so its is possible even to conduct that one rite which Scripture itself deems legitimate when performed outside the "tent of meeting," the Temple. The laws remain valid; the relevant ones require study.

The destruction of the Temple thus is important, in the unfolding of the history of the Mishnah's laws and ideas, principally because of what it does not demarcate. It does not mark a significant turning in the history of the laws of Purities. These unfolded within the generative principles of their own logic. The inner tensions embedded from before 70 in the exercise of locating the unclean on a continuum with the holy and of situating ordinary food in place of that continuum account for what was said after 70. The loss of the Temple, enormous though it was, does not. The expectation that the rites governing agriculture and the disposition of the produce of the Land would remain valid accounts for the evidence we have surveyed, just as that same expectation, that people would eat in a state of cultic cleanness, clearly is in evidence in the character of the laws of Purities between the wars. True, the destruction of the Temple and the supposedly temporary cessation of the cult precipitated thought on laws governing the Temple altar and the priests in the act of sacrifice. That was a natural interest among people who, to begin with, thought that was happened in the Temple formed the center and focus of Israelite life. With the Temple gone, people will naturally have wondered whether some deep flaw in the conduct of its rites might explain the awful punishment Israel suffered in the destruction of the Temple and the hold city. So, in that same, essentially priestly, perspective of the world, it was entirely predictable that sustained thought on the right conduct of the cult should have gotten under way. The themes and detailed principles collected in the Divisions of Agriculture, Holy Things, and Purities, the first and the third continuing from before the war, the second beginning in its aftermath, testify to a continuity of vision, a perpetuation of focus.

The people whose ideas come to full expression and closure in the Mishnah, as we shall see later on, were diverse. But in so far as the definition of the group is concerned, who, before and between the wars, contributed to the ultimate corpus of ideas contained in what was framed after the wars, that definition remains unchanged. They were priests and lay people who aspired to act like priests. These are the ones whose fantasy lies before us in the stratum, A.D. 70 - 135, of the laws of the Mishnah just now surveyed. Yet fresh elements in their thought turn out to have laid the foundations for what, in the end, is truly Mishnaic about the Mishnah, I mean, the Mishnah's message at its deepest structure about the interplay between sanctification, on the one side, and the human will, on the other.

The period between the wars, that is, after 70 and before 135, marks a transition in the unfolding of the Mishnaic law and system. The law moved out of its narrow, sectarian framework. But it did not yet attain that full definition, serviceable for the governance of a whole society and the formation of a government for the nation as a whole, which would be realized in the aftermath of the wars. The marks of the former state remained. But those of the later character of the Mishnaic system began to make their appearance. Still, the systemic fulfillment of the law would be some time in coming. For the system as a whole in its ultimate shape would totally reframe the inherited vision. In the end the Mishnah's final framers would accomplish what was not done before or between the wars: make provision for the ordinary condition of Israelite men and women, living everyday lives under their own government. The laws suitable for a sect would remain, to be joined by others which, in the aggregate, would wholly revise the character of the whole.

The shift would be from a perspective formed upon the Temple mount, to a vision framed within the plane of Israel, from a cultic to a communal conception, and from a center at the locative pivot of the whole. To be sure, this still would be what the cult-centered vision had perceived: a holy nation in a holy Land living out a holy life and deriving sustenance from the source of life, through sanctification set apart from death and uncleanness. But the shift is made. The orbit moved to a path other than what it was. Between the wars the shift is yet to be discerned. But if the orbit was the same as it had been for well over half a millennium, still, we see a wobble in the pivot.

When we take up the changes in this transitional period, we notice, first of all, continuity with the immediate past. What was taking place after 70 is encapsulated in the expansion, along predictable and familiar lines, of the laws of uncleanness, so to these we turn first. If the destruction of Jerusalem and the Temple in 70 marks a watershed in the history of Judaism, the development of the system of uncleanness does not indicate it. The destruction of the Temple in no way interrupted the unfolding of those laws, consideration of which is well attested when the Temple was standing and the cult maintained. Development is continuous in a second aspect as well. We find that, in addition to carrying forward antecedent themes and supplying secondary and even tertiary conceptions, the authorities between the wars develop new areas and motifs of legislation. These turn out to be both wholly consonant with the familiar ones, and, while fresh, generated by logical tensions in what had gone before. If, therefore, the destruction of the Temple raised in some minds the question of whether the system of cleanness at home would collapse along with the cult, the rules and system before us in no way suggest so. To be sure, the destruction of the Temple does mark a new phase in the growth of the law. What now happens is an evidently rapid extension of the range of legislation, on the one side, and provision of specific and concrete rules for what matters of purity were apt to have been taken for granted but not given definition before 70, on the other. So the crisis of 70 in the system of uncleanness gives new impetus to movement along lines laid forth long before.

What happened in the third period of the Mishnah's development, that is, the period beyond the decisive catastrophe of Bar Kokhba's War in 135 to 160 or 170? We begin by reminding ourselves that the destruction of the Temple in 70 left alive the hope for its restoration. After 135, with Jerusalem forbidden to Jews and the Temple mount ploughed over, few could hope for a near-term rebuilding of the Temple and restoration of its bloody cult. So the real work of framing a system in response to the final end of a thousand-year-old mode of social organization fell upon the survivors after 135.

Before the two wars (70, 135) the people whose ideas come to full expression in the Mishnah formed a small group, perhaps to be categorized as a sect. If so, it was a cultic sect, a holiness order, expressing the aspirations of lay people to live as if they belonged to the caste of priests, and of priests to live as if the whole country were the Temple. It is no surprise that those definitive topics of the Mishnah which gain attention early on were the ones having to do with food and sex: how food is raised, the petty obsessions governing its preparation and consumption, and who may marry whom in the constrained circle of those who worried those small, compulsive worries. After the two wars the entire framework of the Mishnah would undergo revision. The range of topics so expanded that laws came to full expression to govern not merely the collective life of a small group but the political and social affairs of a whole nation. What had come from the then-distant past, from the preceding century, would be taken into caring hands and carefully nurtured, as if it mattered. But the fresh and the new challenge of an age of new beginnings would lead to daring choices: laws for real estate and commercial transactions, laws for the scribal profession and the documentation of changes in the status of people and property, laws, even, for the governance of the Temple, then in ruins, and the conduct of its rites throughout the cycle of appointed times and seasons, for the maintenance of the Temple and its caste of priests and Levites, and (of all things) for the design of the Temple when it would be rebuilt and for the conduct of its everyday offering. All of this would follow in that remarkable time of fulfillment and closure which came in the aftermath of the wars.

What was achieved between them? Small things, little steps -- a bridge between that completed statement constituted by the sectarian fantasy framed before the wars, and that also-completed statement about everything and everyone: the political vision, the social policy, the economic program, in full and glorious detail, which would be the closed and ample Mishnah itself. When we consider the beginnings of it all in a narrowly priestly fantasy, acted out by a tight little circle of specialists in uncommon and egregious laws involving the contact of a loaf of bread of a specified status with a deceased reptile, we must wonder what swept the world out of the old and into the new orbit.

For, as I have just now stressed, the priestly vision, with its emphasis on the Temple as the pivot and the world as the periphery, the Temple as guarantor of life, the world as the threatening realm of death, the Temple as the security and strength of Israel, the world as its enemy, and, above all, the unreliable and perpetually threatening character of persons and substances on the borders between Temple and world -- when we contemplate that vision, we must wonder that anyone could share it <u>and yet expand it</u>. That is just what happened. For the priestly component of the ultimate structure of the Mishnah remains paramount. Yet the Mishnah is not a priestly document. It is much more than that. Had the Mishnah come to closure before the wars, it would have consisted of the system of uncleanness, fully exposed if lacking numerous details, a part of the system of agriculture, a system (quite its own) about food preparation, with emphasis upon doing so on special occasions (when the group presumably was able to come together), and, finally, a half-system on suitable marital candidates under special conditions, a set of laws calculated (if observed) to render members of the group unacceptable to non-members as marriage partners. New, that version of the Mishnah spun about the Temple, in a stable orbit around the altar.

And the other Mishnah, the one we now have, pursues its predictable path in quite another orbit. It makes peripheral the Temple and its concerns, as they come to expression in everyday imitation of the priesthood. It treats as central other things entirely: civil and criminal law and political institutions and their power, in the Fourth Division; the conduct of the cult itself, not merely of people wishing to place themselves into relationship with a cult by setting their feet on a single continuous path to the altar, in the Second and Fifth Divisions; the web of documents which encase and protect transfers of persons and property, both in life and afterward, in the Third and Fourth

Divisions; the full articulation of the rules governing the disposition of crops in accord with the holiness inhering in them, and the arrangement of relationships (hitherto remarkably ignored) between virtuosi of the law and outsiders so that all, all together, might constitute a single Israel, this in the First Division and in the Sixth. Now these changes, ultimately realized in the full expression and closure of the Mishnah itself, are no issue of small detail. They cut to the heart of the matter. They shift completely and ultimately the very center of focus of the document itself. They represent, as I said, a Mishnah wholly other than the Mishnah (if we may call it that) which would have taken shape before the wars, if anyone had thought to make one.

But, of course, so far as we know, no one did. So the truly stunning change effected after the wars was the formation of the book itself, the book which brought together the ideas and principles and laws in circulation before its time, and put them all together into something far more than the components, the paltry corpus of conceptions available to the framers of the document. Now we see with full clarity the ponderous movement from one orbit to the other, the shift of the previous culture of, if not a millennium, then at least nearly seven or eight hundred years (from the second century backward to the sixth). That old, reliable, priestly way of life and world view from the Temple mountain came to be subsumed by, and transformed into, a social vision, as I said, framed on the plane of Israel. What is stunning is the shift in perspective, not the change in what was to be seen. Merely seeing the Temple and its altar from a vantage point other than the Temple mount itself is a remarkable movement in perspective. Only framing a code of law framed in rules made of words in place of practice codified in gesture and studied act constitutes an astonishing shift in focus. From interests limited to the home and hearth the opening lens of social thought takes in a larger frame indeed: from home to court, from eating and drinking, beds and pots and pans, to exchanges of property and encounters of transactions in material power. What moved the world on its axis, the ball of earth in its majesty? The answer is self-evident: seventy years of wars and the tumult of wars. These shattered a hope which, to begin with, had had little to do with the Temple at all. There was then a moment of utter despair about things which, from the perspective of the philosophers of the Mishnah, might as well have taken place on yet another planet (but, alas, things wholly within their experience). The previous culture of somewhat less than a millennium spun into another orbit, not because of the gravity of yet a new civilization of impressive density, though.

Having briefly surveyed the main developments in the earliest and formative stages of rabbinic Judaism, from before 70 to after 135, we turn to the social question. We ask, specifically, what groups in Israelite society of the second century find a voice in the Mishnah as we have it. That is to say, what groups speak through the system of earliest rabbinic Judaism?

In so far as the Mishnah is a document about the holiness of Israel in its Land, it expresses that conception of sanctification and theory of its modes which will have been shaped among those to whom the Temple and its technology of joining heaven and holy Land through the sacred place defined the core of being, I mean, the caste of the priests.

In so far as the Mishnah takes up the way in which transactions are conducted among ordinary folk and takes the position that it is through documents with a supernatural consequence that transactions are embodied and expressed (surely the position of the relevant tractates on both Women and Damages), the Mishnah expresses what is self-evident to scribes. Just as, to the priest, there is a correspondence between the table of the Lord in the Temple and the locus of the divinity in the heavens, so, to the scribe, there is a correspondence between the documentary expression of the human will on earth, in writs of all sorts, in the orderly provision of courts for the predictable and just disposition of exchanges of persons and property, and heaven's judgment of these same matters. When a woman becomes sanctified to a particular man on earth, through the appropriate document governing the transfer of her person and property, in heaven as well, the woman is deemed truly sanctified to that man. A violation of the writ therefore is not merely a crime. It is a sin. That is why the Temple rite involving the wife accused of adultery is integral to the system of the Division of Women.

So there are these two social groups, not categorically symmetrical with one another, the priestly caste and the scribal profession, for whom the Mishnah makes self-evident statements. We know, moreover, that in time to come, the scribal profession would become a focus of sanctification too. The scribe would be transformed into the rabbi, locus of the holy through what he knew, just as the priest had been, and would remain, locus of the holy through what he could claim for genealogy. The tractates of special interest to scribes-become-rabbis and to their governance of Israelite society, those of Women and Damages, together with certain others particularly relevant to utopian Israel beyond the system of the Land -- those tractates would grow and grow. Others would remain essentially as they were with the closure of the Mishnah. So we must notice that the Mishnah, for its part, speaks for the program of topics important to the priests. It takes up the persona of the scribes, speaking through their voice and in their manner.

Now what we do not find, which becomes astonishing in the light of these observations, is sustained and serious attention to the matter of the caste of the priests and of the profession of the scribes. True, scattered through the tractates are exercises, occasionally sustained and important exercises, on the genealogy of the priestly caste, upon their marital obligations and duties, as well as on the things priests do and do not do in the cult, in collecting and eating their sanctified food, and in other topics of keen interest to priests. Indeed, it would be no exaggeration to say that the Mishnah's system seen whole is not a great deal more than a handbook of how the priestly caste wished to design its life in Israel and the world. And yet in the fundamental structure of the document, its organization into divisions and tractates, there is no place for a Division of the Priesthood, no room even for a complete tractate on the rules of the priesthood, except, as we have seen, for the pervasive way of life of the priestly caste, which is everywhere. This absence of sustained attention to the priesthood is striking, when we compare the way in which the priestly code at Lev. 1-15 spells out its concerns: the priesthood, the cult, the matter of cultic cleanness. Since we do have divisions for the cult (the fifth) and for cleanness (the sixth) at Holy Things and Purities, we are struck that we do not have this third division: the priesthood.

We must, moreover, be equally surprised that, for a document so rich in the importance lent to petty matters of how a writ is folded and where the witnesses sign, so obsessed with the making of long lists and the organization of all knowledge into neat piles of symmetrically arranged words, the scribes who know how to make lists and match words nowhere come to the fore. They speak through the document. But they stand behind the curtains. They write the script, arrange the sets, design the costumes, situate the players in their place on the stage, raise the curtain -- and play no role at all. We have no division or tractate on such matters as how a person becomes a scribe, how a scribe conducts his work, who forms the center of the scribal profession and how authority is gained therein, the rights and place of the scribe in the system of governance through courts, the organization and conduct of schools or circles of masters and disciples through which the scribal arts are taught and perpetuated. This absence of even minimal information on the way in which the scribal profession takes shape and does its work is stunning when we realize that, within a brief generation, the Mishnah as a whole would fall into the hands of scribes, to be called rabbis, both in the Land of Israel and in Babylonia. These rabbis would make of the Mishnah exactly what they wished. Construed from the perspective of the makers of the Mishnah, the priests and the scribes who provide contents and form, substance and style, therefore, the Mishnah turns out to omit all reference to actors, when laying out the world which is their play.

The metaphor of the theater for the economy of Israel, the household of holy Land and people, space and time, cult and home, leads to yet another perspective. When we look out upon the vast drama portrayed by the Mishnah, lacking as it does an account of the one who wrote the book, and the one about whom the book was written, we notice yet one more missing component. In the fundamental and generative structure of the Mishnah, that is, at the foundations of Judaism, we find no account of that other necessary constituent: the audience. To whom the document speaks is never specified. What group ("class") generates the Mishnah's problems is not at issue. True, it is taken for granted that the world of the Mishnah expresses the sanctified being of Israel in general. So the Mishnah speaks about the generality of Israel, the people. But to whom, within Israel, the Mishnah addresses itself, and what groups are expected to want to know what the Mishnah has to say, are matters which never come to full expression.

Yet there can be no doubt of the answer to the question. The building block of Mishnaic discourse, the circumstance addressed whenever the issues of concrete society and material transactions are taken up, is the householder and his context. The Mishnah knows about all sorts of economic activities. But for the Mishnah the center and focus of interest lie in the village. The village is made up of households, each a unit of production in farming. The households are constructed by, and around, the householder, father of an extended family, including his sons and their wives and children, his servants, his slaves (bondsmen), the craftsmen to whom he entrusts tasks he does not choose to do. The concerns of householders are in transactions in land. Their measurement of value is expressed in acreage of top, middle, and bottom grade. Through real estate critical transactions are worked out. The marriage settlement depends upon real property. Civil penalties are exacted through payment of real property. The principal transactions to be taken up are those of the householder who owns beasts which do damage or suffer it; who harvests his crops and must set aside and so by his own word and deed sanctify them for use by the castes scheduled from on high; who uses or sells his crops and feeds his family; and who, if he is fortunate, will acquire still more land. It is to householders that the Mishnah is addressed: the pivot of society and its bulwark, the units of which the village is composed, the corporate component of the society of Israel in the limits of the village and the Land. The householder, as I said, is the building block of the house of Israel, of its economy in the classic sense of the word.

So, to revert to the metaphor which has served us well, the great proscenium constructed by the Mishnah now looms before us. Its arch is the canopy of heaven. Its stage is the whole Land of Israel. Its actors are the holy people of Israel. Its events are the drama of unfolding time and common transactions, appointed times and holy events. Yet in this grand design we look in vain for the three principal participants: the audience, the actors, and the playwright. So we must ask why.

The reason is not difficult to discover, when we recall that, after all, what the Mishnah really wants is for nothing to happen. The Mishnah presents a tableau, a wax museum, a diorama. It portrays a world fully perfected and so fully at rest. The one thing the Mishnah does not want to tell us is about change, how things come to be what they are. That is why there can be no sustained attention to the priesthood and its rules, the scribal profession and its constitution, the class of householders and its interests. The Mishnah's pretense is that all of these have come to rest. They compose a world in stasis, perfect and complete, made holy because it is complete and perfect. It is an economy -- again in the classic sense of the word -- awaiting the divine act of sanctification which, as at the creation of the world, would set the seal of holy rest upon an again-complete creation, just as in the beginning. There is no place for the actors when what is besought is no action whatsoever, but only perfection, which is unchanging. There is room only for a description of how things are: the present tense, the sequence of completed statements and static problems. All the action lies within, in how these statements are made. Once they come to full expression, with nothing left to say, there also is nothing left to do, no need for actors, whether scribes, priests, or householders.

So the components of the system at the very basis of things are the social groups to whom the system refers. These groups obviously are not comparable to one another. They are not three species of the same social genus. One is a caste; the second, a profession; the third, a class. What they have in common is, first, that they do form groups; and, second, that the groups are social in foundation and collective in expression. That is not a sizable claim. The priesthood is a social group; it coalesces. Priests see one another as part of a single caste, with whom, for example, they will want to intermarry. The scribes are a social group, because they practice a single profession, following a uniform set of rules. They coalesce in the methods by which they do their work. The householders are a social group, the basic productive unit of society, around which other economic activity is perceived to function. In an essentially agricultural economy, it is quite reasonable to regard the householder, the head of a basic unit of production, as part of a single class.

It remains to state, in a few words, the principal point expressed by the coalition of scribe, priest, and householder, for whom the Mishnah speaks.

The Mishnah's principal message, which makes the Judaism of this document and of its social components distinctive and cogent, is that man is at the center of creation, the head of all creatures upon earth, corresponding to God in heaven, in whose image man is made. The way in which the Mishnah makes this simple and fundamental statement is to impute power to man to inaugurate and initiate those corresponding processes, sanctification and uncleanness, which play so critical a role in the Mishnah's account of reality. The will of man, expressed through the deed of man, is the active power in the world. Will and deed constitute those actors of creation which work upon neutral realms, subject to either sanctification or uncleanness: the Temple and table, the field and family, the altar and hearth, woman, time, space, transactions in the material world and in the world above as well. An object, a substance, a transaction, even a phrase or a sentence is inert but may be made holy, when the interplay of the will and deed of man arouses or generates its potential to be sanctified. Each may be treated as ordinary or (where relevant) made unclean by the neglect of the will and inattentive act of man. Just as the entire system of uncleanness and holiness awaits the intervention of man, which imparts the capacity to become unclean upon what was formerly inert, or which removes the capacity to impart cleanness from what was formerly in its natural and puissant condition, so in the other ranges of reality, man is at the center on earth, just as is God in heaven. Man is counterpart and partner and creation, in that, like God he has power over the status and condition of creation, putting everything in its proper place, calling everything by its rightful name.

So, stated briefly, the question taken up by the Mishnah and answered by Judaism is, What can a man do? And the answer laid down by the Mishnah is, Man, through will and deed, is master of this world, the measure of all things. Since when the Mishnah thinks of man, it means the Israelite, who is the subject and actor of its system, the statement is clear. This man is Israel, who can do what he wills. In the aftermath of the two wars, the message of the Mishnah cannot have proved more pertinent -- or poignant and tragic.

II
JUDAISM IN BABYLONIA
THE EVIDENCE OF THE BABYLONIAN TALMUD

By "Babylonian Judaism" we mean that aspect of the rabbinic system of Judaism that comes to full expression in the pages of the Babylonian Talmud. That document, which came to closure in ca. A.D. 600 and in its final form represented the viewpoint of the rabbinical circles of Babylonia, presents a picture of Judaism in no way distinctive to the Iranian satrapy in which it took shape. For, first of all, the Talmud of Babylonia is organized as a dual commentary, with about 60% of the whole, in volume, devoted to the exegesis of the Mishnah, and about 40% of the whole, to the exegesis of Scripture. So in its redactional structure, the document that alone attests to the Judaism of rabbis in Babylonia in no way rests upon foundations unique to Babylonia or particular to its rabbis. Much else -- many large-scale units of discourse -- in the Talmud of Babylonia, moreover, derives from the schools of the Land of Israel. These schools, until the later fourth century, made a solid and continuing contribution to the legal and exegetical studies of the rabbis of Babylonia. It is possible to differentiate only in minor detail that "Judaism" that we find attested in the Talmud of Babylonia from that "Judaism" that we study in the Talmud of the Land of Israel, but the distinctions make very little difference. So far as the basic mythic and symbolic structure of the Judaism of the rabbis of the two countries, the way of life and the world view represented in the writings produced in the one land as against the other, there is no material difference at all.

At the same time, we can point to distinctive characteristics in the unfolding of the religious life of the Jews, particularly sages, in Babylonia, as that life comes to expression in the Talmud of Babylonia. For Babylonia lay well within the great Iranian empire ruled by the Sasanians (226-641), and the stability, orderly rule, characteristic tolerance, and ordinarily wise government of the Iranians under that dynasty (as under the prior one, the Arsacids of the Parthian province of Iran, 240 B.C. - A.D. 226), did allow the Jews much freedom of development. Accordingly, we err if we assume that pretty much everything in the literature of the rabbis of the Land of Israel applies without differentiation or nuance to the description of the Judaism of the rabbis of Babylonia and of their followers in the Jewish community. It follows that, for the present purpose, we may well make use of the Talmud of Babylonia in particular and ask it to make its distinctive contribution to the description of the Judaism represented within its pages. If we read that document by itself, we gain a picture of considerable depth and interest.

The first and most important trait of the Judaism of Babylonia is that, so far as we know about it, it is a Judaism that appears in books. Our main evidence is literary. The only source of that literary evidence is the rabbinical estate or movement itself. The task then is to turn a book by an elite into a document of, testimony about, a religion. We have to ask about the traits of the authors as figures in the expansion and development of a religion. In the case of the Judaism portrayed by the Talmud of Babylonia, then, we turn to the figure of the rabbi, who constitutes the authorship of our document, and inquire into his configuration as a model of the religion, Judaism -- hence, "Babylonian Judaism."

The sage, or rabbi was not merely a lawyer and judge, and the master disciple circle, or rabbinical academy, not merely a law school. The rabbi was much more than a lawyer, however, and the academy was different from a law school. The rabbinate constituted a party or estate in Babylonian Jewish life, the only organized one so far as I can tell, and the estate aimed at a radical reformation of the life of the Jewish people. It was prepared to effect such a reformation through whatever political agencies it could get its hands on. Its purposes however were far more than political, though at first the issues seemed merely to relate to law and, in some measure, sociology, devolving upon who should administer the internal affairs of the Jews, and what law should pertain.

Four forces shaped the history of Babylonian Judaism. First was the Sasanian government, which had power to do exactly as it liked with various groups in the empire, and proved it by the way it solved the Manichaean problem. The Manichaeans posed a severe threat to the Mazdean faith, for they appealed to the same groups upon which the Mazdean church was based, namely the Iranian component in the population of the western part of the empire. Seen by the Mazdeans as dangerous heretics, they could not be tolerated, but had to be expelled, and were driven out as soon as the Mazdean authorities were able to arrange it. The fate of the Manichaeans illustrates what <u>could</u> have been done to the Jews, had the government so desired. But no reason to expel the Jews existed. It was perfectly satisfactory through a loyal agent to oversee their affairs, to collect their taxes, and to leave them pretty much to their own devices.

Through the exilarchate the Sasanians proposed to attend to Jewish affairs, and it thus constituted the second major force in Babylonian Jewish history. Its duty was to govern the Jews and to carry out among them the policies of the Sasanian regime. Having agreed to do so, the exilarch was given a free hand. In his view, his authority was based upon his distinguished ancestry and upon the support quite naturally accorded to him by the Sasanian government. Even more than the Sasanians, he wanted only to keep the peace and maintain a stable and constructive control of Jewish affairs. The scion of David could not ask less of himself, or promise more to the people, than good government. To govern the people, he sought to apply to their affairs the one law they recognized and he with them, as divinely ordained, namely, the Mosaic revelation.

In order to do so, he drew upon the personnel and leadership of the third force, namely the rabbinate. The rabbinical movement had first appeared in Babylonian Jewry after the Bar Kokhba War, when refugees from Palestine established their schools in Nisibis and Huzal, and there carried on the studies they had pursued in Palestine. The Nisibis group, formed by students of Aqiba, eventually returned to Palestine, but the Huzal school, constituted by the leading students of Ishmael, remained in Babylonia, and trained some distinguished rabbis of late second-century Babylonia. The exilarch of the period seems to have made use of these highly motivated lawyers in his administration, even though they could not have constituted the whole of it. Alongside were Jewish upper-class officials, who knew the traditions of Babylonian Jewry and were well acquainted with difficult legal issues. They were well-trained, though we do not know in whose schools or according to what traditions. We know only that they were not educated as rabbis or in rabbinical schools. The one encounter between the rabbinical and the native groups reveals that the latter did not defer to the former, but held the rabbis strictly to their own view of what the law required. By the beginning of the third century, with the foundation of still another school by Rav, and the development of the Nehardean academy by Samuel, the non-rabbinical lawyers no longer could have mattered very much. We can only conjecture that, so far as the exilarch was concerned, the graduates of the rabbinical academies proved quite satisfactory. Since the academies were run by men loyal to himself, he could not have found any reason to curb them, or even to take much interest in what was taught there. In Rav's and Samuel's day, the schools turned out men trained in the Mishnah, recently promulgated in Palestine by Judah the Patriarch, who were dedicated to enforcing that code among Babylonian Jews. As the years passed, it became clear that they had other purposes as well, and the exilarch faced a new problem. He found that the lawyers and judges, administrators and teachers educated in the academies were not of one mind about their service to his government. A few of them openly defied his authority, and many apparently regarded his rule as founded upon inferior right. If it was the "Torah" that was to shape the life of Babylonian Jewry, then its rabbinical masters -- since they alone were privy to the true meaning of Scriptures -- should have the supreme rule, and ought not remain subservient to one who was supposedly their inferior in knowledge of Torah. Whether in fact the exilarch knew less about "the Torah" than they is no issue here. The fact is that they claimed he did, and preserved in their records numerous studies of how he had humbly studied the law with his own rabbinical employees. By the end of the third century, however, the exilarch found that their subversion affected only slightly, if at all, the practical administration of his regime. Leading rabbis, some related to him, including Nahman, Huna, Rabbah b. Abbuha, and others were thoroughly loyal, and clearly rejected the pretensions of other academicians to have a say in government, except upon the basis of exilarchic acquiescence.

The fourth, the largest, and least effective group, was formed by the ordinary people. We have almost no direct knowledge of what they thought about their government and its agents. They had traditions they believed to be both ancient and correct, and these did not conform to the views of the rabbis. But what was more important, people must have responded to the presence of a relatively new group, or class, of religious authorities in their midst in more varied ways than we can now discern. Some part of the ordinary people would have come very much under the influence of local authorities, as in the case of the Nehardeans and Nahman, and the Pumbeditans and Judah. Both of these towns, like Sura, were the sites of major academies, and one may suppose that where the academies were located, there rabbinic influence in one form or another was substantial.

The many major towns in which rabbinical schools were not found, indeed in which even rabbinical courts may not have been permanently situated, must have been another matter entirely. But what made the rabbis an effective group was not alone the power of their courts. They formed a class of religious literati and theurges, distinguished by their behavior and carriage, conforming to rules of conduct not widely observed, or even heard of before the preceding century, but nonetheless claiming to set the standard for popular, and not merely elite, behavior. It was in the streets, as much as in the academies or courts, that the ordinary people were exposed to the rabbi.

These four "forces," the Sasanians, the exilarchate, the rabbinate, and the masses, cannot be compared to one another, for they constituted different entities.

The Sasanian government proved weak and not very effectual. Had it been stronger, it might have become aware of the danger to the lasting power of its agency, the exilarchate, posed by the rabbinate, and might have intervened not only when called upon, but more vigorously and consistently, to eliminate such a threat.

On the other extreme, I do not think the ordinary people constituted a party or a group at all. The foci of their life were the fields and marketplaces, the streets and the synagogue. Whatever leadership they had did not extend beyond the given town or village. They were not a "movement" transcending local lines. Where they lived, there alone did they act. They were, so far as I can see, inert, a great mass to be twisted this way and that, but incapable of guiding or shaping its own growth except in response to events or powers more determined, better organized, and more dynamic than itself. The inertial force of tradition and culture rather than a particular theology or purpose shaped the life of the masses. But we can only guess what that tradition consisted of, beyond Scriptures.

The middle groups -- exilarchate and rabbinate -- cannot be compared to one another. The former was a relatively small and self-contained administration, centered upon the person of the Davidic scion and his police and administrators, and based upon the authorization and active support of the imperial regime.

The latter estate, not centered upon a single man, or dependent upon the recognition of the government, constituted a party based on schools, attracting through active proselytization in the academies and courts alike the support of growing numbers of Jews. These accepted their claim and therefore did the things necessary to carry it out: they went, or sent their children, to the academies; they paid respect to the great men of the party; they supported its cause by observing its bans and honoring its decrees. As a party, the rabbinate could not easily be compared to the inchoate masses upon which it worked, or to the subordinated exilarchate, or to the imperial government. The people were not similarly coherent, the imperial government not so purposefully engaged or single-minded, the exilarch not equivalently motivated. Sporadic persecution would not destroy them, nor was such persecution undertaken to begin with. Occasional setbacks would not deter them. All the while, as the government ignored them, and the exilarch made use of some, perhaps many, of them, for its own purposes, the rabbinate continued to seek every possible means to win over to its particular viewpoint on politics and theology whomever it could, to educate in its schools, and through the exemplars it sent out from them, as many people as possible. So the established forces, the government and its Jewish administration, proved unequal to the task of opposing a fairly well-disciplined, coherent, and certainly well-organized party, which in time -- though not in this period -- subverted the latter and thus rendered the former's choices for the Jews quite irrelevant.

The rabbinate, including its Judaism, represents a singularly successful "party." In the history of mankind, one can find few "parties" which achieved so lasting a success that until this very day, their conception of history and society dominates precisely the group which they intended from the beginning to shape and control. I can think of only one similarly successful group, and that is the Christians, who actively undertook to subvert, and then control, and finally to dominate, the Roman empire, and whose historical role provides an analogy to that of the rabbis. They are not wholly comparable, for the Romans persecuted the Christians, sporadically but ferociously, while the partriarchate in Palestine and the exilarchate in Babylonia actually employed the rabbis. The two parties however thrived by persistence and faith, and in time succeeded in winning the sovereignty to which they aspired, the one to the Roman world, the other to the rule of Israel. It is only in the past two centuries that either has had to face a significant challenge, when the values and ideals of each ceased to shape the groups whom they had dominated for so many centuries.

We have referred to the rabbinate as a party and estate. We shall now seek a valid definition for the rabbinate as an estate, or a recognizable group within Jewish society. It is clear that the rabbinate did not form a caste, for it was not only open to all who qualified, but also actively fostered the conformity of the masses to its paradigms. Everything demanded of the rabbi was <u>equally</u> expected of ordinary people. The rabbinate's social ideal, which stressed the transformation of the lives of <u>all</u> Jews and not merely those of the elite to conform to "the Torah," had nothing in common with the aspirations of a caste. Neither birth nor marriage could help a man achieve status within the party, though both might naturally confer obvious advantages. Second, it is concommitantly clear that the rabbinate did not constitute an economic class, or occupy a single stratum within Jewish society. While many of the most important rabbis emerged from, or became part of, the upper classes, theirs were not intrinsically upper-class values or ideals. They recognized tensions between themselves and the rich and powerful classes. They greatly encouraged the education of poor students. Third, they were not a clerical group. They played no particular role in the liturgical or sacerdotal life of the Jewish community, nor did the synagogue afford them a special platform for their ideas, except when they preached there. They contended in earlier times with the priesthood, which did form a sacerdotal caste, but by this time, the priests were not a significant or influential group within Babylonia Jewry, according to the evidence available to us, but had long since accommodated themselves to a perfunctory and inconsequential place in ritual life alone.

One thing is perfectly obvious: It was not only as men learned in the law or Scriptures that the rabbis set forth their claim against priests, on the one side, and the exilarch, on the other, that is, those sons of Aaron and the seed of David. Had they possessed legal or exegetical learning alone, the superior genealogy of priest and Davidide alike in a community obsessed with genealogy would have proved insurmountable. The priests had earlier had their legal traditions, believed by numerous Jews to be the proper guide to the application of revelation to the current age. The exilarch proved quite able to hire lawyers as bureaucrats, judges, and protagonists. Since none doubted that he had the most distinguished ancestry of all, the claim to superior learning alone could have meant little in the political economy of Babylonia. The rabbi both presented himself as, and was widely believed to be, a holy man, whose charisma weighed at least as heavily as his learning, and whose learning to begin with encompassed far more than a mere collection of ancient traditions of Scriptural exegesis. What was extraordinary about him was his mastery of a body of theurgical learning, the power of which rendered him exceptionally influential in heaven and earth. This learning was called "Torah," but "Torah" comprehended more than merely the Scriptures revealed at Sinai or to the prophets, along with the oral traditions that had accompanied them. If rabbinical knowledge, or gnosis, proved an effective basis for public activities, it was because the rabbis could authenticate it by a wide variety of impressive proofs. No phenomenon above or below proved too hard for their understanding. They were neither wizards nor sorcerers, but their wisdom was such that they could interpret natural phenomena and consort with heavenly beings. They were not physicians, but possessed sound knowledge about healing. The substance and effects of their gnosis sufficiently impressed other Jews that they were seen, by virtue of what they knew, to have been transformed into extraordinary men. Against "Torah," genealogy and politics could scarcely contend, but one must stress, it was "Torah" based as much upon personal charisma as upon knowledge of facts, even of mysteries, that characterized the rabbinical estate.

The rabbi was believed to enjoy more intimate connections with God and the angels, and more searching knowledge of the "mysteries" of the world, than ordinary people. Nonetheless, such knowledge alone would not have set him apart for special respect or veneration. It would, at best, have characterized him as a man of broad learning, a philosopher, but certainly not a "holy man." Much as people may have been impressed by what he knew about the natural world and dreams or about the Torah, they expected something more practical, namely mastery of occult, including healing arts. Without the ability to do extraordinary deeds, the rabbis would hardly have achieved a more significant status than merely that of unusually learned men. The ability to talk to Elijah, or to interpret and explain the phenomena of nature, was by itself hardly sufficient to relieve the rabbis of the obligation to pay for the defense of the cities in which they lived. If the rabbis required no protection, the reason had to do with something more than their learning.

The people looked to the "holy man" for healing, and when he was able to oblige, ascribed his skill to divine favor or heavenly wisdom. The earliest Christian missionaries to Adiabene and Edessa gained a hearing through their ability to perform miraculous cures. For example, when Pekidha, later the first Christian bishop of Arbela, who had been in the service of a Magus, met Addai, he was so impressed by his ability as a physician that he converted to Christianity. Similarly, Mani was expected to act as the physician of the court. Like many many of the rabbis mastered medical traditions, which were part of the normal paraphernalia of any "holy man," along with astrological knowledge. That the holy men of various communities knew something about matters of health ought not to obscure the fact that a medical profession existed. The rabbi knew he himself was not a physician, who, as in other cultures, combined medicine with barbering and sundry other arts. So when a rabbi taught his disciples about matters of health, or prepared an ointment or salve, he did not do so because no one else would. Rabbinical medical "practice" stressed two things, first of all, good advice about maintaining health, and second, occasional preparation of medicines to cure specific ailments. We rarely, if ever, hear of rabbis' actually letting blood or carrying out one of the other commonplace medical or surgical procedures. Medical knowledge, part of "Torah" and quite necessary for the enforcement of parts of the law, represented partially esoteric learning, which was not to be widely shared. I should thus understand the place of medicine in the schools. The ordinary people had different expectations. They were sick, and if the physicians could not help, why not turn to God, or to "holy men" who had a closer relationship to him -- if Jews, they might have phrased it in terms of "learning" -- than other people? After Rav died, people used to take the dirt from his grave and made it into poultices, for application on the first day of an attack of fever. If so, the person, and not merely the learning, of the rabbi must have been seen as "holy" by the plain people. So the people would have understood the rabbis' medical knowledge and traditions as signifying mastery of divine mysteries. The rabbis, by contrast, regarded medicine as a perfectly normal segment of "Torah."

Of far greater interest than rabbinic theurgy is rabbinic liturgy. The Talmud of Babylonia is rich in prayers made up by rabbis. Some of these clearly find their natural provenance in the master-disciple circle, for example, asking for divine favor for the act of study of Torah. Other prayers do not appear limited to the concerns of masters and disciples.

Both rabbi and ordinary person believed that God and angels heard and answered prayers, though preferably those said in Hebrew, according to the following authorities:

> Rav Judah held that one should not ask his needs in Aramaic, and R. Yohanan said that if he did, he could not be heard by the angels, who do not understand Aramaic.
>
> (b. Shab. 12b)

Since the language of the ordinary people was Aramaic, the insistence of the rabbis upon the Hebrew language required the support of such a warning: If you want the help of the angels, you had better pray in a language they understand. Nonetheless, while numerous formal differences between academic and popular prayer are evident, one can hardly distinguish between the prayerful spirit of the academies and the piety of the streets. In both instances, prayer was regarded as a puissant act. The teachings of the rabbis concerning prayer stressed proper attitude, dress, and conduct, but these teachings could not have run contrary to popular sentiment. Since the rabbi was seen as a holy man, the way in which he prayed and the effectiveness of his prayers would have elicited popular emulation and credulity. Rav Judah would dress himself before he prayed; R. Sheshet would, at the appropriate places, "bow like a reed and rise like a serpent." The earlier rabbis' manner of prayer was remembered.

A number of rabbis composed prayers. R. Sheshet's prayer after fasting was as follows:

> "Lord of the aeons, It is fully revealed before you that in the time when the Temple was standing, a man would sin and offer a sacrifice, and they would present of it only the fat and blood, and it would make atonement for him, and now, I have sat in a fast and diminished my fat and blood. May it be pleasing before you that my fat and blood, which have been diminished, be seen as if I have offered it to you on the altar, and may you be reconciled to me."
>
> (b. Ber. 17a)

Mar Uqba contributed the following prayer for a time of crisis:

> R. Hisda in the name of Mar Uqba said, "Even in the hour that you are as filled with wrath concerning them as a pregnant woman, may all their needs be before you." Some say, R. Hisda in the name of Mar Uqba said, "Even in the time that they are transgressing matters of Torah, may all their needs be before you."
>
> (b. Ber. 29b)

Rav Judah's Tanna recited the following:

> If a man was standing and saying the Tefillah and he broke wind, he waits until the odor passes and begins with the following prayer, "Sovereign of the Universe, You have formed us with various hollows and vents. Well do you know our shame and confusion, that our latter end is worms and maggots." And he begins from the place where he stopped.
>
> (b. Ber. 24b)

This prayer is not described as composed by Rav Judah, but rather as recited before him by the Tanna of his school. It was not widely known, and may have been originally written in his academy. We have several compositions attributed to, or cited by, Rav Judah:

What is the blessing of betrothal? Both Rabin b. R. Adda and Rabbah b. R. Adda in the name of Rav Judah say, "Blessed are you, O Lord, our God, king of the universe, who has sanctified us by his commandments and commanded us concerning forbidden relations, forbidding to a betrothed women and permitting us a woman through marriage by means of canopy and sanctification." R. Aha b. Rabba in the name of Rav Judah completed it as follows: "Blessed are you, Who sanctifies Israel by the wedding canopy and sanctification."

(b. Ket. 7b)

The passage continues:

[Our Rabbis taught: The blessing of the bridegrooms is said in the presence of ten people all seven days.] Rav Judah said, "That is only if new guests come." What does one say? Rav Judah said, "Blessed are you, O Lord, our God, king of the world, who has created all things for his glory ... the creator of man ... who has made man in his image, in the image of the likeness of his form, and has prepared for him out of himself an eternal building [Gen. 2:22, 3:30]. Blessed are you O Lord, creator of man. May the barren greatly rejoice and exult [Is. 54, 61:10, 57:5] when her children will be gathered in her midst in joy [Is. 54:1-3]. Blessed are you, O Lord, who makes Zion rejoice through her children [Is. 62:3-4]. May you make these beloved companions greatly to rejoice even as in ancient times you delighted your creatures in the Garden of Eden. Blessed are you, O Lord, who delights the bridegroom and the bride. Blessed are you, O Lord our God, king of the universe, who made joy and gladness, bridegroom and bride, rejoicing, song, mirth and delight, love, brotherhood, peace and friendship. Quickly, Lord our God, may there be heard in the cities of Judah and in the streets of Jerusalem the cry of joy and of gladness, the cry of the bridegroom and the bride, the cry of the singing of bridegrooms in their canopies, and of youths from their feast of song. Blessed are you, O Lord, who delights the bridegroom with the bride."

(b. Ket. 7b-8a)

For the Day of Atonement, two confessions were cited:

What is the Confession ... Rav Hamnuna said, "My God, before I was created I was unworthy, and now that I have been created, it is as if I were not. I am dust in my life, and more so in my death. Behold I am before you like a vessel filled with shame and humiliation. May it be pleasing before you that I should not sin, and my former sin erase in mercy but not by suffering."

> Rav Judah said, "Our inequities are too many to count, and our sins too numerous for numbering."
>
> (b. Yoma 87b)

Rav Judah's betrothal blessing follows the form, now more widely accepted than ever, of the <u>Berakhah</u>. The brief reference to "his" confession may indicate merely that such was the prayer, among many available, which he selected; or that he composed the brief sentence, contrasting to the confession of Rav Hamnuna. The blessing for betrothal seems more clearly ascribed to Rav Judah, in which case one wonders whether a blessing was said for betrothal before his time, or whether he was in fact adding to the betrothal ceremony. Rav Judah also provided a text for the blessing of the new moon:

> Rav Judah gives it thus: "Blessed ... who created the heavens with his word, and all their hosts with the breath of his mouth. He appointed unto them fixed laws and times, that they should not change their way. They rejoice and are glad to do the will of their maker. They do his work truthfully, for their action is truth. The moon he ordained that she should renew herself as a crown of beauty for those whom he sustains from the womb, and who will be renewed in the future, and magnify their maker in the name of the glory of his kingdom. Blessed are you, O Lord, who renews the moons."
>
> (b. Sanh. 42a)

R. Hisda cited a prayer for the traveler:

> R. Jacob ... in the name of R. Hisda said, "Whoever sets out on a journey should say a prayer for the journey. What is it? 'May it be your will, O Lord my God, to lead me forth in peace, and direct my steps in peace, and uphold me in peace, and deliver me from the hand of every enemy and ambush by the way, and send a blessing on the works of my hands and cause me to find grace, kindness, and mercy in your eyes and in the eyes of all who see me. Blessed are you, O Lord, who listens to prayer.'"
>
> (b. Ber. 29b)

R. Hisda held, according to R. Jacob, that the prayer should be said at the moment that he starts out, but it is permissible to say it until he has gone a parasang. He should say it standing still, though R. Sheshet said he may say it while moving.

Our interest transcends the question of whether or not a given generation made significant contributions to the development of liturgy. What is of greater interest is, What kind of religion is to be inferred from the prayers and rules of praying here considered? One needs first to note the ways in which the rabbis and the ordinary people together shared a common faith. These become most obvious in the compositions of prayers. The rabbis' prayers centered upon four major images, first, the Temple and its cult, second, the wrath of God which was revealed in an hour of crisis, third the humility and helplessness of man, and finally, the corpus of ideas and symbols embodied in the sacred history of Israel.

The spiritual situation of both rabbis and the masses may be described as follows: "We are absolutely worthless, and are now deprived even of the former ways of finding favor with You. Once there was a Temple, and we could offer sacrifice there, but now it is no more, so we must give the sacrifice of our flesh and blood. But who are we to propitiate, who are of no consequence and have no future? We are nothing, except that we are <u>Israel</u>, the children of men you loved, and bearers of the revelation you delivered. And so, even in the most private moments of life, we are not alone, but are surrounded by the merits of the fathers and the presence of memories of the sacred moments of our history. Nor are we hopeless, because we look forward to the fulfillment of the promises made to the prophets in olden times. So we are sanctified in all which we do out of love and loyalty to you. In the hour of our greatest private joy, at the marriage canopy, we remember both the public sorrow and the coming joy of Zion, and recall not only its destruction, but what was said by Jeremiah when it was destroyed, that it will be rebuilt. So if we are sinners, we lie in the hands of a God of great mercy. Even the passage of the seasons, which we witness regularly month by month, testifies to your enduring sovereignty. Just as the moon keeps your laws, so do we, and just as it testifies to the greatness of its maker, so would we. So when we find ourselves in a time of danger, we turn to you and beseech your blessing."

I see no detail in which ordinary people would have either not comprehended, or not believed in the faith of the rabbis as here expressed. While the prayers concerning study of the Torah and the discussions of proper procedures in the academies or of benedictions may not have been understood by the people, the spiritual situation revealed by the rabbis' prayers was precisely congruent, so far as I can tell, to theirs. They too were "Israel," and they revered the Scriptures, and remembered its lessons. They too longed for the coming of the Messiah, and though unable to express their yearnings in the evocative and noble language of the rabbis, they could surely have adopted the rabbinical liturgies without the least difficulty.

The precise and detailed discussions of how and when to pray, the proper blessings to say over one thing or another, the conditions for interrupting prayer and the like -- these represent, more narrowly academic concerns. I doubt that ordinary people were much bothered by the issues posed to the masters, nor did the instruction imparted to the disciples reach a broad audience. To learn the proper way of saying grace proved terribly difficult for many students, and outsiders could scarcely have comprehended all the rules. Indeed, knowing and keeping them was one of the important significations that a person had entered the rabbinical estate. Yet one must not suppose that the issues of the common faith were divorced from the rabbinical discussions, or that the legalistic rabbis really had no very vivid spiritual life. The prayers they composed testify to the contrary. But so too does the seriousness with which they considered the whole matter of prayer. It was precisely <u>because</u> they believed as fervently as ordinary people in prayer that they thought one should pray with at least the decorum and respect shown to an earthly king of kings, and that they seriously inquired into the proper and improper procedures for praying. In this sense, the rabbis' laws represent the continuation of popular faith: if the people believed that prayer mattered, then the rabbis -- who were, after all, lawyers -- set out the rules of conduct and procedure which would conform to such a belief.

Above all, I am struck by the intensity of Rav Judah's prayers concerning the Messianic kingdom. In the liturgy for the marriage ceremony, the center of attention focused upon the coming joy of Zion, which was even one prefigured by the delight of bridegroom and bride. Just as the one loved the other, and rejoiced in that love, so in time would God again espouse Israel in Zion, and rejoice in her. The most private joy of life was thus seen to be paradigmatic for the most public event of coming history. It was the Messianic hope which became most vivid in times of difficulty. If the academic discussions of when the Messiah might come and who he might be seemed less fervent than earlier, still the very deep and abiding longing for his coming characterized master, disciple, and outsider alike. However they might accommodate themselves to the conditions of the current life, the Jews saw it as merely transitory and impoverished. In time to come, the advent of the true and permanent age would inaugurate a time of fulfillment and completion. However private, personal, and ahistorical seem the prayers and discussions of these years, they must be seen against the broader framework of faith in which they found a place. Within the humble affairs of Israel's life here and now, one might, though darkly, discern the shadowed reflections of a great illumination that was to come. Both in and for that light, Jews prayed.

Like other "holy men," the rabbi thus played political, religious, and cultural roles. Just as the Magus was involved in the administration of the local community, in the maintenance of cultic life, and in the study and teaching of Mazdean beliefs and possibly, by this time, Scriptures, so too was the rabbi. While the Magus, however aspired to serve as a significant and influential part of its administration and to constitute its religious arm, the rabbis wanted independently to exercise quite direct and substantial power over the Jewish community.

A more significant parallel is to be drawn to the Christian "religious," the monastic figures who dominated the Christian faith east of the Euphrates and shaped its character. Unlike the Christian monks, however, it was the aspiration of the rabbi <u>not</u> to form a separate society. He kept to himself very little. He did not live in a tight little eschatological community, confidently awaiting the day on which the sinners would know that he was right and they were wrong. He did not, for all his sense of forming part of an elite, look upon the rest of the community as outsiders or less "elect" than himself. At many important points he shared the fundamental convictions of the broader community. What he most wanted was to teach the people how to live up to these convictions as <u>he</u> understood them. So if he was not a sectarian, the reasons was that he aspired to a wider influence than others. He wanted all the Jews to become rabbis. He asked <u>nothing</u> of himself that he felt inapplicable to others, and nothing of others that did not pertain to himself. Herein lies a paradox of the rabbinical "estate." On the one hand, it was separate and, by its own standard, superior. On the other, it hoped to obliterate the distinctions between the rabbinate and other Jews, and believed that every Jew was equally able to achieve "superiority." So its aspiration to political power, at once so partisan and subversive of existing authority, represented a perfectly natural extension of its self-understanding. It was through politics that people might be changed. Through the courts and collaboration with the regime that set them up, the most effective influence might be attained. Indeed, when one seeks to locate the points of contact between the rabbi and the town, he finds them less in the marketplace, synagogue, or in the streets, though the rabbis did not avert their eyes from what happened there, than in the lawcourts. The court is most usefully to be compared to the Southern U.S. county court, that is to say, not only a place of litigation, but also of administration of all manner of affairs. To direct the court represented the most convenient and efficient way of doing what the rabbinate wanted. And yet, as I have emphasized, what the rabbinate wanted was not to <u>control</u> others, who would permanently remain essentially outside its circle, but rather to win others to the viewpoint of its estate, to transform the community into a replica of the academy. The rabbi wanted to bring all Israel closer to their "Father in Heaven," and his traditions provided a very full program on how to do so -- and what to do then.

The ultimate issue, therefore, was not politics, but piety: What must one do to serve God in heaven? Piety was manifested by right action in society, and right knowledge of what right action consisted of, by continual study and reflection upon revelation which defined right from wrong, and by acts of devotion. If the rabbi was the object of divine or angelic favor, that was not authenticated by the miracles he supposedly could perform, though these clearly mattered to everyone, but, in the end, by the rightness of the ideals he advanced in Jewish society. Such was admittedly <u>his</u> viewpoint. And in studying the history of Babylonian Jewry in this or any other period, we know for certain only that viewpoint. As we turn to consider the relationship between the culture of the academies, and the life of the people, we may well keep in mind the conviction of Rav Judah:

> Rav Judah said, "He who would like to be a man of piety (<u>hasida</u>) should carry out the matters of <u>torts</u> (<u>neziqin</u>)."
>
> (b. BQ. 30a)

That is to say, the real issues of faith are truly settled in the civil courts and by law. Doubtless ordinary people would greatly have differed, for their concerns would have centered quite naturally upon the private anguish of common people in any generation: how to sustain life, provide for children, die an easy, dignified death, and achieve "immortality," or a "portion in the world to come," or in some other way to triumph over personal extinction. But paradoxically it was this most private and personal concern which opened the heart of the ordinary man to the message of the rabbis, for they claimed they knew how to attain that last, least accessible hope, through "Torah."

How and in what aspects did the rabbinate actually succeed in achieving its broad social aspirations? Forming an elite of religious and civil leaders, the rabbis combined a tradition of learning with considerable charismatic and magical influence, legal and administrative functions with theological and metaphysical convictions partially expressed in, but much transcending, matters of law. It becomes important to find what analogies may help to illuminate the functioning of the rabbinate among the Jews. The Christian communities in the fourth century began to witness the formation of monasteries and the development in them of a religious elite which served some, but not all, of the functions of the rabbinate. A comparison between the Jewish academy and the Christian monastery is made possible by the researches of Arthur Vööbus, proves that the monastic movement of Syria and Iran developed by the end of the third century, quite independently of the contemporary institutions of Egypt and elsewhere. So it is a particularly appropriate phenomenon for consideration at this point. Both the academy and the monastery constituted the institutions which comprehended the religious virtuosi in their respective communities. In both cases, the participants thought of themselves as embodying the highest and most noble ideals of the faith. Both, furthermore, set themselves up for the emulation of the masses, in the Jewish instance by the very practical exercise of public authority, in the Christian by laying stress upon the sanctity and piety of the encratites, anchorites, and other kinds of monks, who were revered. Both were cultural centers for their respective communities. Vööbus describes the monastic movement as the formative element in oriental Christianity. Predominating in the monasteries was a profound devotion to asceticism. Their huts, cells, and monasteries provided essential social services. The chief contribution of the ascetic movement was its establishment of schools and cultivation of learning and scholarship. It is here that I find the most striking parallel. The monasteries were the intellectual center of Iranian Christianity, and it is their legacy, and practically no other, which comes down to us today. Similarly, whether or not the academies dominated Judaism in their own day or not, it is quite evident that their legacy shaped it from Talmudic times onward.

A detail of some interest is the stress in Christian discourse upon military terminology, involving the use of words such as struggle, fight, battle, and war, a vocabulary shared in the academies, which spoke of the "war of the Torah," meaning, the academic discourse itself. Distinguishing patterns of proper behavior including (in the Jewish case) mourning rites, grace after meals, clothing, conduct with other disciples and with the master, and the like -- all of these find their counterpart in the distinctive behavior-patterns required of the Christian ascetics. The central monastic ideals were, first, virginity including the belief that sexual intercourse in marriage (or otherwise) is unclean; second, stress on other kinds of continence, including avoiding any kind of direct contact with woman. Vööbus says, "In general the ascetics do not accept any service of hospitality from women, regardless of whether they are virgins, single or married, Christian or heathen, the ascetics accept service only from men ... [they] do not stay in a place where there is only one women." All these trends, Vööbus notes, ended in misogyny. These values appear similar to those of the rabbis. Other ascetic practices included scanty food, the menu of Thomas, for instance, consisting of only bread and salt. They did not eat meat or drink wine. Fasting played an important role. The ascetics did not hold possessions, and wore ragged garments; were homeless and frequently vagrants. They abhorred sleep, and ignored hygiene. They had a profound sense of dissociation from the world. The Christian was a warrior against the world, again Vööbus, "In their war and contest they saw something which was working towards the consummation of the cosmic upheaval, something which helped to accelerate the realization of the coming of the Kingdom of God." The ascetics and monks were called "benai qeima" or "benat qeima," sons or daughters of the covenant.

Though it was only later that the monastic schools came into being, the monasteries became great centers for teaching and learning. Postulants were both instructed in Scriptures, particularly Psalms, and initiated into ascetic ways. The schools, Vööbus says, appear as training centers in biblical knowledge. But hagiography, as much as biblical studies, was cultivated. The director of instruction supervised the foundation of schools for children and adults alike. A further monastic concern was to counter dissidence and heresy. Of greatest interest are Vööbus's remarks about the role of monasticism in the religion of the people. The monks were highly influential, both because of their exemplification of the faith, and because of their protest against lax morality and "impure belief." So they were the chief embodiment of the Christian life. "Primitive Christian enthusiasm found refuge in monastic circles." The monastic example kept alive among Eastern Christians a sense for the transience of the world. Their residences attracted great crowds, and their blessings were eagerly sought. The human want and suffering of their lives deeply influenced the religion of the masses. As did the Jews with rabbis, in time of trouble, people would turn to the monks, and trusted in their prayers to do wonders and avert calamities. As martyrs, their remains were especially prized, and the numerous fourth-century monastic martyrdoms produced a cult of relics. The monks were seen as counselors, spiritual fathers, even as mediators who could conciliate God with their prayers. The monks led the movement to liquidate pagan cult objects and places. They made every effort to reach the masses, through public teaching in the streets as well as in the monasteries. These schools enforced a rigid discipline, and all who came to them had to carry out the ascetic standards of the place for the time of their residence.

The academy played an approximately similar role in Jewish community life. But the differences are striking. First of all, it is clear that the monks were not the only Christian religious leaders, for the pastors and hierarchy, extending to the bishops, had equally important roles to play. On the other hand, I know of no evidence that Babylonian Jewry's formal religious leadership included other than rabbis in this period. Second, and more fundamental, the ascetic emphasis of the monasteries finds only superficial parallels among the rabbis. Fasting, as we have seen, was resorted to in time of need, but was never regarded by rabbis as a normal form of piety. Property was not abhorred. While the attitude toward women was the same, marriage was greatly honored, and never is licit sexual intercourse regarded as anything but of the highest value. Indeed, not marrying is much condemned. So the content of monastic ideals was naturally very different from that of the Jewish academies. While both were centers for learning and transmission of authoritative traditions, the specific forms of learning were quite different. In the monasteries books were written and libraries created. Among the academicians, notebooks or brief, unofficial notes existed, but nothing like a library. The exegetical works of the monasteries were written down by single masters or monks. The hagiographic literature took a more central place in monastic writings. The monastic curriculum was considerably broader. Students concentrated on the Bible, but also studies philosophy, including Aristotle, and other fields of Greek learning, history, science, geography, and rhetoric. The rabbis, by contrast, did not write books, but their literature was produced much later on, and in very different forms. The "Tanna" of the academy was a kind of living book, and the stories told of the deeds of the rabbis mostly concerned how they had exemplified one or another legal teaching. The miracle-stories we have noted occupied a very insubstantial part of the corpus of rabbinic traditions. And most fundamental of all, nothing is so characteristic of rabbinic Judaism as its affirmation of the world, and it was upon a fundamental rejection of this world that the monasteries were founded.

The similarities appear to have been mostly functional and neutral. Both were, as I said, centers of study, and their adepts equally embodied piety. The rabbi and the monk served in the imagination of the masses as persons closer to God than ordinary people, and therefore were supposed to be able to entreat God's favor, or mobilize through prayer or superior knowledge of occult sciences natural forces to serve the people's needs. The fantasies of the masses endowed both rabbi and monk with formidable power, and neither did much to dissuade the people from believing in them. Indeed, since each believed that his was the way God really wanted men to live, both probably thought that whatever powers they were believed to have they in fact <u>ought</u> to possess. Rigid patterns of distinctive behavior set apart both rabbi and monk from the masses, and doubtless each was rendered a still more impressive figure on account of such bizarre behavior. In both cases, the political leaders of the respective communities made use of the virtuosi. When a convert showed promise, the bishop normally sent him directly to the monastery for study, and in other ways, the <u>catholicus</u> employed the forensic skills and popular influence of the monks to control the Christian community. The exilarch similarly used the academies to prepare the needed lawyers and bureaucrats. Neither the <u>catholicus</u> not the exilarch wholly subjected himself to the discipline of the academies. The academy and the monastery thus <u>functioned</u> within their respective communities in much the same way. So the obvious differences derived from their respective religious traditions, and the similarities from their equivalent setting and social functions.

Vööbus compares the monastic communities to the Jewish sectarian groups of the pre-Christian centuries, and draws numerous specific parallels between the oriental monks and those who lived at Qumran and the Essenes in general. The rabbinical academies derived quite directly from the Pharisaic academies of the same period. Just as in former times, the Pharisees aspired to enforce their views of law and theology among the masses, so now did the rabbis do the same. Formerly the Pharisees were prepared to cooperate with any government which would place into their hands the actual administration of Jewry, taking a neutral position on matters not directly concerned with day-to-day affairs, much as now the rabbis would cooperate with the exilarch, and by inference, with the Sasanian regime, so long as they could do what they wanted in their courts and schools. By contrast, the sectarian attitudes persisted in the Christian monasteries, which saw themselves not as the practical leaders of "the people of God" but as forming the covenanted community which would attain salvation. They left in the hands of others the everyday management of Christian affairs, so long as they could in the end constitute the highest embodiment of the faith. Despite public preaching, they did not make the effort to come to grips with the life of the ordinary Christians. Their rigid, Manichaean prohibition against marriage, for one thing, made it absolutely necessary for another body of Christians to maintain the natural continuity of the church. He who entered the monastery left the ordinary life of the Christians, and while he hoped that others would join him, he did not return to the "world," but resigned himself to exemplify the right way of life mostly outside of it. So the most striking contrast between monastery and academy lies in the deeply sectarian quality of the former, by comparison to the broad, public concern of the latter. The academy sent its rabbi back to live in "the world," to teach, judge, and bear witness in the streets and marketplace to the doctrines of the school. The monastery sought no such continuing place in the common life, though individual monks did teach outside its walls. The difference is one of focus and normative intent. The academy did not retain its disciples, but always intended for them to go back to the community, which it never supplanted in their lives. Though a school, its books were the people it educated, and its disciples did not copy manuscripts, but men, and sought to make their imprint upon the lives of others. In later times, it would call back student and disciples to leave the villages and attend periodic lectures at the schools. Its literature was produced almost by force of circumstance. The traditions it sought to preserve were scattered abroad, and supposed to be made permanent by their constant impact upon the shape and form of ordinary life.

Conclusion: The rabbis constituted a relatively small group of religious virtuosi, some of whom were appointed by the exilarch to administer Jewish law for the semi-self-governing Jewish millet. These laws primarily concerned marriage, inheritance, transfer of property between members of the community, and validation of documents necessary for these legal transactions. The rabbis further used their influence, which far transcended their practical authority, to persuade the community to consult them on matters of ritual slaughter, menstrual separation, and Sabbath observance.

The area over which the rabbis exerted substantial influence was probably limited to Babylonia itself. It was there that the exilarch possessed authority. While we have references to other exilarchs in Nisibis, and in Apamea in the south, no evidence pertains to rabbis in the latter community, and, for this period, none to the former either. We are explicitly told that Elam produces students, but no rabbis. Furthermore, the intense dislike of the Babylonian rabbis for the Jews in Mesene, Elam, and elsewhere in the south and east suggests that their decrees were roundly ignored, if they were known there to begin with. Whoever decided in the south and east the kinds of legal questions brought to the rabbis in Babylonia, they certainly were not "learned masters of Torah" as the rabbis understood it. I should imagine the Mesenian and Elamite Jews possessed a corpus of law, perhaps developing, as had Babylonian Jewish law before the rabbis arrived, upon the basis of ad hoc Scriptural exegeses and local traditions. That law differed in important ways from the rabbis', which accounts for the prohibition of intermarriage between Babylonian and Mesenian Jews. The Jewish governments elsewhere would have had their own legal experts and apparatus for enforcing the law. If so, one must assume that the Sasanians or local satraps established administrations for other Jewish communities similar to the exilarchate in Babylonia. Each region would have enjoyed complete autonomy, being answerable only to the Persian government. This would explain the fact that "Isaac the exilarch" was quite unknown in Babylonia. Mar Uqba and the other Babylonian exilarchs were probably just as little known elsewhere. It is striking that the Palestinian data contain few, if any, references to inquiries emanating from outside of the Babylonian academies, nor are emigré disciples mentioned who were educated elsewhere than in Babylonia. the Jews outside of Babylonia would have had no direct connections to the Palestinian schools, because, in the absence of rabbis, the Mishnah of R. Judah the Patriarch, which was taught in the rabbinical academies in both Babylonia and Palestine, was not enforced among them. With neither a law in common, nor authorities who looked to Palestine for guidance, the Mesenians, Elamites, and others had no good reason to turn to Palestine and its patriarchate.

The Babylonian rabbis thus constituted primarily a new school of legal interpretation, present in Babylonia from the second century onward. They formed a new school because of the Pharisees' adoption first of Greek methods of legal exegesis, and then of Roman methods of codification. This school was introduced originally by persons close to the Babylonian exilarch. They won his approval, and then were given control of Jewish community courts under his sponsorship by his appointment of persons expert in Mishnaic law as judges. They then used their position, influence, charisma, and legal powers to propagate their opinions in other fields than property and personal status. Their prestige as interpreters of the texts helped them. Extension to other fields came later, both because elsewhere there was no such obvious biblical basis, and because established usage stood in the way. The specific range of rabbinic influence, the political foundations of which we have outlined, can be determined only by a search for the evidences on which of the laws were enforced. While in matters of religion, the rabbis exerted influence, in the courts, their word was law.

PART TWO

THE HISTORICAL STUDY OF FORMATIVE JUDAISM

III

THREE PICTURES OF THE PHARISEES: A REPRISE

The Pharisees formed a group of indeterminate classification (political cult?) in the Jewish nation in the Land of Israel in the century or so before A.D. 70. They are of special interest for two reasons. First, they are mentioned in the Synoptic Gospels as contemporaries of Jesus, represented sometimes as hostile, sometimes as neutral, and sometimes as friendly to the early Christians represented by Jesus. Second, they are commonly supposed to stand behind the authorities who, in the second century, made up the materials that come to us in the Mishnah, the first important document, after Scripture, of Judaism in its classical or normative form. Hence the Mishnah and some related writings are alleged to rest upon traditions going back to the Pharisees before A.D. 70. Whether or not that is the case need not detain us. What is of interest is what we know about the Pharisees and how we know it. The answer is that we have three discrete sources that refer to Pharisees, in order of conclusion (1) the Gospels, (2) the writings of Josephus, and (3) the later rabbinic compositions, beginning with the Mishnah, hence, in time of closure, ca. A.D. 70-90, ca. A.D. 90-100, and ca. A.D. 200-600, respectively. In the end, therefore, we cannot say precisely who the Pharisees were. We have no writings produced by them or descriptions of them as a group deriving from writers of the time in which they flourished, whether in the first century B.C. or the first century A.D. All we do know is what later writers said about them.

Our task is to make critical use of three separate bodies of information: first, the historical narratives of Josephus, a Jewish historian who, between 75 and ca. 100 A.D., wrote the history of the Jews from the beginnings to the destruction of Jerusalem, including the war against Rome which had led to the destruction; second, biographical traditions about, and sayings attributed to, Jesus, assembled in the nascent Christian community between ca. 50 and ca. 90 A.D.; third, the laws and sayings attributed to pre-70 Pharisees by their successors and heirs, the rabbis of late first and second century Palestine.

These separate sources are quite different in character. The first is a systematic, coherent historical narrative. The second is a well-edited collection of stories and sayings. The third consists chiefly of laws, arranged by legal categories in codes and commentaries on those codes. Moreover, the purposes of the authors or compilers of the respective collections differ from one another. Josephus was engaged in explaining to the Jewish world of his day that Rome was not at fault for the destruction of the Temple, and in telling the Roman world that the Jewish people had been misled, and therefore not to be held responsible for the terrible war. The interest of the Gospels is not in the history of the Jewish people, but in the life and teachings of Jesus, to which that history supplies background. The rabbinical legislators show no keen interest in narrative, biographical, or historical problems, but take as their task the promulgation of laws for the government and administration of the Jewish community.

The several sources concerning pre-70 Pharisaic Judaism were generally shaped in the aftermath of the crisis of 70 A.D. With the Temple in ruins it was important to preserve and, especially, to interpret, the record of what had gone before. Josephus tells the story of the people and the great war. The Gospels record the climactic moment in Israel's supernatural life. The rabbis describe the party to which they traced their origin, and through which they claimed to reach back to the authority of Moses at Sinai. The issue in all three cases was: What is the meaning of the decisive history just passed? To Josephus the answer is that Israel's welfare depends upon obedience to the laws of the Torah as expounded by the Pharisees and upon peaceful relationships with Rome. The Gospels claim that, with the coming of the Messiah, the Temple had ceased to enjoy its former importance, and those who had had charge of Israel's life -- chief among them the priests, scribes, and Pharisees -- were shown through their disbelief to have ignored the hour of their salvation. Their unbelief is explained in part by the Pharisees' hypocrisy and self-seeking. The rabbis contend that the continuity of the Mosaic Torah is unbroken. Destruction of the Temple, while lamentable, does not mean Israel has lost all means of service to the Creator. The way of the Pharisees leads, without break, back to Sinai and forward to the rabbinical circle reforming at Yavneh. The Oral Torah revealed by Moses and handed on from prophet to scribe, sage, and rabbi remains in the hands of Israel. The legal record of pre-70 Pharisaism requires careful preservation because it remains wholly in effect.

The theological side to Pharisaic Judaism before A.D. 70, however, is not easily accessible, for the pre-70 beliefs, ideas, and values have been taken over and revised by the rabbinical masters after that time. We therefore cannot reliably claim that an idea first known to us in a later rabbinical document, from the third century and afterward, was originally both known and understood in the same way. For pre-70 Pharisaic Judaism, our sources of information tell little of theological interest. A number of books in the Apocrypha and Pseudepigrapha of the Old Testament are attributed to Pharisaic writers, but none of these documents positively identifies its author as a Pharisee. Secure attribution of a work can only be made when an absolutely peculiar characteristic of the possible author can be shown to be an essential element in the structure of the whole work. No reliance can be placed on elements which appear in only one or another episode, or which appear in several episodes but are secondary and detachable details. These may be accretions. Above all, motifs which are not certainly peculiar to one sect cannot prove that sect was the source. No available assignment of an apocryphal or pseudepigraphical book to a Pharisaic author can pass these tests. Most such attributions were made by scholars who thought that all pre-70 Palestinian Jews were either Sadducees, Pharisees, Essenes, members of the "Fourth Philosophy," or Zealots, and therefore felt obliged to attribute all supposedly pre-70 Palestinian Jewish works to one of these four groups. That supposition is untenable. I omit all reference to apocryphal and pseudepigraphical literature. Perhaps when scholarly progress in the study of that literature permits, we may expand our conceptions about pre-70 Pharisaism.

But for now, the only reliable information derives from Josephus, the Gospels, and rabbinical literature, beginning with the Mishnah, the law-code of Judah the Patriarch. As is clear, none of these gives contemporary account of Pharisaic theology before 70. Josephus concentrates on political questions, and the theological teachings to which he does allude are primarily of a general philosophical character. The Gospels have no interest in Pharisaic theology, and rabbinical attributions of theological sayings to the Pharisaic masters before 70, which are not likely to be reliable, constitute little more than a collection of sage comments, commonplaces of practical wisdom.

At the outset of our inquiry it is best that we seek perspective on the Pharisaic sect in its own setting. Josephus tells us that "more than 6,000 Pharisees" refused to take an oath of loyalty to Herod:

> There was also a group of Jews priding itself on its adherence to ancestral custom and claiming to observe the laws of which the Deity approves, and by these men, called Pharisees, the women of the court [of Herod] were ruled. These men were able to help the king greatly because of their foresight, and yet they were obviously intent upon combating and injuring him. At last when the whole Jewish people affirmed by an oath that it would be loyal to Caesar and to the king's government, these men, over six thousand in number, refused to take this oath, and when the king punished them with a fine, Pheroras' wife paid the fine for them. In return for her friendliness they foretold -- for they were believed to have foreknowledge of things through God's appearances to them -- that by God's decree Herod's throne would be taken from him, both from himself and his descendants, and the royal power would fall to her and Pherora and to any children that they might have....

(Josephus, Jewish Antiquities 17:41-4, trans. Ralph Marcus [Cambridge: Harvard University Press, 1963], pp. 391, 393.)

What was the position of these 6,000 Pharisees in relationship to the mass of the Jewish population?

Morton Smith, the great historian of antiquity, points out that the man who was a Pharisee was not primarily a Pharisee all the time. He presumably played many roles in society. Gamaliel is described in Acts 5:34 as a Pharisee in the council of the Temple. Was he appointed to the council because he was a Pharisee, and thus represented the party or sect there? Or was he a Pharisee who also happened for some other reason, perhaps social distinction or political and economic power, to be appointed to the Temple? Was he then a Temple councillor who also happened to be a Pharisee? What was the meaning of "being a Pharisee" in the lives of various sorts of people? It seems most likely that to be a Pharisee was not a profession, but an avocation.

Pharisaism was, in terms of ancient civilization, a sect within the "philosophy" of Judaism. Smith stresses:

> ...Judaism to the ancient world was a philosophy. That world had no general term for <u>religion</u>. It could speak of a particular system of rites (a cult or an initiation), or a particular set of beliefs (doctrines or opinions), or a legal code, or a body of national customs or traditions; but for the peculiar synthesis of all these which we call a "religion," the one Hellenistic word which came closest was "philosophy." So when Judaism first took shape and became conscious of itself and its own peculiarity in the Hellenized world of the later Persian Empire, it described itself with the Hellenic term meaning the wisdom of its people (Deut. 4:6). To the success of this concept within Judaism the long roll call of the wisdom literature bears witness. Further, the claim was accepted by the surrounding world. To those who admired Judaism it was "the cult of wisdom" (for so we should translate the word "philosophy" which they used to describe it), and to those who disliked it was "atheism," which is simply the other side of the coin, the regular term of abuse applied to philosophy by its opponents.

(Morton Smith, "Palestinian Judaism in the First Century," in <u>Israel: Its Role in Civilization</u>, ed. Moshe Davis [New York: Harper Row, Publishers, 1956], pp. 67-81.)

The Pharisees claimed to be authoritative because they taught a philosophy that derived from Moses at Sinai. They therefore preserved a "chain of tradition" reaching back from their own day to the authority of remote antiquity. Their piety was centered on the revelation of Moses. Smith says:

> It is... not surprising that Jews living, as Palestinian Jews did, in the Greco-Roman world, and thinking of their religion as the practice of wisdom, should think of the groups in their society which were distinguished by peculiar theories and practices as different schools of the national philosophy [pp. 79-80].

Thus Palestinian Judaism overall, and the Pharisaic sect in particular, are to be seen as Jewish modes of a common, international cultural "style" known as Hellenism. To see Palestinian Judaism outside of its context within world civilization is to misinterpret the meaning of its accomplishments. The Jews were not an isolated or provincial people, and their "philosophy" was not incomprehensible, at least in form, to the rest of civilized mankind. The Jews, on the contrary, responded to the challenge of Hellenism by shaping a uniquely Jewish form of that common culture. Nor was this merely in generalities. The

Pharisees, for one, exhibited numerous traits familiar to Hellenistic culture, as Smith points out:

> Not only was the theory of the Pharisaic school that of a school of Greek philosophy, but so were its practices. Its teachers taught without pay, like philosophers; they attached to themselves particular disciples who followed them around and served them, like philosophers; they looked to gifts for support, like philosophers; they were exempt from taxation, like philosophers; they were distinguished in the street by their walk, speech, and peculiar clothing, like philosophers; they practiced and praised asceticism, like philosophers; and finally -- what is, after all the meat of the matter -- they discussed the questions philosophers discussed and reached the conclusions philosophers reached.

> Here there is no need to argue the matter, for Professor Wolfson, in his... classic study of Philo, has demonstrated at length the possibility of paralleling a philosophic system point by point from the opinions of the Rabbis. Now one, or two, or two dozen parallels might be dismissed as coincidental: all men, by virtue of mere humanity, are similar and life presents them with similar problems; it is not surprising, therefore, that they should often and independently reach the same answers.

> But parallels of terminology are another matter, and here we come... to Professor Lieberman's demonstration that some of the most important terms of Rabbinic Biblical exegesis have been borrowed from the Greek. This is basic.... The existence of such borrowings can be explained only by a period of profound Hellenization, and once the existence of such a period has been hypothecated it is plausible to attribute to it also the astounding series of parallels which Professor Wolfson has shown to exist between the content of philosophic and Rabbinic thought.

> In sum, then, the discoveries and research of the past twenty-five years have left us with a picture of Palestinian Judaism in the first century far different from that conceived by earlier students of the period. We now see a Judaism which had behind it a longer period of thoroughgoing Hellenization -- Hellenization modified, but not thrown off, by the revival of nationalism and nationalistic and antiquarian interest in native tradition and classic language (an interest itself typically Hellenistic). As the Greek language had permeated the whole country, so Greek thought, in one way or another, had affected the court and the commons, the Temple... the school and the synagogue.

> If there was any such thing, then, as an "orthodox Judaism," it must have been that which is now almost unknown to us, the religion of the average "people of the land." But the different parts of the country were so different, such gulfs of feeling and practice separated Idumea, Judea, Caesarea, and Galilee, that even on this level there was probably no more agreement

between them than between any one of them and a similar area in the Diaspora. And in addition to the local differences, the country swarmed with special sects, each devoted to its own tradition. Some of these, the followings of particular prophets, may have been spontaneous revivals of Israelite religion as simple as anything in Judges. But even what little we know of these prophets suggests that some of them, at least, taught a complex theology. As for the major philosophic sects -- the Pharisees, Sadducees, and Essenes -- the largest and ultimately the most influential of them, the Pharisees, numbered only about 6,000, had no real hold either on the government or on the masses of the people, and was, as were the others, profoundly Hellenized.

This period of Palestinian Jewish history, then, is the successor to one marked by great receptivity to outside influences. It is itself characterized by original developments of those influences. These developments, by their variety, vigor, and eventual significance, made this small country during this brief period the seedbed of the subsequent religious history of the Western world [p. 81].

We learn from Smith's characterization that the Pharisees were a small group within Palestinian Judaism, a philosophical school with a particular set of beliefs and religious practices. They claimed the right to rule all the Jews by virtue of their possessing the "Oral Torah" of Moses, that is, the body of traditions not written in Scriptures, but revealed to Moses at Mount Sinai along with the written Torah. They referred to a list of masters extending back to Moses, whom they later called "our rabbi." In their own setting, however, the Pharisees were much like any other Hellenistic philosophical school or sect.

Their importance in later times derives from two facts. First, they play a large role in the Gospels' accounts of the life of Jesus. Second, they produced the rabbinical masters who, after 70 A.D., defined the law and doctrine that became normative for the Judaic tradition. Judaism as it is now known begins with the Pharisees of the two centuries before the destruction of Jerusalem and the Temple in 70 A.D.

As to the Pharisees in the Gospels, we may forthwith turn to Morton Smith's summary and conclusions on the matter (in his <u>Jesus the Magician</u> [N.Y., 1978: Harper & Row], p. 157, reprinted in Jacob Neusner, <u>From Politics to Piety. The Emergence of Pharisaic Judaism</u> [N.Y., 1979], pp. 155-159):

> This review of the Gospels' references to the Pharisees has left us with very little material that is likely to come from Jesus' lifetime. From Q we learn that Jesus <u>may</u> have ridiculed their neglect of moral obligations in favor of tithing herbs and cleaning utensils, from Mark, that they <u>may</u> have criticized him and his disciples for violating the Sabbath, and <u>may</u> have questioned him about giving tribute to Caesar. The saying about their leaven, since it connects them with a Herod, is not likely to be genuine. The Herod

Jesus knew was in Galilee, and there is strong evidence that there were practically no Pharisees in Galilee during Jesus' lifetime. A generation later, when the great Pharisee Yohanan ben Zakkai lived there for eighteen years, only two cases were brought to him for decision; he reportedly cursed the country for hating the Law -- it was destined to servitude. Y. Shabbat XVI.8 (15d, end). The story may be a legend -- the curse looks like a prophecy ex eventu of the results of the later revolt -- but at least the legend shows that the Pharisees remembered Galilee before 70 as a land where they had few followers. More important is the evidence of Josephus; it is clear from War II. 569-646, and even more from his Vita (28-406 and especially 197f.), that as late as 66 Pharisees might be respected in Galilee for their legal knowledge (though Josephus' suggestion of this is suspect as part of his pro-Pharisaic propaganda), but they were certainly rare: the only ones Josephus encountered were sent from Jerusalem, and had been chosen to impress the Galileans by their rarity. Thus the synoptics' picture of a Galilee swarming with Pharisees is a further anachronism. John at least avoided this, his Pharisees all appear in Jerusalem, and Jesus goes to Galilee to get out of their reach (4.1ff.).

Josephus's first work, the War, presents a picture of the Pharisees as a political party, active in the court affairs of the Maccabean state. To understand Josephus's account, we must review the history of the Maccabees. The Maccabees, a family that became a dynasty founded an independent Jewish state in Palestine in 165 B.C., and ruled until 63 B.C., when the Romans conquered the country. They came to power as head of a Jewish revolt against Antiochus IV Epiphanes, King of Syria (including Palestine), by whose orders the Temple at Jerusalem had been desecrated and turned into a pagan sanctuary. Antiochus had further decreed that Jews no longer observe the commandments of the Mosaic revelation, the Torah. They could not circumcize their sons, sanctify the Sabbath, and worship one God alone. The animal Jews regarded as most repulsive, the pig, was offered as a sacrifice on local altars and in Jerusalem. The biblical Book of Daniel, written during the period of persecution, tells us that a nameless seer felt the end of time was at hand. Only God's direct intervention could save Israel. In the winter of 166 B.C., the king's agents came to Modin, near Lydda, and set up the pagan altar. When the first Jew came out to offer the sacrifice, Mattathias, a priest, killed him and the king's agent as well. Mattathias and his followers undertook a guerilla war against the Syrian-Greek rulers. Shortly thereafter, Mattathias died, and his son, Judah the Maccabee ("hammer") took over. Owing to his successes, the Syrian government rescinded the persecution of Judaism, and in 164 granted the Jews their former rights.

Judah ignored the decree, retook Jerusalem, purified the Temple, and fortified the city. After a protracted struggle, Judah succeeded in establishing himself and his family as the legitimate regime. When he died in 160 B.C., his brothers carried on the government and made the country independent. In 142 B.C., Simon, the last of the brothers, obtained Israel's complete freedom from tribute. His son, John Hyrcanus, succeeded in

134. John's mother had been a war captive who later married the priest, Simon, though this was contrary to law, since captive women usually were ravished and therefore prohibited to the priesthood.

John "became a Hellenistic prince like his contemporaries and rivals." Each prince strove to expand his frontiers. For his part, John conquered the coastal plain, and, later on, Galilee, Samaria, and Idumea (the biblical Edom). His son Alexander Jannaeus ruled from 104 to 76 B.C., with power extending from the Egyptian border to Mount Carmel, and from the Mediterranean to Trans-Jordan.

The Pharisees at this time, in Josephus's narrative, constituted a political party which sought, and for a time evidently won, domination of the political institutions of the Maccabean kingdom. In other words, however they might hope to <u>teach</u> people to conform to the Torah, they were prepared to coerce them to conform through the instruments of government. Bickerman says, "Early Pharisaism was a belligerent movement that knew how to hate."

When Alexander Jannaeus died, his wife Alexandra Salome succeeded. Here is the point at which Josephus's Pharisees first enter the picture in <u>War</u>, because Alexandra Salome put the government in their hands. They thereupon executed Jannaeus's counselors, who had been their enemies, and exercised power with a high hand. The anti-Pharisaic opposition at this time was led by the queen's second son, Aristobulus. When the queen died in 67 B.C., Aristobulus won the throne. His brother, Hyrcanus, allied to Antipater the Idumean, father of Herod, besieged Aristobulus in the Temple of Jerusalem. The Roman general in the Near East, Pompey, intervened and supported Aristobulus, but he found reason to change his mind and preferred Hyrcanus. The Romans then took Jerusalem in the fall of 63, and the independent government of the Maccabean dynasty came to an end. A few years later, Herod was entrusted with the rule of Judea.

The Pharisaic position was that foreign domination was acceptable, so long as the Torah was the binding law on the Jews. Since the Pharisees also claimed that they themselves determined the substance of the Torah, this position constituted not merely a religious, but also a political claim. In effect they were saying, "We shall rule the country, in collaboration with whatever foreign power is willing to make possible our dominion over the inner life of Israel." We may now understand what Josephus has to tell us in <u>War</u>. The Pharisees occur in three important passages. First, without being introduced or extensively described, but standing without a history, they suddenly make an appearance as the dominant power in the reign of Alexandra Salome. They are later alluded to in connection with the court affairs of Herod. Finally, in Josephus's long account of Jewish sectarianism, the Pharisees receive requisite attention.

In 95 A.D., 20 years after he wrote <u>War</u>, Josephus greatly expanded his picture, adding important details to familiar accounts and entirely new materials as well. To understand the additions, we must recall that at the same time he wrote <u>Antiquities</u>, Josephus was claiming he himself was a Pharisee. Pharisees who survived the destruction of Jerusalem in 70 spent the next 20 years establishing themselves as the dominant group. Led by Yohanan ben Zakkai, they had created a Jewish administration at the coastal town of Yavneh. This administration assumed those powers of self-government left in Jewish hands by the Roman regime. By A.D. 90, the head of the Yavnean government, Gamaliel II, grandson of the Gamaliel mentioned as a Pharisee in the Temple council in Acts 5:34, and son of the Simeon ben Gamaliel alluded to in Josephus's Life as a leader of the Jerusalem government in A.D. 66, had negotiated with the Roman government for recognition as head of Palestinian Jewry. The basis for settlement was the Yavneans' agreement to oppose subversion of Roman rule in exchange for Roman support of the Yavneans' control over the Jews -- the same agreement offered to Pompey in 63 B.C. The Yavnean authorities, called rabbis -- hence "rabbinical Judaism" -- thus continued the Pharisaic political and foreign policies initiated at the end of the Maccabean times. This time, however, the Pharisees met with no competition. The Herodian dynasty had long since passed from the scene. The Essenes were wiped out in the war. The Sadducees, who had controlled the country through their power in the Temple government, lost their power base with the destruction of the Temple and evidently ceased to constitute an important political force.

If one read only War without knowledge of the Life, one might suppose Josephus took most keen interest in the Essenes and certainly sympathized with their ascetic way of life. That surprise would receive support if we knew that he spent three years of his adolescence with Bannus, whose way of living corresponded in important ways to that of the Essenes, though Josephus does not call him an Essene. So one might expect that the great historian regarded the Essenes as the leading Jewish "philosophical school." But he does not. The Essenes of War are cut down to size; the Pharisees of Antiquities predominate. Josephus now says that the country cannot be governed without their cooperation, and that he himself is one of them. Josephus was in fact part of the pro-Roman priestly aristocracy before the war of 66-73. But nothing in his account suggests he was a Pharisee, as he later claimed in his autobiography.

Antiquities has two "philosophical school" passages. The first is brief, interrupting the narrative of Josephus's account of Jonathan Maccabee's agreement with Rome of ca. 140 B.C. The second coincides, as in War, with the beginning of procuratorial government, in the beginning of the first century A.D. Josephus here alludes to a rebellion led by Judas, a Gaulanite, and Saddok, a Pharisee who started a "fourth school of philosophy" in addition to the three already known, namely, a school of people who sought the destruction of Roman rule. The passage thus corresponds in position and function to War 2:162-166. The first of the two accounts is as follows:

> Now at this time there were three schools of thought among the Jews, which held different opinions concerning human affairs; the first being that of the Pharisees, the second that of the Sadducees, and the third that of the Essenes. As for the Pharisees, they say that certain events are the work of Fate, but not all; as to other events, it depends upon ourselves whether they shall take place or not. The sect of Essenes, however, declares that Fate is mistress of all things, and that nothing befalls men unless it be in accordance with her

decree. But the Sadducees do away with Fate, holding that there is no such thing and that human actions are not achieved in accordance with her decree, but that all things lie within our own power, so that we ourselves are responsible for our well-being, while we suffer misfortune through our own thoughtlessness. Of these matters, however, I have given a more detailed account in the second book of the Jewish History.

(Josephus, Antiquities, trans. R. Marcus [Cambridge: Harvard University Press, 1957], 13:171-73, pp. 311, 313.)

Fate, or providence, is thus the primary issue. The three "schools" take all possible positions: fate governs all; fate governs nothing; fate governs some things but not everything. The Pharisees enjoy the golden middle. In the War the Pharisees are given the same position, but there the issue of the immortality of the soul is also introduced.

The second "philosophical school" account is as follows:

The Jews, from the most ancient times, had three philosophies pertaining to their traditions, that of the Essenes, that of the Sadducees, and, thirdly, that of the group called the Pharisees. To be sure, I have spoken about them in the second book of the Jewish War, but nevertheless I shall here too dwell on them for a moment.

The Pharisees simplify their standard of living, making no concession to luxury. They follow the guidance of that which their doctrine has selected and transmitted as good, attaching the chief importance to the observance of those commandments which it has seen fit to dictate to them. They show respect and deference to their elders, nor do they rashly presume to contradict their proposals. Though they postulate that everything is brought about by fate, still they do not deprive the human will of the pursuit of what is in man's power, since it was God's good pleasure that there should be a fusion and that the will of man with his virtue and vice should be admitted to the council-chamber of fate. They believe that souls have power to survive death and that there are rewards and punishments under the earth for those who have led lives of virtue or vice: eternal imprisonment is the lot of evil souls, while the good souls receive an easy passage to a new life. Because of these views they are, as a matter of fact, extremely influential among the townsfolk; and all prayers and sacred rites of divine worship are performed according to their exposition. This is the great tribute that the inhabitants of the cities, by practising the highest ideals both in their way of living and in their discourse, have paid to the excellence of the Pharisees.

The Sadducees hold that the soul perishes along with the body. They own no observance of any sort apart from the laws; in fact, they reckon it a virtue to dispute with the teachers of the path of wisdom that they pursue. There are but few men to whom this doctrine has been made known, but these are men of the highest standing. They accomplish practically nothing, however. For whenever they assume some office. though they submit unwillingly and perforce, yet submit they do to the formulas of the Pharisees, since otherwise the masses would not tolerate them.

(Josephus, Antiquities, trans. L. Feldman [Cambridge: Harvard University Press, 1965], 18:11-17, pp. 9, 11, 13, 15.)

This considerable account adds to the Pharisees' virtues their simple style of living -- the asceticism Josephus had admired -- and deference to the elders; earlier he said the Sadducees were boorish. The issues of providence and life after death, last judgment, and reward and punishment for deeds done in this life are alluded to.

What is entirely new is the allegation that the townspeople follow only the Pharisees, and that the Temple is conducted according to their law. Of this we have formerly heard nothing. With the Temple in ruins for a quarter of a century and the old priesthood decimated and scattered, it was now possible to place the Pharisees in a position of power of which, in Temple times, they had scarcely dreamed. The Sadducees, moreover, are forced to do whatever the Pharisees tell them, for otherwise the people would ignore them -- an even more extreme allegation. Later we shall hear that the followers of Shammai, the rival in Pharisaic politics to the predominant leader, Hillel, knew that "the law really follows Hillel," and therefore all their decisions were in accord with Hillelite doctrine. The allegation of Josephus is of the same order, and equally incredible.

In War Alexandra listened to the Pharisees "with too great deference," and they took advantage of her. They ran the government, but she paid. They wreaked terrible vengeance on their enemies, so many had to flee. In Antiquities 13:399-418 we have Alexander Jannaeus, archenemy of the Pharisees, telling the queen to put the Pharisees in power! Since everyone follows them, she can govern the country effectively if she can win their support. Josephus waxes lugubrious on this very point. No longer do the Pharisees take advantage of the woman's ingenuousness. Now they are essential for her exercise of power. Even Alexander Jannaeus himself would have had a better time of it had he won their support. He advises her to let them dishonor his corpse if necessary, and above all to do anything they tell her. In place of a credulous queen, we have a supine one; in place of conniving Pharisees, we have powerful leaders of the whole nation. The Pharisees are won over, and they win over the masses, even to the extent of eulogizing Jannaeus. What do the Pharisees do with their power? They teach the people to live in accordance with "the tradition of their fathers." John Hyrcanus's and Alexander Jannaeus's work is undone, exiles are called back, prisoners are set free. To be sure, the queen organized a professional army. Josephus adds that the Pharisees sought to avenge themselves upon their enemies, killing one of them and then more, and so the account of Aristobulus's protection of the Pharisees' enemies is included. Somehow, the Pharisees fall away from the account. The mass slaughter of War, in which the Pharisees killed anyone they wanted, is shaded into a mild persecution of the Pharisees' opposition.

The Pharisees now have a different, and more important, place in the account of Herod's reign. They have foresight, and seek to oppose Herod. No one takes for granted that the Pharisees can be bribed. Their foresight, not their love of money, warned them that Herod's family was destined for a bad end (which everyone knew by 95 A.D.). The Pharisees are accused of corrupting people at court, not of being corrupted. Some of them are put to death on that account.

How shall we make use of the materials supplied by Josephus? First we must ask what details may we account for by reference to Josephus's own interests? What does Josephus tell us because he wants to make a particular case? What is credible in Josephus's picture?

> In the War, written shortly after the destruction of Jerusalem, Josephus still favors the group of which his family had been representative -- the wealthy, pro-Roman section of the Priesthood. He represents them... as that group of the community which did all it could to keep the peace with Rome. In this effort he once mentions that they had the assistance of the chief Pharisees, but otherwise hardly figure on the scene. In this account of the reign of Salome-Alexandra he copies an abusive paragraph of Nicholas of Damascus, describing the Pharisees as hypocrites whom the queen's superstition enabled to achieve and abuse political power.
>
> In his account of the Jewish sects he gives most space to the Essenes. (Undoubtedly he was catering to the interests of Roman readers, with whom ascetic philosophers in out-of-the-way countries enjoyed a long popularity.) As for the others, he merely tags brief notices of the Pharisees and Sadducees onto the end of his survey. He says nothing of the Pharisees' having any influence with the people, and the only time he represents them as attempting to exert any influence (when they ally with the leading priests and other citizens of Jerusalem to prevent the outbreak of the war), they fail.
>
> In the Antiquities, however, written twenty years later, the picture is quite different. Here, whenever Josephus discusses the Jewish sects, the Pharisees take first place, and every time he mentions them he emphasizes their popularity, which is so great, he says, that they can maintain opposition against any government. His treatment of the Salome-Alexandra incident is particularly illuminating: he makes Alexander Jannaeus, Salome's husband and the lifelong enemy of the Pharisees, deliver himself of a deathbed speech in which he blames all the troubles of his reign on the fact that he had opposed them and urges the queen to restore them to power because of their overwhelming influence with the people. She follows his advice and the Pharisees cooperate to such extent that they actually persuade the people that Alexander was a good king and make them mourn his passing!

What motivated Josephus's rewriting of War so as to place the Pharisees into a position of nearly absolute power in later Maccabean times? Smith answers this question:

> It is almost impossible not to see in such a rewriting of history a bid to the Roman government. That government must have been faced with the problem [after 70 A.D.]: Which group of Jews shall we support?... To this question Josephus is volunteering an answer: The Pharisees, he says again and again, have by far the greatest influence with the people. Any government which secure their support is accepted; any government which alienates them has trouble. The Sadducees, it is true, have more following among the aristocracy... but they have no popular following at all, and even in the old days, when they were in power, they were forced by public opinion to follow the Pharisees' orders. As for the other major parties, the Essenes are a philosophical curiosity, and the Zealots differ from the Pharisees only by being fanatically anti-Roman. So any Roman government which wants peace in Palestine had better support and secure the support of the Pharisees.
>
> Josephus's discovery of these important political facts (which he ignored when writing the Jewish War) may have been due partly to a change in his personal relationship with the Pharisees. Twenty years had now intervened since his trouble with Simeon ben Gamaliel, and Simeon was long dead. But the mere cessation of personal hostilities would hardly account for such pointed passages as Josephus added to the Antiquities. The more probable explanation is that in the meanwhile the Pharisees had become the leading candidates for Roman support in Palestine and were already negotiating for it....

(Morton Smith, "Palestinian Judaism in the First Century," in Israel: Its Role in Civilization, ed. Moshe Davis [New York: Harper & Row, Publishers, 1956], pp. 75-76.)

The picture of the War therefore contains two important facts. First, the Pharisees had been a political party, deeply involved in the politics of the Hasmonean dynasty. They were opponents of Alexander Jannaeus, but we do not know why, and supported Alexandra Salome, who put them into power, but we do not know for what purpose. In the first century A.D., individual Pharisees remained active in political life. Simeon ben Gamaliel and other Pharisees certainly took a leading role in the conduct of the war. But, strikingly, Josephus makes no reference to the group's functioning as a party within the revolutionary councils. We may conclude that Simeon and others were members of the group, but not the group's representatives, any more than Judah the Pharisee represented the Pharisaic group in founding the Fourth Philosophy. The Pharisees then probably did not constitute an organized political force. Evidently the end of the Pharisaic political party came with Aristobulus, who slaughtered many of them, and was sealed by Herod, who killed even more. From that point forward, so far as Josephus is concerned, the Pharisees as a group no longer played a role in the politics and government of Jewish Palestine.

Second, the Pharisees also constituted a philosophical school. Smith's observation that Jews thought of groups in their society which were distinguished by peculiar theories and practices as different schools of the national philosophy helps us understand the foundations of the Pharisaic polity. As a political party, the Pharisees presumably stood for a particular perspective within the national philosophy. They probably claimed they ought to rule because they possessed true and wise doctrines. The specific doctrines alluded to by Josephus, however, seem quite unrelated to the political aspirations of the group. It is not clear why people who believed in fate and in the immortality of the soul should rule or would rule differently from those who did not, nor is it clear how such beliefs might shape the policies of the state. But evidently what characterized the group -- these particular beliefs -- and what rendered their political aspirations something more than a power-grab were inextricably related, at least in the eyes of their contemporaries.

This brings us to the rabbinic traditions, the third and most voluminous corpus of references to authorities before A.D. 70 believed to have been Pharisees. The reason those who are mentioned in what follows are associated with the Pharisaic group is that at least two of the named authorities of the chain of "Fathers" of M. Abot 1:1-18, Gamaliel and his son, Simeon, are specified as Pharisees by documents external to the literature of the rabbinic movement, Gamaliel by Acts 5:34 and his son, Simeon b. Gamaliel, by Josephus (Life 190-191).

The statements concerning authorities before A.D. 70 contained in the sizable corpus of writings of rabbis of A.D. 200 and beyond generally deal with issues of the inner life of a sect, a table-fellowship group. Other sayings in the vast rabbinic corpus deal with many other matters, and some of these too may represent the views held in a distinctive way by Pharisees before 70. But while that possibility commonly surfaces in writing about the Pharisees, no one has systematically demonstrated it. We are on firm ground in describing solely on the basis of attributions to authorities before 70 what the later rabbis had to say about their predecessors before 70. These in general are assumed to have been Pharisees. Self-evidently, everything we know about the Pharisees before 70 is not exhausted by these sayings. But they do form a coherent and important body of evidence, demanding description, analysis, and interpretation in their own terms.

The rabbinic traditions about the Pharisees before 70 thus are pericopae in the Mishnah and later rabbinic writings in which we find names of either pre-70 masters or the Houses of Shammai and Hillel. Pre-70 masters are the men named in the chains of authorities down to and including Simeon b. Gamaliel and masters referred to in pericopae of those same authorities. Traditions of others who were evidently presumed by the Tannaitic tradents both to have lived before 70 and to have been Pharisees do not add up to much; the traditions are mostly concerned with the masters named in the Pharisaic chains. Few others are known. Authorities who began teaching before 70 but whose traditions derive chiefly from Yavneh, rather than pre-70 Jerusalem, are excluded.

What did the rabbinic traditions have to say about, or attribute to, pre-70 Pharisaic masters? The rabbinic traditions about the Pharisees before 70 A.D. consists of approximately 371 separate items -- stories or sayings or allusions -- which occur in approximately 655 different pericopae. Of these traditions, 280, in 456 pericopae, pertain to Menahem, Shammai, Hillel, and the Houses of Hillel and Shammai; these make up approximately 75% of all. A roughly even division of the materials would give twenty-three traditions in forty pericopae to each name or category, so the disparity is enormous. Exact figures cannot be given, for much depends upon how one counts the components of composite pericopae or reckons with other imponderables. The following approximate figures suffice to indicate that the disproportionately greater part of the rabbinic traditions of the Pharisees pertains to Hillel and people involved with him:

Master	Number of Traditions		Number of Pericopae	
Simeon the Just	10		30	
Antigonus of Sokho	2		2	
Yosi b. Yoezer	4		10	
Yosi b. Yohanan	6		13	
Joshua b. Perahiah	3		6	
Nittai the Arbelite	2		2	
Judah b. Tabbai	7		26	
Simeon b. Shetah	13		38	
Shemaiah-Abtalion	11		18	
Shammai	15		25	
Menahem	2		3	
Hillel	33	61	89	156
Shammai-Hillel	11		39	
Gamaliel	26		41	
Simeon b. Gamaliel	7		13	
Houses of Shammai and Hillel	219		300	
	371		655	

Approximately 67% of all legal pericopae deal with dietary laws: ritual purity for meals and agricultural rules governing the fitness of food for Pharisaic consumption. Observance of Sabbaths and festivals is a distant third. The named masters normally have legal traditions of the same sort; only Gamaliel greatly diverges from the pattern, Simeon b. Shetah somewhat less so. Of the latter we can say nothing. The wider range of legal topics covered by Gamaliel's legal lemmas and stories goes to confirm the tradition that he had an important position in the civil government.

The rabbinic traditions about the Pharisees as a whole may be characterized as self-centered, the internal records of a party concerning its own life, its own laws, and its own partisan conflicts. The omission of records of what happened outside of the party is not only puzzling, but nearly inexplicable. Almost nothing in Josephus's picture of the Pharisees seems closely related to much, if anything, in the rabbis' portrait of the Pharisees, except the rather general allegation that the Pharisees had 'traditions from the fathers,' a point made also by the Synoptic storytellers. The rabbis' Pharisaic conflict-stories moreover do not tell of Pharisees' opposing Essenes, Christians, or Sadducees, but of Hillelites' opposing Shammaites. Pharisaic laws deal not with the governance of the country but with the party's rules for table-fellowship. The political issues are not whether one should pay taxes to Rome or how one should know the Messiah, but whether in the Temple the rule of Shammai or that of Hillel should be followed in a minor festal sacrifice.

From the rabbinic traditions about the Pharisees we cannot reconstruct a single significant public event of the period before 70 -- not the rise, success, and fall of the Hasmoneans, nor the Roman conquest of Palestine, nor the rule of Herod, nor the reign of the procurators, nor the growth of opposition to Rome, nor the proliferation of social violence and unrest in the last decades before 66 A.D., nor the outbreak of the war with Rome. We do not gain a picture of the Pharisees' philosophy of history or theology or politics. We should not even know how Palestine was governed, for the Pharisees' traditions according to the rabbis do not refer to how the Pharisees governed the country -- the rabbis never claim the Pharisees did run pre-70 Palestine, at least not in stories told either about named masters or about the Houses -- nor do they tell us how the Romans ran it. Furthermore, sectarian issues are barely mentioned, and other sects not at all. The rabbis' Pharisees are mostly figures of the late Herodian and Roman periods. In the rabbinic traditions, they were a non-political group, whose chief religious concerns were for the proper preservation of ritual purity in connection with eating secular (not Temple) food, and for the observance of the dietary laws of the day, especially those pertaining to the proper nurture and harvest of agricultural crops. Their secondary religious concern was with the proper governance of the party itself.

By contrast Josephus's Pharisaic records pertain mostly to the years from the rise of the Hasmoneans to their fall. They were a political party which tried to get control of the government of Jewish Palestine, not a little sect drawn apart from the common society by observance of laws of table-fellowship. Josephus's Pharisees are important in the reigns of John Hyrcanus and Alexander Jannaeus, but drop from the picture after Alexandra Salome.

But the Synoptics' Pharisees appropriately are much like those of the rabbis; they belong to the Roman period, and their legal agenda are virtually identical: tithing, purity laws, Sabbath-observance, vows, and the like.

The rabbinic tradition thus begins where Josephus's narrative leaves off, and the difference between them leads us to suspect that the change in the character of Pharisaism from a political party to a sect comes with Hillel. If Hillel was responsible for directing the party out of its political concerns and into more passive, quietistic paths, then we should understand why his figure dominates the subsequent rabbinic tradition. If Hillel was a contemporary of Herod, then we may commend his wisdom, for had the

Pharisees persisted as a political force, they would have come into conflict with Alexander Jannaeus. The extreme rarity of materials of masters before Simeon b. Shetah, except those of Yohanan the High Priest = John Hyrcanus, suggests that few survived Jannaeus's massacres, and that those few did not perpetuate the policies, nor, therefore, the decisions of their predecessors. Hillel and his follows chose to remember Simeon b. Shetah, who was on good terms with Salome, but not his followers, who were almost certainly on bad terms with Aristobulus and his descendants, the leaders of the national resistance to Rome and to Antipater's family (see Josephus's story of Aristobulus's protection of the Pharisees' victims). As Herod's characteristics became clear, therefore, the Pharisees must have found themselves out of sympathy alike with the government and the opposition. And at this moment Hillel arose to change what had been a political party into a table-fellowship-sect, not unlike other, publicly harmless and politically neutral groups, whatever their private eschatological aspirations.

All this is more than mere conjecture, but less than established fact. What is fact is that the vast majority of rabbinic traditions about the Pharisees relate to the circle of Hillel and certainly the best attested and most reliable corpus, the opinions of the Houses, reaches us from that circle's later adherents. The pre-Hillel Pharisees are not known to us primarily from the rabbinic traditions, and, when we begin to have a substantial rabbinic record, it is the record of a group very different from Josephus's pre-Hillelite, pre-Herodian party.

We have three chains of Pharisaic tradition, that is lists of names of authorities in succession, to each of which names is given an opinion. The first (M. Hag. 2:2) is a list of six pairs, Yosi b. Yoezer and Yosi b. Yohanan, Joshua b. Perahiah and Nittai the Arbelite, Judah b. Tabbai and Simeon b. Shetah, Shemaiah and Abtalion, Hillel and Menahem, Shammai and Hillel; the opinions are to lay or not to lay hands on the festival offering before slaughter on the Sabbath. The subscription assigns to the first the office of patriarch, to the second the office of "father of the court." The latter office is never elsewhere referred to in the rabbinic traditions about the pre-70 Pharisees. The former occurs only with regard to Hillel's rise to power in the Temple.

Meir and Judah refer to the list. Meir knew nothing of the Hillel-Menahem clause. Meir's list is a secondary development. Instead of Hillel-Menahem, he has Hillel-Shammai.

The second lists, on uncleanness, have only six names, three pairs: Yosi b. Yoezer and Yosi b. Yohanan, Simeon b. Shetah and Judah b. Tabbai, and Shammai and Hillel. The form calls for decreed uncleanness plus objects: land of the peoples, metal utensils, uncleanness on hands, respectively.

The moral sayings of M. Avot 1:18 are explicit in linking Yohanan b. Zakkai, or Gamaliel and Simeon b. Gamaliel, to Hillel. They take for granted that the latter two were his heirs and successors, although nothing in the early traditions of any links him to Hillel through either stories or citations of legal teachings. Simeon b. Gamaliel was represented by his son, Gamaliel II, as a Shammaite. It looks to me as if the predominance of Hillelites later on called for the establishment of a relationship between Hillel and the authorities who came between him and the Yavnean Hillelites, so Gamaliel I was made his son, Simeon b. Gamaliel his grandson, and -- in a different circle -- Yohanan b. Zakkai into his successor (still later, his outstanding disciple).

Simeon the Just appears in ten traditions occurring in thirty pericopae. The Simeon-traditions relate primarily to the Jerusalem Temple and cult: he prepared a red-heifer sacrifice; heard in the holy of holies that a decree was annulled; saved the Temple in the time of Alexander; served forty years as high priest; and predicted his own death on the basis of his supernatural experience in the cult. His son founded the Temple of Onias. Only the story of the guilt-offering of a worthy Nazirite stands apart -- but not far -- from Temple-materials. The Nazir-story is told in the first-person, a unique narrative in the rabbinic traditions about the Pharisees. Simeon appears in a pericope attested by Meir, referring to the heifer-sacrifice. He made a new ramp for each offering; since he was a good high priest, the practice was not extravagant.

No Simeon-pericope reveals forms that might derive from before 70 A.D. M. Par. 3:5, for example, is in the form given it by Judah the Patriarch on the basis of a dispute of Meir and the sages. But the heavenly message, though said to have come in Aramaic, then is translated into Hebrew and is attested in Josephus -- but not for Simeon the Just. It may represent an old tradition taken over in Tannaitic times and assigned to Simeon. The pericope in which it occurs is composite and was formed no earlier than Ushan times, if then.

For the rabbis Simeon the Just marked the end of the legitimate priesthood. From his time on some priests were, and some were not, acceptable. The Tannaic tradition about him is wholly narrative, primarily "historical"; it contains no legal or exegetical materials, nothing to indicate Simeon was other than a high priest admired by Pharisees.

Antigonus of Sokho has one tradition in one pericope. Apart from his appearance in M. Avot 1:3, Antigonus occurs only in ARN Ch. 5, where the theological question is explored, Why is there no reward in the world to come? The beginnings of the Sadducees and Boethusians are traced to dissension about this problem among Antigonus's disciples.

Yose b. Yohanan occurs only with Yose b. Yoezer, in four traditions, which come in ten pericopae: (1) the end of the grapeclusters, augmented by the tradition on the reproach against the grapeclusters; (2) the decree on the uncleanness of the land of the peoples and of glassware; (3) laying on of hands on the sacrifice; and (4) the sayings in M. Avot 1:4-5. Yose b. Yoezer occurs alone in an additional six traditions, occurring in a total of thirteen pericopae, for a total of ten traditions in twenty-three pericopae. Yose b. Yoezer's uncleanness-saying is attested at the very beginning of the Yavnean stratum by Eliezer b. Hyrcanus. It is simply a list of three rulings, which probably circulated as a group, as in M. Ed. 8:4: the ayil-locust is clean, liquids in the Temple shambles are clean, and touching a corpse makes one unclean. This list seems to me to supply a model for Pharisaic legal traditions before the Yavnean revisions, one of two available examples of a pre-Yavnean formulation of laws; the other is Yohanan the High Priest's abrogations. It is a brief list, on a single subject -- uncleanness rules -- and appears without an exegetical foundation, but rather with the name of an authority. Perhaps other Pharisaic legal materials came down in much the same form, namely, as brief lists of related laws attributed to an important authority. The list contains no contrary opinions, no discussion, and no generalizations. The use of Aramaic is uncommon; DKY should be THR, SB should be TM. The words occur only here in the rabbinic traditions about the Pharisees. But they are not rare in the Mishnah, especially in M. Bekhorot. The Qumran laws, given without attributions to authorities, are similarly arranged in little lists on a single theme.

Other materials pertinent to both Yoses consist merely of references to the two masters. They stand at the end of the grapeclusters, a theme of importance to Ushans, and Yose is called the most pious of the priesthood.

His disinheriting his son is a tradition consisting of two sentences tied fore and aft to a story bearing no relationship to that tradition, about his son's gift to the Temple. The tradition would be represented by the sayings, Yosef b. Yoezer had a son who did not behave properly and Yosef b. Yoezer brought in one and his son took out seven. The story told in between these two sayings has to do with the son's exemplary behavior in giving to the Temple a substantial sum of money. The story should tell of how Yose's son had deprived the Temple -- or someone -- of money which his father had originally donated. Whatever story we should have, the one we do have exhibits no relationship to the key sentences and evidently is told by someone who has no direct knowledge of whatever tradition is 'encapsulated' in the fixed lemmas. This then gives us a hint as to the way in which generalized traditions, perhaps conveying themes of some sort or other, might produce specific, but quite novel, accounts. The fixed traditions prove of little, if any, help in formulating those accounts. The story of Yaqim of Serurot, Yose's "nephew" may have been assigned to Yose because he and Yaqim derived from (or are assigned to) the same town. Otherwise there is no relationship to Yose. But on account of Yose's origin in Serurot, Yose is made to be carried out to be hanged. Thus stories of how Jewish martyrs, presumably of the Bar Kokhba period, died brave deaths, while those who looked on without sympathy either died ignominious ones or committed suicide, might be told of Yose as well. The whole is a mélange of late themes and clichés; the historical Yose has contributed only his name.

Yohanan the High Priest is nowhere identified as John Hyrcanus. For the rabbis he was both a high priest and a Pharisee. He has six traditions in fifteen pericopae. The most important of these concerns his cultic abrogations of the confession and of certain questionable procedure in slaughtering. The heavenly-echo story, which Josephus assigns to John Hyrcanus, is given by the rabbis in closely similar form to Yohanan. The other four traditions are all mere allusions to Yohanan's name: he prepared a red-heifer; he is mentioned by Yohanan b. Zakkai (the sole reference of Yohanan b. Zakkai to a pre-70 Pharisee); he ended up a Sadducee after eighty years in the high priesthood, a conclusion that evidently followed from Yohanan b. Zakkai's calling him a Sadducee; and the medieval Scholion to Meg. Ta. has a little story of Yohanan the High Priest as a well-meaning but inept legislator. So the 'Pharisaization' of Yohanan the High Priest comes down merely to the record of his abrogations, which produces the assumption that he was a good rabbi, and further leads to the development of other materials around his name. The pericope in M. M.S. 5:15 containing the abrogations is a simple list of 'three things' he did, in historical language; it recalls the Yose-uncleanness-ruling pericopae, and, as I said, may reflect the way in which pre-70 materials were formulated and transmitted before the Yavnean stage.

Nittai the Arbelite occurs only alongside Joshua b. Perahiah, in two traditions in two pericopae, M. Avot and M. Hag. Joshua in addition has three traditions in six pericopae, a saying on wheat from Alexandria, on the difficulty of giving up high office, and the flight to Alexandria at the time of Yannai's murder of the Pharisees. This last makes him a contemporary of Simeon b. Shetah, then not <u>nasi</u>, and involves him with his disciple Jesus, thus further making Jesus into a rabbinical disciple of the second century B.C., or Joshua into a rabbi of the first century A.D. The Jesus-story has an attached tradition, <u>Jesus practised magic</u>, etc., which does not refer to Joshua, and none of the details of the Joshua-Jesus story is alluded to in the summary-sentence, <u>Whoever sinned and caused others to sin</u> etc.

A tradition that Joshua was a great magician persisted, but left no trace in rabbinic literature. That both he and Jesus were connected with magic probably explains why Jesus was made his disciple. This tradition reached Jews in Babylonia, who called upon Joshua's name to exorcise demons. His appearance on the Jewish magical bowls of Nippur, written in the sixth or seventy century A.D., is unwarranted by rabbinic stories about him, which make him a standard rabbinical figure.

Judah b. Tabbai similarly appears only along with Simeon b. Shetah; he has no traditions for his own and sometimes is dropped from Simeon-materials where he should appear, in favor, for example, of Shelomsu the Queen. Simeon-Judah traditions are seven, counting sayings in M. Avot 1:8-9 and M. Hag. 2:2; these occur in twenty-six pericopae. Two Simeon-Judah traditions are closely related, first, putting a man to death illegally, second the anomaly of the law with respect to circumstantial evidence. The role of each in the Pharisaic government was debated. Judah is sent to Alexandria, instead of Joshua b. Perahiah; and the uncleanness decree on metalware is credited to him, though not in all versions of that chain.

Simeon has in addition thirteen traditions, occurring in thirty-eight pericopae. Of these, two are similar to Josephus's stories about John Hyrcanus and the Pharisees and Herod and the Pharisees, the former so close as to suggest dependency. Clearly, later rabbis supposed Jannaeus and Simeon were contemporaries. Abbaye identified Jannaeus with John Hyrcanus, which would account for the use of a Hyrcanus-story with Simeon. Of the thirteen traditions, Simeon is central in the ones about hanging eighty women in Ashqelon, the decree on the marriage contract, the story of Simeon, Yannai, and the Nazirites, the trial of Yannai for his slave's murder, and the vanquishing of the Sadducees, a medieval fantasy. In the others Simeon contributes merely a name: it rained heavily in his time, he rebuked Honi, in his day property litigations came to an end, he decreed children should go to school, and he returned a pearl to a Saracen. What is striking is that while Simeon appears, in all, in twenty traditions, the matter of Hillel makes an impression on none of these. Simeon-traditions form an independent corpus. While many of them obviously are rather late (e.g. the hangings in Ashqelon) or certainly derivative (e.g. the Yannai-materials), some of them are both centered upon Simeon and important, e.g. the Nazirites and Yannai, the decrees on the marriage-contract, and other legal matters. Simeon therefore stands as an independent authority, and not a minor one, in the mind of the rabbinic historians. But the exact nature of his legal traditions was not clear. Most of Simeon's materials are "historical," rather than legal. He has no standard legal lemmas or significant exegetical traditions.

After Simeon b. Shetah, the figure of Hillel nowhere is wholly absent from traditions of important Pharisaic masters. Of the eleven Shemaiah-Abtalion traditions in eighteen pericopae, Hillel is present in, or glossed into, three; M. Avot and M. Hag. account for two more, and the latter certainly leads to Hillel-Shammai. So we are left with six traditions in which Hillel is absent; of these, a legal item, on setting apart an animal or a bird for festival use, pertains to a matter of law discussed by the Houses of Shammai and Hillel. A saying on Heave-offering, cited by Yose, and a precedent on administering the bitter-water rite to a suspected adulteress stand independent of the Hillel-corpus. In addition we have an important Scriptural exegesis, on the faith that merited the splitting of the Red Sea; the story of the high priest who insulted Shemaiah and Abtalion, and the allegation, glossed into a pericope from which the two were originally absent, that they were descended from Sennacherib. One enigmatic tradition has Judah b. Dortai, otherwise unknown, criticize S + A for not ruling as he thought they should. The two masters are rarely separated at all. In this respect they carry to an extreme the tendency of materials on earlier authorities to be attributed jointly to the two regnant authorities; while Joshua and Simeon in several traditions stand separately from their colleagues, S + A have only one.

The Honi-the-Circler-corpus consists of the M. Ta. 3:8 story about his rain-making, which is developed in various later versions, but not substantially changed. Nothing in that version makes him into a Pharisee, and the traditions do not allege that he was a Pharisee.

Menahem occurs only in M. Hag. 2:2 and produces an additional gloss, in both Talmuds, about what happened to him after he "went forth."

Shammai by himself has fifteen traditions in twenty-five pericopae. Hillel stands in the background of many of these. Shammai appears by himself and as a fully respectable authority primarily in respect to Sabbath-rulings. Nearly all narratives about Shammai form part of the Hillelite polemic. Shammai is represented as subordinated to the authority of 'the sages'; his precedents are made into private preferences, without legal weight. His legal sayings are juxtaposed to those of his House in such a way as to suggest either that Shammai and his House differ, or that Shammai is more stringent than his House, or that Shammai is a crypto-Hillelite. He is further shown to be weak, unable to accomplish desirable changes in the law. The tendency to revise materials into hostile accounts continues into Amoraic times. A favorable story about Shammai and Jonathan b. Uzziel, told in Palestine, is turned into a very unfriendly account in the Babylonian circles of Pumbedita, though I think the reason has to do with the politics of Babylonian rabbinic

Judaism, not with the historical Shammai. So Shammai-traditions apart from Hillel and the matter of the Houses are not much different in quantity or character from those of earlier, pre-Hillel Pharisaic masters, Joshua b. Perahiah or Judah b. Tabbai. Simeon's corpus is substantially richer than those Shammai-materials which reflect a neutral or favorable opinion about him. Hillel's tradents, presumably at Yavneh and afterward, denied to Shammai more than a negligible position in the traditions, except on Hillelite terms. This makes all the more striking the immense and balanced picture of the traditions of the House of Shammai handed on by the Yavnean tradents.

Hillel by himself has thirty-three traditions in eighty-nine pericopae. Hillel's materials include legal traditions and exegeses, exegeses turned into narratives; legal precedents; biographical traditions; and a huge corpus of moral and theological logia, which, except for M. Avot 1:1-18, far outweighs all moral and theological logia assigned to all other masters put together. The traditions center on the theme of Hillel's rise to power, Hillel as paragon of virtue, model for legal and moral behavior, and authority in legal and exegetical matters, particularly with reference to ritual cleanness, tithing, and keeping agricultural rules and taboos. Hillel's emigration from Babylonia is everywhere taken for granted, but we have not story about when or why he came.

The Hillelite indictment of Shammai and his House primarily pertains to non-legal matters. In legal pericopae Shammai and Hillel are treated as equals, just as are the Houses. The historical and biographical materials are another matter. Here Shammai's vice serves as a foil to Hillel's virtue. Shammai lacked power. He differed from his House. Shammaites were violent and prevailed, when they did, only because of their superior numbers and force. Good Shammaites knew the law was really as taught by the House of Hillel. A bad Shammaite was called the first-born of Satan. Shammai's precedents are dismissed either because they apply only to Shammai himself, or because they prove the law is correctly taught by the House of Hillel. Because of their superior rationality and moral character, the Hillelites sometimes change their views and follow the reasoning of the Shammaites. The Shammaites never do so. When Hillelites do, to be sure, it is because the change is to a position in consonance with other Hillelite opinions, or is in fact no change at all, or because the Shammaites explicitly accept Hillelite precedents. In the end the Hillelites triumphed because they were kindly, modest, and open-minded, also because Heaven itself announced that the law follows Hillel.

Shammai and Hillel appear together, as I said, in a few legal pericopae, in which the two are fairly balanced, and otherwise, in polemical materials directed against Shammai and his House. In all, the two masters share eleven traditions in thirty-nine pericopae. The legal materials pertain to uncleanness and agricultural matters. Later tradents explain that the source of the disputes between the Houses was inadequate study with Shammai and Hillel. They develop the laying on of hands dispute into narratives in which Hillel obeys the Shammaite law because he is forced to. The striking omission is of the Temple priests, who actually ran things. We are told that the internal politics of the Pharisaic sect dominated even the cult. Either Shammaites or Hillelites ran -- and would run -- the cult, but not the priests and Sadducees to whom it was supposedly entrusted.

The Romans are unrepresented in the mob-scenes, but a single Shammaite put matters right, a fantastic picture. Shammai-Hillel decrees pertain to uncleanness of the hands; they argue about, or agree on, the uncleanness off vintaging grapes for the vat. Otherwise the corpus consists of stories in which Shammai's vices contrast to Hillel's virtues, or Shammai's rules are shown inferior to Hillel's. One beraita makes Simeon Gamaliel and Simeon Hillel's sons and heirs. This takes for granted the M. Avot sequence and the descent of the patriarchate from Hillel, therefore it must be relatively late in the formation of the traditions.

Gamaliel I occurs in twenty-six traditions in forty-one pericopae, some of which may not refer to him, but to his grandson. The Gamaliel-corpus consists primarily of stories and allusions to Gamaliel, not of rulings in standard legal form. His place in the traditions is not infrequently merely within the redactional formula. While most of his predecessors rule on uncleanness laws and agricultural matters, Gamaliel also has important rulings about receiving testimony on the New Moon, marriage and divorce rules and procedures, preparing a Targum for Job, letters on the leap-year, permitting the use of drinking vessels which had been used for gentile wine, and other matters outside of the legal framework established by the antecedent materials. Some of these legal materials, e.g. family law, are congruent to the figure of a Pharisaic master who also held a position in the Sanhedrin, as Acts reports of Gamaliel. That Gamaliel was a Pharisee is attested in the same place, so it is unlikely that he was an outsider anachronistically and retro-actively 'Pharisaized', like Honi or possibly Hanina b. Dosa. Gamaliel may have been the conduit through which rulings on matters formerly outside of the range of Pharisaic legal interest entered the party's traditions. A number of stories place him in the Temple or in Jerusalem. Several fables about Gamaliel with a king or the king and the queen may relate to Gamaliel I; telling such fables may rest upon a generalized tradition that Gamaliel, like Simeon b. Shetah, had something to do with the court or the government; their absence may reflect the (accurate) view that other figures, such as Hillel, did not. Simeon b. Gamaliel has seven traditions in thirteen pericopae, including the Avot-sayings. All materials are stories about him: how he lowered the price of doves, how he gave peah, how he dealt with a non-believer with respect to the eruv, how he juggled, blessed a pretty gentile woman, and the like. His son, Gamaliel II, further tells stories of his house's conformity to the rulings of the House of Shammai.

Clearcut and well-defined forms were used for the transmission of the Houses-ma-terials, Hillel-pericopae, and related data. The single striking formal characteristic of the whole corpus is, of course, attribution to named authorities; this applies throughout -- by definition. The form developed for such attributions, namely, X says, produces the dispute-form (Statement of problem, X says... Y says...), the debate form (They said to them... They said to them...), and related forms. All are well-attested at early Yavneh and are used primarily for Houses-materials, secondarily for the masters standing behind the Houses, finally for later first-century authorities. The Houses-form (The House of Shammai say... The House of Hillel say...) comes when the Houses are of roughly equal strength, so that the form used for the transmission of their opinions will give parity to both sides. This seems to derive from early Yavneh, both because it is attested in the earliest Yavnean stratum, and because it is at that point that the Houses came together evidently as equals to reconstruct the tradition, both at the same strength. Before then, Shammaites prevailed, afterward, Hillelites. The whole corpus of earlier materials characteristic of the respective Houses was transmuted into the joint Houses-form, with the Houses' opinions given on a mutually determined agenda of legal problems, and with an antithetic relationship preserved throughout.

A second Yavnean form used for Pharisaic material is the ordinance, appropriate for Yohanan b. Zakkai-decrees, but entirely inappropriate for most Pharisaic pericopae to which it is applied.

The testimony-form seems primarily the creation of the circle responsible for M. Ed., though it would seem that the form had appeared before the second half of the second century, at which time finished pericopae of disciples of Aqiba were included in M. Ed., forming the foundations of that tractate.

Chains and lists, so far as these may be regarded as forms, are presumably old but are preserved at the earliest from the time of Shammai and Hillel.

Precedents do not exhibit a single fixed form; they function in a well-defined way, but that is not the same thing.

Techniques of story-telling and other narratives are of a different order; they are not forms and characterize the whole range of materials before us.

Forms for the citation of Scripture seem primarily redactional in origin; they differ from one document to the next and are consistent within the respective compilations. Where we do have a well-defined form for Scriptural pericopae, it appears primarily in Hillel-materials. Thirty-three of thirty-five exegeses for legal purposes are attributed to Hillel, Shammai, or the Houses.

Not only do most of the forms we are able to isolate derive from Yavneh, specifically from the circles responsible for the redaction of the Houses' antithetic pericopae, but evidence of mnemonic techniques first occurs in precisely the materials produced by those same circles. First, as I said, the form of the apodoses of Houses-pericopae invariably is: House of X say... House of Y say... Furthermore, the actual opinions of the Houses normally are balanced opposites, or other mnemonic devices are used to set up the same balance. Some of the patterns derive from a balanced number of syllables. Others are conventional syzygies, such as unclean/clean. Still others involve fixed changes in morphological or syntactical elements. Approximately 105 pericopae do not exhibit any sort of mnemonic formula or pattern; approximately 82 exhibit some sort of pattern, generally external to the substance; and 314 pericopae contain small units of tradition or other highly disciplined mnemonic forms. In all, Houses' and Hillel-Shammai-pericopae normally exhibit mnemonic patterns or are balanced in some way or other. Pericopae of other named masters are apt not to be balanced or to exhibit other mnemonic patterns. Thus the evidence indicates that, although these forms and patterns were used in pericopae produced by later masters, the Yavnean tradents in clearcut literary forms and who created the common lemmas in such a way as to facilitate memorization and transmission.

This does not prove that the Yavnean materials originally were orally formulated and orally transmitted. Part of the corpus seems to me to have been ritually shaped according to the myth of how Moses orally dictated, and Aaron memorized, lemmas, namely, those in the Aqiban Mishnah. But the allegation that the present rabbinic material about the pre-70 Pharisees consists of the written texts of traditions originally orally formulated and orally transmitted is groundless. The only allegation we find about pre-70 Pharisees is that they had traditions. Nothing is said about whether these traditions come from Moses, nor about whether they were in oral form. They generally are ascribed to the 'fathers,' and their form is not specified. No mention of an Oral Torah or a dual Torah occurs in pre-70 pericopae, except for the Hillel-and-the-convert story, certainly not weighty evidence. Moreover the Pharisaic laws contain no instructions on how materials are to be handed on, nor references to how this actually was done. Allegations that Moses dictated an Oral Torah to Aaron in much the same way as rabbis taught Mishnah first occur with Aqiba, who in fact undertook exactly that process in the formulation of his Mishnah. The myth of oral formulation and oral transmission is first attested by Judah b. Ilai, although a dispute between Eliezer and Aqiba presupposes oral formulation and transmission in Yavnean circles.

We are moreover able to verify the existence of the larger part of the Houses-corpus both at Yavneh and Usha. The verifications exhibit a uniform pattern. Types of laws attributed to the Houses at Yavneh are the same types attributed to them at Usha. The Houses-form was not used as a mere mnemonic device, to facilitate the memorization of traditions of any sort, but was reserved for the redaction of materials on a few themes on which the Yavneans and Ushans evidently believed the Houses actually legislated. This further justifies our attribution of the forms and mnemonic patterns to Yavnean tradents. But we cannot suppose that a great part of the rabbinic tradition has been left in its pre-70 form. On the contrary, I take it for granted that the individual Houses preserved records of their own opinions not in juxtaposition to the opinions of the opposing House, just as did Qumranians. The model would be the uncleanness-saying of Yose b. Yoezer, perhaps also the three abrogations of Yohanan the High Priest. But the Shammai-Hillel-Houses-corpus of laws follows a single form, and that is, the dispute -- even using it where the opinions of the Houses do not differ. It follows that the people responsible for the Houses-dispute-form and the mnemonic small units inserted in it also recast the whole of the antecedent tradition in this form, obliterating the earlier forms of whatever materials they had. This makes it all the more striking that the earliest, and substantial verifications come from the disciples of Yohanan b. Zakkai and their contemporaries, at the very outset of the Yavnean tradition.

If Yavneans and Ushans were meticulous in reporting the Houses' disputes, they were not equally careful to preserve a balanced picture of the period from Hillel to the destruction of the Temple. The picture they produced is the work of Yavneans more than of Ushans. It reflects intense competition between Yavnean Hillelites and the Shammaite opposition. Evidently the Hillelites predominated at Yavneh but had to overcome the common recollection of Shammaite predominance before the destruction. This they accounted for through a number of vicious stories about Shammaites' use of force and even murdering their Hillelite opponents. It is striking that the generation (if not the same tradents) responsible for the carefully balanced disputes also produced entirely unbalanced stories. The thematic authenticity of the laws seems to me beyond doubt. The historical accuracy of the stories is similarly to be affirmed, for their picture of pre-70 politics seems to me plausible, albeit prejudiced. Along with the latter, however, goes the body of anti-Shammaite polemic, much of it Yavnean, and most of it probably grossly exaggerated if not wholly false. We may conjecture that the legal material with its fixed forms is the official product of the Yavnean academy in which the parties, under Yohanan b. Zakkai's leadership and the pressure of necessity, cooperated, and that the stories and propaganda, in less fixed forms, represent what was then the private gossip of the Hillelite party, and only later, with the triumph of that party, got into the official tradition. But this is only conjecture.

Our picture of the rabbinic traditions about the Pharisees therefore is clear. Perhaps beyond those traditions we may even gain a perspective on part of pre-70 historical Pharisaism. The traditions pertain chiefly to the last half-century or so before the destruction of the Temple -- at most, seventy or eighty years. Then the Pharisees were (whatever else they were) primarily a society for table-fellowship, the high point of their life as a group. The laws of table-fellowship predominate in the Houses-disputes, as they ought to -- three fourths of all pericopae -- and correspond to the legal agenda of the Pharisees according to the Synoptic stories. As we saw, some rather thin and inadequate traditions about masters before Shammai-Hillel persisted, but these do not amount to much and in several cases consist merely of the name of a master, plus whatever opinion is given to him in the chain in which he appears. The interest of the non-legal materials concentrates on the relationships of Shammai and Hillel, on the career of Hillel, and related matters. Materials on their successors at best are perfunctory, until we come to men who themselves survived to work at Yavneh, such as Hananiah Prefect of the Priests and, of course, Yohanan b. Zakkai. The chief interest of Hillel-tradents, apart from the preservation of favorable stories of Hillel and the attribution of wise sayings to him, was Hillel's predominance in Pharisaism. After the Houses-disputes ceased to matter much, by the Bar Kokhba War, the growth of Hillel-materials was undiminished. The rise to power-stories then begin, very likely at Usha, and are rapidly glossed by patriarchal and anti-patriarchal hands, so that by Judah the Patriarch's time everyone knows Hillel is the ancestor of the patriarchate in general, and of Judah in particular. The attribution of a Davidic ancestor to Hillel naturally means that the patriarch Judah also derives from the Messianic seed. The work of Yavneh consisted, therefore, in establishing viable forms for the organization and transmission primarily of the Houses-materials. The Ushans continued to make use of these forms, and further produced a coherent account of the history of the Orah Torah from Moses onward. The Yavneans probably showed greater interest in the development of stories about the relationships between the Houses than did later masters, for whom the disputes were less interesting. The Ushans may have augmented the traditions of other early masters, besides Shammai-Hillel, and otherwise broadened the range of interests.

So, in all, we have from the rabbis a very sketchy account of the life of Pharisaism during less than the last century of its existence before 70, with at most random and episodic materials pertaining to the period before Hillel. We have this account, so far as it is early, primarily through the medium of forms and mnemonic patterns used at Yavneh and later on at Usha. What we know is what the rabbis of Yavneh and Usha regarded as the important and desirable account of the Pharisaic traditions: almost entirely the internal record of the life of the party and its laws, the party being no more than the two factions that predominated after 70, the laws being mainly rules of how and what people might eat with one another.

IV
THE HISTORY OF A BIOGRAPHY
YOHANAN BEN ZAKKAI IN THE CANONICAL LITERATURE OF FORMATIVE JUDAISM

This name occurs with authorities of Judaism who are assumed to have flourished both before and after A.D. 70, so R. Yohanan ben Zakkai is associated with that period as well. We have no reliable information at all about him, because he left no writings of his own, and contemporaries and disciples also produced no records redacted in his lifetime or shortly after his death. A sequence of references to him in much later writings, beginning with the Mishnah (ca. A.D. 200), fills out a picture in diverse ways. What we do know, therefore, is what later authorities, beginning with his disciples, are alleged to have said about him or imputed to him. Any picture of the man, his doings and doctrines, therefore, finds detail in portraits drawn by others, on the basis of their interests and concerns.

Among these, we may point, in particular, to such near-contemporaries as Eleazar b. Arakh and his circle, Eliezer b. Hyrcanus and his, and Joshua b. Hananiah, to all of whom are attributed sayings or stories involving Yohanan ben Zakkai. One must treat as part of the picture also the views of representatives of the priesthood who had survived the destruction of the Temple, on the one side, and surviving followers of the house of Hillel, on the other. Yet another, somewhat later group, is constituted by the authorities who flourished after the Bar Kokhba War, ca. A.D. 135-160, and, finally, for the period in which the Mishnah was closed and brought to publication, authorities around the figure of Judah the Patriarch. Let us now survey what each of these sets of authorities, within the first century and a half of Yohanan ben Zakkai's lifetime, had to tell about him.

<u>Eleazar b. Arakh (Emmaus)</u>: Eleazar's circle concentrated on the mystical and moral side of Yohanan's teachings. The <u>Merkavah</u> vision based on Ezekial 1, (without the substance of the mystery, to be sure), the good way-evil way sayings, and words of comfort when Yohanan's son died -- these are the substance of Eliezer's contribution. Exegeses, legal sayings, Yavnean decrees, stories of Yohanan's life and work -- none of these occurs. The Yohanan ben Zakkai of Emmaus was a mystic and a homilist, a moralist and a visionary. He was neither a lawyer nor a teacher nor a judge. He played no part in great historical events. Eleazar himself likewise seems to have conformed to this view of the master. While his students do not preserve stories of "how the master did so and so, just like <u>his</u> master Yohanan," in the manner of Eleazar's school, nonetheless we discern a striking resemblance between Yohanan ben Zakkai and Eleazar, the moral master, the mystic visionary, who came to Emmaus rather than struggling in Yavneh.

<u>Eliezer b. Hyrcanus</u>: For Eliezer b. Hyrcanus's circle, the master and the master's master, Yohanan, were much the same. Both played an important role in the legislative

activities of the day. The work of Yavneh was advanced by Yohanan, "just as did Eliezer his disciple after him;" the legislation of Yohanan himself as well as his legal traditions were carefully preserved. But the Yohanan who saw the Merkavah and heard voices calling him to heaven -- of that Yohanan ben Zakkai we hear not a single word. Eliezer was no mystic. He was a lawyer, judge, staunch defender of the traditions he received. And the Yohanan of Eliezer ben Hyrcanus's circle set the precedent. The law of tithing came from Moses; the priests required careful instruction on the law; a few important exegeses of legal and theological interest were likewise handed on. Yohanan, and Eliezer after him, never said anything his master had not said first; he never neglected his tefillin; and he never saw the Merkavah; he probably never played a great role in historical events; but faithfully, against all odds, preserved the true traditions of the law.

Joshua b. Hananiah (Yavneh): Joshua's traditions stand between the mystical and moral Yohanan of Eleazar on the one side, and the traditional, legal conservative Yohanan of Eliezer on the other. Joshua's Yohanan saw the Merkavah, but also taught important laws, exegeses, and moral rules which only later on were recognized as valid. He was responsible for the Yavnean ordinances about the lulab and Day of Waving and struggled with the priesthood. In all, like Joshua himself, Joshua's Yohanan never withdrew from, but took a vigorous part in, political life, gladly facing up to the opposition and overcoming it. Like Joshua, Yohanan lived a deep and mystical inner life. He served as lawyer and judge; and above all, he attended to the needs of the day through the Yavnean legislation.

The Yohanan of the several disciples' schools or circles thus conformed to the lives the several disciples actually lived later on. This rather general judgment requires refinement in closer study of the lives of Joshua and Eliezer, in particular; since Yohanan appears in almost all Eleazar-materials, we are on firmer ground in comparing the disciple's view of the master to the later disciples' traditions about the disciple, Eleazar himself.

Hostile priests and/or Hillelites: A number of stories may have been given their primary form by priests hostile to Yohanan, by Gamaliel and his friends, or by both. Among these stories were those about the garments in which the heifer is sacrificed, and about how "Ben Zakkai" conducted a murder trial. The hostile-priestly tradition, later revised by both of Yohanan's chief disciples in several ways so as to reflect credit on him, thus was concerned with the heifer-ceremony. I imagine that in the years immediately preceding the war of 66, some ceremony took place in the Temple, and a Pharisee presumably criticized the conduct of a ceremony, saying the priests did not do it according to "the whole Torah." The priests would then have paid slight attention. But after the war, the incident must have been remembered and dramatized by priestly circles to demonstrate the incapacity of even Yohanan ben Zakkai himself to claim to have directed the cult, or to direct once again what would be done in the Temple. If the story was told, it was quickly taken up by Yohanan's circle, as I said, and then given a far more satisfactory form.

It is striking that Hillelites (Gamaliel II, for instance) never seem to have shaped stories about Yohanan as did the disciples Eliezer, Eleazar, and Joshua. We indeed do not have a single statement handed on by Yohanan in Hillel's name. Since, at least according to Eliezer, Yohanan never said anything he had not first heard from his master, and since his master was supposedly Hillel, that fact is striking. It would suggest that no one was interested in attributing to Yohanan any sayings in Hillel's name. The Hillelite house would have been the obvious candidate for the preservation, fabrication or invention of such attributions. Those friendly to Jonathan b. Uzziel and hostile to the Hillelites said Yohanan was Hillel's youngest, or least, disciple and passed silently by the actual heirs of Hillel: Simeon b. Gamaliel, Gamaliel, and Simeon b. Gamaliel. The Hillelites, in the persons of Gamaliel II, Simeon b. Gamaliel II of Usha, and Judah, as well as the circles of masters close to the patriarchate -- these important authorities said nothing whatever.

But it is equally important that none of Yohanan's disciples claimed Yohanan ever quoted Hillel. This must mean that in the context of Yavneh, after A.D. 70, they did not choose to link their master's authoritative statements to those of any former master whatever, including Hillel. It was one thing to assert Yohanan received the Torah, that is, normative authority, from Hillel. It was quite another to admit that anything Yohanan ever said required anterior precedents, and this the disciples never confessed. On the contrary, Eliezer advised the consistery of "that day" not to doubt its rightness, for Yohanan taught him -- in the name of Moses, but not of Hillel! -- just what they had concluded.

I think the circles that might have cited Hillel-Yohanan sayings failed to do so for opposite reasons. Both the disciples of Yohanan and the heirs of Hillel either suppressed what they had or failed to fabricate what they did not have. The former must have preferred to ignore their master's alleged dependence on Hillel, thus avoiding the inference that they now should subordinate themselves to Hillel's heir. The latter must have wanted to avoid any unnecessary reference to the "fact" that Hillel had neglected their own forebears in favor of their present (or, immediately past) competition for authority in Yavneh. Further study of the formation of the Hillel sayings may make clearer the original context in which Hillel's sayings actually were handed on.

The generation of Usha (ca. 140-180) is represented in sayings imputed to Yohanan by Judah b. Ilai and Joshua b. Qorha. Both men concentrated on the Yavneh ordinances. We may safely say that interest in the Yavnean laws was greater now than earlier. Since authorities of Usha, after 135, were responsible for issuing a number of new taqqanot in the manner of Yohanan, the sages probably devoted more attention to the study -- possibly including fabrication -- of what Yohanan had done in the earlier disaster. But I see no direct connection between the content of the decrees now attributed to Yohanan and the circumstances of Usha. It is probably the more general need to issue taqqanot, rather than any search for specific precedents for what the Ushans actually needed to do, that accounts for their increased interest in Yavnean decrees. Perhaps, additionally, Judah's interest in Yohanan's Galilee experience, reflected in the Arav materials, was provoked by the establishment in Galilee of rabbinical centers. A search for early precedents for the new situation may have elicited concern for the Yohanan of Arav.

Sayings attested by <u>Judah the Prince and his circle</u> (ca. A.D. 170-210) all make the same point: Yohanan had great authority in the Temple. He furthermore was friendly with Judah's ancestor, Gamaliel (whether the first or second was intended hardly matters), certainly a new fact. Thus Yohanan's role in Jerusalem before 70 was of special interest to Judah. Judah's and his circle's interest in that particular question probably was provoked by the possibility that the Temple might in fact be restored. We do not know whether Judah was really friendly with "Antoninus," but we do know that he achieved excellent relations with the Romans. It is not out of the question that Judah hoped to use his influence with the imperial government to secure permission to restore the Temple, now that the after-effects of Bar Kokhba's war had been forgotten. He may well have maintained that while the Romans could not entrust the project to revolutionaries, they could well trust Judah, their proven friend, and the sages around him. And this would certainly have solidified his rule over the Jews, for what war had failed to accomplish, the Hillelite heir would have won. Indeed, since Judah claimed to descend from David -- and was worried about the equivalent claim of the Babylonian exilarch -- his expected success in rebuilding the Temple would have been widely interpreted, with his encouragement, to mean that he was the Messiah. We do not know whether he openly sought permission to restore Jerusalem, but it is beyond doubt that he would have profited from doing so and would have been unwise to fail to consider the consequences for Jewish government.

It therefore was useful to point to the role of Yohanan in the earlier war. Even then, had the Romans placed into power a wise sage such as Yohanan, he could have prevented the great upheavals. With this in mind, Judah may have further stressed that if and when the Temple is rebuilt, he and the subordinated rabbis, not the ancient priesthood, would in fact run it, just as Yohanan ben Zakkai had done one hundred fifty years earlier. That may be why the bulk of the new material in the Mishnah and Tosefta, of which Judah was sponsor, pertains to this issue.

Babylonians played so great a role in Judah's court that a <u>homer</u>-explanation, attributed to Yohanan, of how Babylonian Jews came to Babylonia in the first place, must have easily been provoked. It was not a very friendly exegesis: Jews are there only because their ancestors played the whore, so were sent back where they came from -- where they belonged. The exegesis appears nowhere else and may be pseudepigraphic in origin.

It is difficult to know whether Judah's circle or some later students bear responsibility for any of the <u>Fathers According to R. Nathan</u> (ARN) materials. The collection of sayings about the need to plant a sprout before receiving the messiah, avoiding pride, and the sins of the householders, is all quite new, and if the sayings have no roots in earlier materials, and if ARN also dates from this period, then it would not be farfetched to suppose Judah's circle is in some degree responsible for the sayings. It would be easy enough to trace the anti-Messianic saying to Judah's court, for it is quite congruent to

Judah's interests and policies. But is equally useful in earlier and later settings, and for much the same reasons. The other sayings could be related to Judah's interests. The escape-story obviously conforms to the patriarch's Roman policy.

The principal documents beyond the Mishnah and its closely associated writings comprise the two Talmuds, the one of the Land of Israel, the other of Babylonia. If we now ask what stories and sayings about Yohanan ben Zakkai first occur in these and related documents, that is, of the third and fourth centuries and beyond, we find a number of fresh details.

Authorities of the rabbinical circle in the town of Pumbedita, a center of Talmudic literary activity in the fourth century, from start to finish took a remarkably keen interest in Yohanan ben Zakkai. Yohanan-traditions cited at Pumbedita and nearby Mahoza pertained to bringing food to the Sukkah, with Gamaliel; the eighty disciples of Hillel; the family of Eli saved by Yohanan's advice; the struggle with the Bene Bathyra; the decrees on the Day of Waving and Lulab; Gamaliel's acceptance of Yohanan's rule that one does not call into session courts to deal with priestly marriage practices; Yohanan's approval of Hanan's ruling; praise of Yohanan's court (this may not be Pumbeditan, but the pertinent Mishnah paragraph certainly was discussed there); Yohanan's procedure in examining witnesses at a murder trial; the prince's sin-offering; the Ben Bukhri dispute about the priests' paying a sheqel; Yohanan's practice of greeting everyone in a friendly way; Yohanan's teaching in the Temple mount's shadow; the Shiur Qomah saying; the escape story (b. Git. 56a-b); and the dispute about the census.

We may thus describe the Yohanan ben Zakkai of Pumbedita-Mahoza: He was closely associated with Hillel, as the leading disciple, and with Gamaliel (I). Gamaliel II accepted his authority. His decrees at Yavneh and his disputes with the priests about their offerings to the Temple show that he was the leading authority over priests and patriarch alike. He was obeyed and respected not only by the Hillelites, but also by the assembled sages of Yavneh. In Temple times, he could give the stamp of his approval to the decrees of the "sons of the high priests." His court was worthy of special praise, and his court-procedures elicited close interest. His mysticism may have attracted some attention because of a Pumbeditan, Raba's, interest in similar doctrines. The escape story was subjected to Joseph's criticism, but Yohanan's escape was nonetheless regarded as the means by which some small salvation was achieved in the debacle of 70. He held princes (Jewish rulers) should confess even unwitting sins.

The Yohanan of Pumbedita was, therefore, primarily a political figure, a judge and administrator, rather than a mystic, moralist, or legislator. What interested the Pumbeditans was, specifically, Yohanan's relationships with the Hillelite house and the priesthood, his discipleship at Hillel's school, his subsequent position of equality with Gamaliel I and dominance over Gamaliel II. If we did not know that the Pumbeditans were involved in a bitter struggle with the Davidic stoic of Babylonia, the exilarch, we might have supposed some such difficulty lay at the root of the Pumbeditans' interest in Yohanan. But, in fact, what is known about Pumbedita is precisely this: its half-century effort to raise its own funds and to preserve its independence from the exilarchate. The stories and references to Yohanan conform to that effort and serve its cause. Simply translating Gamaliel, Hillel, and the like to <u>the Davidic exilarch</u>, we find that the rabbi, or collegium of rabbis, is here alleged in times past to have been superior to the exilarch; to have even been selected disciple of the Davidide to the exclusion of the exilarch; to have proved equal to the high priest of old; to have judged at the best court of the day; to be worthy precedent in murder trials (and the only known murder trial of Babylonian Jewish history came toward the end of this period). The prince-exilarch is to be praised if he confesses his unwitting sin and brings a sin-offering, and happy the generation whose prince does so (-- would that ours did!). Torah and good deeds avert the curse of the house of Eli -- that and not the blessing of the priest or king-messiah. The rabbi, not the exilarch, decrees what is to be done about troublesome priests. In other words, Yohanan-sayings and stories served the Pumbeditans as important precedents in their struggle with the exilarch, for it is clear that his relationship to Hillel and the Hillelites provided a vital example of what ought even now to be the case in Babylonia.

It seems to me that the disproportionate interest in Yohanan at Pumbedita in the same period had no equivalent provocation in Palestine, or, if it did, the issues were argued in a different way. In any event, it is a fact that Pumbedita bears by far the largest -- practically sole -- responsibility for the Yohanan-references in the Babylonian Talmud, and Pumbeditans may even have formed some of the <u>beraitot</u> as we now have them. So far as I can tell, no similar interest in Yohanan was localized at any other Babylonian or Palestinian academy.

No element in the unfolding tradition on Yohanan b. Zakkai is without historical consequence, but the significance is for different issues. If we ask, Who was Yohanan ben Zakkai? What did he do? How did he respond to the events and issues of his time? Then we must turn primarily to the early second-century data. That does not mean we find unequivocal and unambiguous answers, for we have no writings of Yohanan, no sayings demonstrably redacted under his authority and transmitted at his instructions, no eye-witness accounts of historians, biographers, or other relatively reliable informants. But it does mean that, standing among the chief disciples, not long after the master's death, while the issues of his actual life and times still lived, we may listen to the recollections of men who knew what they were talking about and whose motives in saying what they did in a measure may be discerned. The first collections of materials, therefore, present responses both to the man and to the times of those who made the collections. The later ones respond to their own setting but contain little, if anything, derived from Yohanan's life and context. They contain exact and entirely valuable information on the mind of the later schools and how later masters found it pertinent and meaningful to tell about Yohanan. A critical biography of Yohanan ben Zakkai would have to rely mainly on the former; an intellectual history of talmudic Judaism on the latter as well.

Relying on the former, however, the biographer will still not gain much. The earliest materials, in Mekhilta, Sifra, Sifre, Mishnah, and Tosefta, are generally not very primitive, but already show the marks of considerable development. Rarely do the earliest components of the tradition appear to stand pretty much in their original state. For instance, "the whole stones/iron" homilies occur in both Aqiban and Ishmaelean forms; the Aqibans clearly altered the tradition to suit their view of war and the Torah. Yohanan's essential idea was that peace-makers perform the function of the altar; the Temple and its instruments can be replaced by human virtues. This, I assume, is Yohanan's original message. But it occurs only in the document of a school fifty years after the event (or more). Early exegeses of Scripture normally were taken up and given dramatic settings, a sign of later development. "Events" in Yohanan's life, such as his forgetting Temple laws, turn out to have been stories told about him by hostile parties, then revised by friendly ones. Many such stories reveal more about partisan politics at later Yavneh, Usha, and Beth Shearim than about Yohanan in Jerusalem or in early Yavnean times. Yohanan's homilies show independent development of an original anecdote; sometimes we can isolate the original element. We are never able to demonstrate that the element was how things actually happened. On the contrary, not infrequently even the original element reveals signs of development. Some materials, to be sure, seem to have come from pre-70 Jerusalem, but they survive in so generalized a form that the original setting and polemic have been removed or lost.

Two themes seem to me historically well founded on the actual life of Yohanan ben Zakkai, first, the opposition to the war of 66-73, second, the promulgation of decrees afterward. These decrees clearly were meant to take account of the destruction of the Temple. The former so permeates the traditions that it attains the status of an axiom. If Yohanan really did not oppose the war of 66-73, then he contributed his name, if nothing else, to the formation of traditions about a man who did. The second is better founded on form-critical analysis, for the traditions about the Yavnean decrees include some decrees, innocuous in content to be sure, in most primitive and undeveloped form; these appear in the earliest documents in that form, recurring unchanged later on, and were discussed, even emulated, from the end of the first-century onward.

Two further themes seem to me probably related to Yohanan's own life and thought, the Merkavah vision and the homer-exegeses. That Yohanan was a mystic is attested by the apparent competition shown by their revision of Hillel-stories to denigrate Yohanan's role and highlight Jonathan's. This fact and the preservation of the Merkavah stories in Aqiban circles and afterward constitute two different and unrelated sorts of evidence pointing toward the same conclusion. The homer-materials, while highly formalized, lay a strong claim to historical relationship to Yohanan. Both the content and peculiarities of form suggest so.

The relationship of Yohanan to Aqiva dominated the formation of traditions in the first century after Yohanan's death. Aqiva recurs in numerous items in the early tradition, shaped not around what Yohanan said, but rather around what Aqiva said about what Yohanan said. As noted, important early stories are revised in Aqiva's school to conform to the policies of the later master.

The second-century materials, while on the whole not interrelated, thus evolved not at random or episodically, but in relationship to living traditions about the master and to genuine concern for what he had said and done. Later on, the Yohanan-tradition developed into the Yohanan-legend: stories were invented out of whole cloth, exhibiting little or no relationship with what had gone before. The most striking invention is the story of Yohanan's escape from Jerusalem, which first occurs in Amoraic times, possibly very late. The sole "fact" we should have known had we access only to Tannaitic collections was that Yohanan opposed the war. Within a century or so, this had become the elaborate account, replete with conversations and dramatic episodes, of b. Git. 56b and elsewhere. The beraitot are another achievement of this stage. Also characteristic of the second stage in the formation of the Yohanan-story was discussion of materials in the first stage; talmudic masters studied some of the materials, e.g. from the Mishnah-Tosefta, in their final form. So the second stage was marked by two quite different sorts of activity, first telling accounts fabricated out of, but independent from, older materials, second, discussing quite old, entirely completed ones.

The third and final stage is constituted by the materials in which Yohanan was merely a name, to be used for the purposes of pseudepigraphy. The escape story related to the fact of Yohanan's opposition to the war and was probably necessitated by the question, How did Yohanan survive the destruction? The stories of Yohanan's evaluation of the red-heifer sacrifice and his encounter with Temple authorities, but contrast, exhibit no similar relationship to what had gone before. The later midrashic collectors either took over without much alteration what existed in earlier collections or made up, without any attention to "facts", whatever they liked. The old was copied without discussion: the new was fabricated without manifest concern for the existing corpus of materials.

The historical question is not the only one of interest. On the contrary, three sorts of "lives" of Yohanan ben Zakkai are possible, and all are interesting. The first is the account of the actual man: What can we say with some certainty about his life and opinions? The answer is meager but not unavailable. The second is the story of the life of the man after his death: What importance did he have in the mind of the immediate disciples and those who followed in later schools and communities? The answer consists of a considerable corpus of facts, for the sources accurately testify to the mind of the schools of the second, third, and fourth centuries that produced them. The third is a composite portrait of the first two, done for the purposes of characterizing the phenomenon that produced the whole: Who was a hero to the rabbis of late antiquity? How did they preserve their views? What religious values are revealed? What reality did their imagination perceive, then shape? The third kind of biography in a measure depends upon the results of the first two, but really constitutes a quite different historical statement. It is a statement given in the context of the history of religions, for the study of which the question, Did these things "really" happen? is not important. What is important is the question, What view of reality shaped the minds of men who told these stories, lived by these laws, believed these myths? Each of the three "lives," to be sure, is critical, but the criticism in each instance is different. All of them together may contribute in the end to the interpretation of both the data and the men who created them.

V
WHEN TALES TRAVEL
THE INTERPRETATION OF MULTIPLE APPEARANCES
OF A SINGLE SAYING OR STORY IN TALMUDIC LITERATURE

I
The Problem

Some sayings and stories pass from one document to the next. They gain or lose weight as they make the journey. At hand is a substantial problem, perhaps still more complex than the relationship of books of the Bible that go over the same matters, for instance, Deuteronomy as against parts of Genesis through Numbers, or Chronicles as against Samuel and Kings, not to mention the four Gospels' use of material in common. What do the changes indicate and what do they mean?

In another age the problem of parallel versions of what we now think was a single event (or, more accurately, a single original tale) found an easy solution. If we have three versions, then we know about three events. Hence in the received Gospels' scholarship comes the famous postulate that, in addition to the Sermon on the Mount, Jesus preached a Sermon on the Plain. In the Hebrew Scriptures, the slightly diverse versions of the Ten Commandments kept long generations of preachers gainfully employed. The several versions of creation and of human and Israelite history supplied by J, E, P, and D challenged the wits of harmonizing exegetes for many centuries. The theory of simultaneous enunciation of the Ten Commandments in Exodus and in Deuteronomy ("Keep" and "Remember" the Sabbath day being stated by a single voice at a single moment!) kept at bay inappropriate doubt for so long as people did not give way to doubt. But what began as a serious answer to a challenge to faith in the literal and linear historicity of the biblical tale long ago had come to signify poetry and theology, no longer to allow people to write history.

In the rabbinical canon, by contrast, historians even now take several versions of a story to indicate one of three possibilities.

Either the sage at hand went around saying the same thing a lot. Thus if the same saying occurs in four passages but in the same sage's name, that sage said it four times ("he often used to say"). If the same saying is placed into the mouths of two different sages, then "X and Y agreed that ...."

Or several versions of a saying or story demand integration and harmonization to supply the single reliable and accurate account of what really happened. That is to say, when we can reduce the versions to their "original" form, we not only account for the (possibly later) revisions. More important, we know pretty much accurately what had actually been said or done.

Or (very commonly nowadays) we account for the inclusion of each detail of a saying or story -- among a variety of diverse details -- by making up a theory on where and how, by whom and for what purpose, a given detail "might" or "would" have been added. Let me spell out this third approach to the problem of the thrice-told tale, because it is characteristic of the last century of scholarship and stands as the foundation of much work even now. When we have a long sequence of versions of a single matter, for instance the vision of the chariot described by Ezekiel as that vision was interpreted by Eleazar b. Azariah to Yohanan b. Zakkai, each successive shift and change in the version appearing in the earliest document to contain it will demand, and receive, a manufactured explanation.

The first of these three theories of the meaning and historical significance of the peripatetic saying serves mainly among the yeshiva-primitives and the Israeli Talmudic historians. It hardly demands serious scrutiny. It falls into the class of marvels and wonders, along with "Keep" and "Remember" in a single act of speech. Theologians and decisors of law harmonize, drawing on all sources to make one point. Others do not have to do so. People interested in the formative history to which stories and sayings attest had best not do so. Our work demands studied description, analysis, and interpretation -- and not a leap of faith.

The second theory is a datum, mostly among the same circles. It hardly contradicts the first but depends on the same fundamentalism.

The third proves popular among the more critical and up-to-date historians of the Jews in late antiquity and of the law and religion, Judaism, in that same period. It is, to say the least, premature, because it rests on infirm foundations. How so? The assumption that each detail testifies to a given historical event or moment, different from other details in the same literary construct, assumes two things. First, the details -- it is postulated -- represent things that really happened. So the premise reveals that same literalist fundamentalism that the allegedly modern historians reject. Second, it is assumed that the text at hand from the beginning was preserved exactly as it was written. Any change exhibited by a later version of a saying or story has, therefore, to find its explanation in a later event or a fresh setting. Changes do not just happen, they are made, and therefore for reason. The people who make them do so for reasons that the scholar can report (as we shall see, commonly on the basis of no evidence whatsoever). Nothing lacks "significance" of the present sort, and everything demands its explanation. No explanation covers everything; each item demands an ad hoc interpretation of its own. So the text is studded with histories, each supplied for its distinct occasion, none proposing to harmonize with or relate to the last or the next. Accordingly, it is theorized, people took a text and rewrote it as new things happened or in new circumstances. They then handed it on to others who did the same.

This literary theory awaits any sort of sustained argumentation, not to mention documentation. But it generates such scholarship as now flourishes on the problem at hand, alas. In connection with the third theory of how to interpret the shifts and turnings of a single story or saying in its movement across the canon, I take up a current example of "incremental history" and show how it actually works. The example derives from the newest generation, the work of an autodidact. So I cannot be accused of calling up ghosts or invoking long-repudiated approaches to refute an abandoned theory. What I think becomes clear is that the theory I call "incremental history," is "talmudic" in the worst sense. That is, it is <u>ad hoc</u> merely made up, just as the Talmud itself makes up history to explain several versions of one saying. Indeed, for all its claim to think in fresh and free ways, the newest generation, as represented here, botches the work. In its bungling, the latest Talmudic historians, as exemplified in what follows, display an intellectual incompetence rarely matched in the earlier, in other ways more credulous and more primitive, age of learning.

II
Incremental History
"When He Was a Student ... and When He Grew Up ..."

Sages of ancient times recognized that sayings and stories appeared in diverse versions. They too proposed explanations of how a given saying or story could come down in more than a single statement. The principal approach to the question posited that each detail represented a different stage in the history of the story, or of the life of its hero in particular, with one version characteristic of one such stage, and another version attesting to a different, and later one. So the successive versions of a saying or story supply a kind of incremental history. How so? Each version tells something about concrete events and real lives (biographies) that earlier versions did not reveal.

The classic Talmudic expression of the incremental theory takes up a passage of the Mishnah in which Rabban Yohanan ben Zakkai is called merely "Ben Zakkai:"

<u>The precedent is as follows: Ben Zakkai examined a witness as to the character of the stalks of figs [under which an incident now subject to court procedure was alleged to have taken place].</u>

Mishnah Sanhedrin 5:2B

As we shall now see, at paragraph N in the following talmudic analysis, exactly the same story is reported, on Tannaite authority. Now <u>Rabban Yohanan</u> ben Zakkai is alleged to have made exactly the same ruling, in exactly the same case. The item is worded in the same way except for the more fitting title. Then, at P-Q, the two versions are readily explained as facts of history. The one of Ben Zakkai was framed when he was a mere disciple. When, later on, he had become a recognized sage, the story was told to take account of that fact. So the theory I call "incremental history" is simple: <u>each story related to, because it derives from, historical moments in a linear progression</u>. The Talmudic passage is as follows:

IX.
A. Who is this "Ben Zakkai"?
B. If we should propose that it is R. Yohanan ben Zakkai, did he ever sit in a sanhedrin [that tried a murder case]?
C. And has it not been taught on Tannaite authority:
D. The lifetime of R. Yohanan ben Zakkai was a hundred and twenty years. For forty years he engaged in trade, for forty years he studied [Torah], and for forty years he taught.
E. And it has been taught on Tannaite authority: Forty years before the destruction of the Temple the sanhedrin went into exile and conducted its sessions in Hanut.
F. And said R. Isaac bar Abodimi, "That is to say that the sanhedrin did not judge cases involving penalties."
G. Do you think it was cases involving penalties? [Such cases were not limited to the sanhedrin but could be tried anywhere in the Land of Israel!]
H. Rather, the sanhedrin did not try capital cases.
I. And we have learned in the Mishnah:
J. <u>After the destruction of the house of the sanctuary, Rabban Yohanan b. Zakkai ordained ... [M. R.H. 4:1]</u>. [So the final forty years encompassed the period after the destruction of the Temple, and Yohanan could not, therefore, have served on a sanhedrin that tried capital cases.]
K. Accordingly, at hand is some other Ben Zakkai [than Yohanan b. Zakkai].
L. That conclusion, moreover, is reasonable, for if you think that it is <u>Rabban Yohanan</u> ben Zakkai, would Rabbi [in the Mishnah-passage] have called him merely, "Ben Zakkai"? [Not very likely.]
M. And lo, it has been taught on Tannaite authority:
N. There is the precedent that Rabban Yohanan ben Zakkai conducted an interrogation about the stalks on the figs [so surely this is the same figure as at M. 5:2B].
O. But [at the time at which the incident took place, capital cases were tried by the sanhedrin and] he was a disciple in session before his master. He said something, and the others found his reasoning persuasive, [41B] so they adopted [the ruling] in his name.
P. When he was studying Torah, therefore, he was called Ben Zakkai, as a disciple in session before his master, but when he [later on] taught, he was called Rabban Yohanan ben Zakkai.
Q. When, therefore, he is referred to as Ben Zakkai, it is on account of his being a beginning [student] and when he is called Rabban Yohanan b. Zakkai, it is on account of his status later on.

The relevance of the Talmudic passage is simple, as I shall now explain.

Modernist scholars have claimed to explain diverse versions of a single saying or story by much the same thesis as we see before us. That is to say, they allege that they know why a given detail is added here, dropped there, changed in the third place, built up and augmented in the fourth, and on and on. Accordingly, the modern, critical scholars accomplish a kind of incremental history. This is the history of what might have actually happened to account for changes in versions of a story, based on a theory of what might have impelled an author to add or revise a given detail. Indeed, practitioners of the incremental approach have not hesitated to declare that they know an entire history for which the text at hand supplies no evidence whatsoever. They then refer to this (entirely undocumented) history in order to explain shifts and changes in versions of a story.

The single best example of the fantasy at hand is supplied by David J. Halperin, <u>The Merkabah in Rabbinic Literature</u> (New Haven, 1980: American Oriental Series 62). Halperin refers to the Merkavah-materials. He posits that, prior to the first written version there was an entire cycle of such stories ("presumably oral" !). He knows that one of these stories had a narrative framework, then lost a miraculous element, then got that miracle reinserted later on. This literary history, claiming to explain shifts and changes in the sequence of stories we saw earlier, derives from not a shred of evidence of any kind. There is <u>no</u> version of these stories at all. The author just made it up and wrote it down, then the American Oriental Society printed it. True, as we shall note, Halperin introduces appropriate qualifications and caveats. But he pays little attention to them; they are mainly formalities.

Here is how he states his conclusions (pp. 138-9):

1. I postulate the following development for the <u>merkabah</u> tradition involving R. Johanan b. Zakkai: (1) A cycle of <u>merkabah</u> stories, presumably oral, recounted the miracles that accompanied the expositions of one or another of R. Johanan's disciples; the stories of this cycle contained little beside the miracles. (This stage is purely hypothetical, and is not attested by any literary source.) (2) One of these stories, which involved R. Eleazar b. Arakh, was given a narrative framework, which suggested that R. Eleazar exemplified the "scholar" of M. Hag. 2:1 (<u>Mek. Rashbi</u>). (3) The miraculous element was "censored" from the story of R. Eleazar, possibly by the compiler of the mystical collection (Tosefta). (4) Miraculous details were reinserted, and stories of other disciples added, on the basis of the old <u>merkabah</u> stories (PT, BT)....

3. If my hypothesis is correct, the <u>merkabah</u> tradition is rooted in a cycle of miraculous legends. Some historical reality may hide behind these legends, but it is nearly inaccessible. Instead of trying to recover it, we should focus on what the legends can teach us about (<u>maaseh</u>) <u>merkabah</u> and the image of those reported to have been expert in it.

Halperin's exposition of his own theories omits all reference to whatever he holds as a fundamental thesis on the character of the literature and the history of its formation, if he has any. Yet even on the surface, it is clear, he proposes to make up explanations for diverse versions of the Merkavah-story. Each detail has its day. None is spared the ravages of Halperin's imaginative reconstruction of its individual life-history. Everything means something somewhere -- and to Halperin it does not matter where. It follows that the theory of "incremental history," assigning a particular event or motive or other explanation for each change in a story as it moves from document to document finds exemplification in Halperin's treatment of the Merkavah-story.

A systematic picture of what Halperin has done and why it is founded on false premises (or on no premises other than an undisciplined imagination) derives from William Scott Green's review of Halperin's book.

In his review (the Second Century, 1983, 3:113-115) Green observes:

> For reasons never specified, Halperin tends to construe each literary unit, each manuscript variant, and each textual version as a discrete historical moment. He then constructs his history by arranging these textual moments into chronological sequence. By adopting this strategy, Halperin forces himself into the grueling exercise of determining the relative dates of decontextualized literary segments. Much is at stake in these demonstrations; the very possibility of Halperin's history depends on their rigor and cogency. Halperin uses a wide range of criteria to date his materials, and he sometimes deploys these inconsistently. That is, he established his chronologies on the basis of the differences among versions of a passage. But the variables he deems decisive are not systematically applied. Rather, they seem to shift from case to case. This sort of unevenness undermines Halperin's demonstrations of chronology and makes at least some of them appear arbitrary. The problems of particular chronologies aside, Halperin's method limits the kind of history of rabbinic, merkabah speculation he can write. His catenae of textual events result in schematic accounts that flip and flop, sparse chronicles of unexpected reversals and inversions in which discrete passages undergo marked, sometimes radical shifts of meaning. He argues, for instance, that the Mishnaic rule that the merkabah may not be expounded "by an individual [variant: to an individual], unless he is a scholar, understanding on his own" (M. Hagigah 2:1) had three distinct meanings before the time of Tosefta's redaction (ca. A.D. 250). When the passage circulated independently, it allowed the sage, but not the disciple, "to undertake on his own an exegesis of Ezekiel's vision" (p. 35). When it was redacted into the Mishnah and incorporated into a list of other biblical passages whose exposition is restricted, "the effect was to reverse the other biblical passages whose exposition is restricted, "the effect was to reverse the meaning of the merkabah ruling; solitary study of the merkabah was no longer the object of the restriction, but a

concession granted to certain exceptional individuals" (p. 36). Still later, the meaning of the rule was changed again to make it "refer to instruction" (p. 36), an alteration reflected in the variant reading. This final meaning is apparent in a story about Yohanan b. Zakkai and Eleazar b. Arakh at T. Hagigah 2:1, which, ironically, preserves the earliest version of the Mishnaic rule.

This kind of lean and linear history disappoints because it does not account for the changes it describes. Even if Halperin's textual sequences are correct, they leave too much unexplained. For instance, to whom within rabbinism were these changes important? Did the different meanings supersede one another or exist simultaneously? Are these changes literary, or do they reflect deeper theological, religious, and social diversions within rabbinism? Are such changes, particularly the reversal of meaning, accidental or deliberate, the result of misunderstanding or of manipulation? Without some theory of rabbinic culture and society, of textual transmission and tradition, and of literary tendencies, Halperin's textual sequences lead nowhere. They are merely chronologies masquerading as history.

In singling Halperin out, my intent is only to show what people are doing now. I do not want anyone to suppose that I have taken a particularly weak example of an otherwise vital theory. On the contrary, Halperin presents us with as capable an exercise of the incremental-historical theory as is in print -- alas. For it seems he is talking to himself, in the privacy of his study. He clearly is not engaging in reasoned arguments with the generality of interested participants in the inquiry. Only by that theory can I explain how anyone can make up a "cycle" of Merkavah-stories ("presumably oral"), tell us what was in them, then what was removed from them -- and only then relate the whole pre-history of unavailable sources to the actual sources at hand. The theory that details in successive versions of a saying or story bears historical meanings deserves better than it has gotten to date.

The approach that seeks to account for shifts and changes by reference to the interests of later authors, tradents, and redactors, remains entirely open. Indeed, in due course we may look forward to the rehabilitation of the theory at hand. My criticism, like Green's, is that, so far as Halperin exemplifies the theory, he provides yet another instance of the dreary approach of made-up explanations, never subjected to tests of falsification or validation. That approach, suitable for talmudic exegesis, does not serve for historical and literary work in our day. While both the theory that "he often used to say ..." and the claim that there is an "original" "tradition," promise little for the future, the one at hand awaits rigorous attention.

III

A Documentary-Historical Theory

The reader will not find surprising the allegation that the authors of later documents in the canon of Judaism in a fairly consistent way fill holes in stories and sayings received from earlier ones. When, therefore, we wish to explain why details are added or dropped, the first appeal will carry us to the matter of rhetoric. We ask whether we are able to explain why a detail makes a first appearance by asking about the relative relationship of the document in which it surfaces to other documents in which it is absent. If we can show that the document bearing the fresh fact comes later in the formation of the canon than the one lacking it, we may appeal first of all to the claim that the later authors' sense of rhetoric, their larger aesthetic theory, precipitated their making up and including that detail. That hypothesis will gain substantial credibility if we can show that, in general, authors of the document at hand did pretty much the same thing with whatever they received.

Yet the theory at hand, which I call the documentary theory, marks the beginning, not the ending, of the matter. For aesthetics, including rhetoric, in a system brings to expression the fundamental and generative character of the system as a whole. Aesthetics constitutes a cultural indicator and relates in a contingent way to the culture -- in this case, the textual community -- at hand. To invoke a theory of aesthetics by itself as explanation of why rhetoric takes one form rather than some other simply is to beg the question. Why so? Because in a truly integrated community of culture, such as the canon of Judaism attests to the sages of late antiquity, each detail addresses the whole. Each one in some small way expresses the character of the entire system. The sages' own convictions about the utter harmony of the whole, the congruity of law to theology, of meal-time to bed-time and of conduct in the toilet to behavior in the synagogue, reenforce the claim at hand. Indeed these commonplace allegations bring it to explicit expression. It must follow that, when we appeal to a rhetorical explanation for the facts at hand and therefore treat the matter as an essentially literary problem, we have only succeeded in restating the question, not resolving it. Aesthetics, including rhetoric, adds up to little more than making something out of interesting arrangements of words into patterns. By itself it constitutes a formalist inquiry into formalism, a quest for trivial explanations of small things.

The fact that later sages rewrote in their own way what earlier sages had handed on to them looms as an enormous presence in the interpretation of the formative age of Judaism. The sages at hand surely do not conform to the definition of traditionalism ordinarily imputed to their culture. For while they faithfully handed on what they had received, it never was never intact, if in their view it always was unimpaired. Why so? Because they saw for themselves a role in the process of formation of what would be "the tradition." That role proved inventive, therefore creative. It must follow that the facts of rhetorical preference and the configuration of a larger sense of aesthetics in important ways convey definitive traits of the system at hand. But describing and analyzing those traits, interpreting them in context for what they reveal about the larger system -- these labors only now begin.

The theory I have called "incremental history" fails not because it lacks merit, but because it lacks successful exemplars. If we are to move on, the route must carry us not from one detail to the next, but to a height affording a perspective overall. Once we have a theory of how to proceed and a thesis worth testing, then, but only then, we move to the details, from large to small, in proper and proportionate succession. Beginning from the outside and systematically working our way within, we first seek large and definitive traits. These then will tell us what to discern in the small field of an individual story.

The incremental-historical theory then undergoes an appropriately rigorous exercise of falsification. How so? We must ask whether details conform to the main point. The alternative is that, like Halperin, we make things up as we go along, text by text and detail by detail. But a useful theory will prove its worth if we are able to explain and even predict the course of matters in a consistent and cogent way. The ultimately useless result of Halperin's work, surveyed just now, derives not from the rather private and subjective character of the results, his meditations on this and that. Even though it is easy to dismiss as mere subjectivity Halperin's power of making up version after version of a tradition no one has ever seen, then appealing to hypothetical version A to explain what is lost in imaginary version C, that is not the main point. It is the methodological inconsistency, the made-up character of the whole approach, not merely the manufactured quality of the individual parts that requires us to dismiss Halperin's work as hopeless. A useful and plausible theory works wholesale, not retail. It cannot come tailor-made but has to come right off the plain pipe rack, so to speak. Halperin's exemplification of all that can go wrong with the incremental theory therefore should not lead to the dismissal of the theory. What we have to do is more thoughtfully consider how to proceed from the documentary facts, awaiting discovery, to the explanation of the documents' preferences, overall, and then _also_ to details of a given story (such as the Merkavah-one), in proper sequence.

Fifteen years ago I attempted such a program in Development of a Legend. Studies on the Traditions Concerning Yohanan ben Zakkai (Leiden, 1970). What I proposed to do was explain why a story appeared with one set of details in one document, and with a different set of details in another. I used two methods. First, I compared versions of the same story as they appeared in successive texts. Second. I asked about the larger tendencies of the framers of the texts, viewed whole and one by one. So the two approaches I advocate here to the problem of sorting out and making sense of diverse versions of a saying or a story -- documentary, then incremental-historical -- find ample illustration in Development of a Legend. The main point is that I appealed to the then-established facts that one document came from one school among the talmudic sages, another and parallel document from a different school, with its distinctive viewpoint. I took the view that traits (at that time) pretty well known to characterize one school and its documents might also guide me to explain why that same school would tell a story in one way and not in some other. This I did for the entire corpus of sayings and stories concerning Yohanan ben Zakkai.

In context and in intellect the book failed for a host of reasons. In that naive period of my life, I assumed books get read, authors' theories get taken up. I did not know that people could dismiss a book by looking for some minor detail and determining that they did not agree with it (hence: an error), or that the fact was a fact but had already been seen to be a fact before, a claim made without reference to the service said fact had earlier contributed to some other book (hence: ho-hum). The one serious review the book got recognized its contribution to the study of Yohanan ben Zakkai, but did not take up the larger methodological theory I had tried to define. So much for context. The intellectual failure lay not with the audience but with the author. I never made explicit the methodological experiment I then proposed to carry out. I left matters inarticulate and inchoate. My guilt lay, and it commonly does for me, I admit, in the assumption that things are ineffably obvious. What came to me as self-evident and beyond need for articulation I imagined would prove equally commonplace to everyone else in the world. It has taken me many years to accept the fact that the world is not made up of mind-readers, any more than, in the field in which I work, it is made up of book-readers. It is what it is. If it is to be made better, the work will have to be done one day at a time, and in one book at a time.

Yet these lessons of age, requiring me now to restate in clear and simple terms things I then feared I had said in an all-too-obvious way fifteen years ago, do not lead me to dismiss the project. On the contrary, <u>Development of a Legend</u> and the books that carried forward its basic inquiry, <u>Rabbinic Traditions about the Pharisees before 70</u> and <u>Eliezer ben Hyrcanus. The Tradition and the Man</u>, did invoke the two modes I advocate here for explaining why sayings and stories change as they move. That is to say, I did ask systematically (1) whether the authors of a document made changes in received sayings and stories for reasons characteristic of their document as a whole, that is the documentary theory. And I did ask systematically (2) what we learn about the historical context and viewpoint of the authors of a document that revealed in received sayings and stories that is, what I call the incremental-history-theory.

Let me therefore provide a reprise of how I originally exemplified these two quite distinct approaches to our problem, and then explain what I think is wrong, and remains right, with each of them.

First let me show how one might ask about the tendencies of documents' authors. Specifically will what is established overall allow us to account for shifts and changes in versions of discrete sayings and stories? For this purpose we deal with two collections of scriptural exegeses on the book of Exodus, one attributed to the school of Ishmael, the other to the school of Aqiba. I reproduce both passages, together with my discussion of them, as they originally appeared in <u>Development of a Legend</u>. In what follows as a comment, I.i.2 refers to Ishmael's version, I.ii.1 to Aqiba's, of the Mekhilta. That is, the former I.i.2, derives from the Mekhilta of Ishmael, the latter I.ii.1, from the Mekhilta of Simeon b. Yohai, who is supposed to have been a disciple of the school of Aqiba. With these facts in hand, the passages will be reasonably accessible.

2(a) <u>For If Thou Lift Up Thy Sword upon it</u> (Ex. 20:25). In this connection R. Simon b. Eleazar used to say, "The altar is made to prolong the years of man and iron is made to shorten the years of man. It is not right for that which shortens life to be lifted up against that which prolongs life."

(b) R. Yohanan b. Zakkai says, "Behold it says: <u>Thou shalt build ... of whole stones</u> (Deut. 27:6). They are to be stones that establish peace.

(c) "Now, by using the method of <u>qal vahomer</u>, you reason: The stones for the altar do not see nor hear nor speak. Yet because they serve to establish peace between Israel and their Father in heaven, the Holy One, blessed be he, said, <u>Thou shalt lift up no iron tool upon them</u> (ibid., v.5). How much the more then should he who establishes peace between man and his fellow-man, between husband and wife, between city and city, between nation and nation, between family and family, between government and government, be protected so that no harm should come to him."

(Mekhilta of R. Ishmael, Bahodesh 11, ed. and trans. J. Lauterbach, II, p. 290)

On this passage I commented:

I.ii.1, the Aqiban version given presently, substitutes <u>sons of Torah</u> for <u>peacemakers</u> who escape punishment; it omits the <u>altar</u>, and the <u>sword shortens life</u> becomes the <u>sword as a sign of punishment</u>. The <u>altar</u> does not prolong life but <u>atones</u> for Israel. I.ii.1 thus shows what the Aqiban party made of this midrash, which was none too palatable to them. The essential element was the exegesis on whole stones/peace. The function of the altar was that of making peace. Therefore peace-makers in this world perform the function of the altar -- and more so! This is Yohanan's essential idea; the functions performed by the Temple and its instruments can be replaced by human virtues. So the <u>qal vehomer</u> preserved in the Ishmaelean tradition I.1.2 and I.ii.5 is also originally from Yohanan, and the saying of Simeon b. Eleazar in I.i.2 shows an early development of Yohanan's idea in its original spirit: war is bad, peace is good. The Aqibans therefore omitted the exegesis of peace/whole stones; revised the <u>qal vehomer</u> to make the essential virtue <u>not</u> peace-making but study of the Torah; revised Simeon's saying to make both the sword and the altar symbols of the attributes of the divine nature -- judgment and mercy, thus making the sword a good thing too; and attributed all of their revised complex to Yohanan. And they did an amazingly good job -- their revised version looks so much like the original that the careless reader would think them nearly identical. It is only when one looks closely that he sees the reversal of the implications.

We proceed to the version of the same saying as presented in what I then thought was the Mekhilta to be attributed to the school of Aqiba:

> This is what Rabban Yohanan ben Zakkai says, "What was the reason iron was prohibited more than all [other] metals [for use in building the tabernacle (Ex. 20:25)]? Because the sword is made from it, and the sword is a sign of punishment, but the altar is a sign of atonement. A sign [means] of atonement.
>
> "And is this not a matter of <u>qal vehomer</u>? Stones, which neither see nor hear nor speak -- because they bring atonement between Israel and their father in heaven, the Holy One blessed be he said [concerning them] <u>Thou shalt lift upon them no iron tool</u> (Deut. 27:5). Sons of Torah, who are an atonement for the world, how much the more so that none of all the harmful forces in the world should ever touch them!"
>
> (Mekhilta of R. Simeon b. Yohai, Yitro 20:22, ed. Epstein-Melamed pp. 157-8, 1.29-31, 1-4)

On this passage I said:

> We have two separate sayings. The first is Yohanan's, that metal is prohibited because the sword is made of metal and is a sign of punishment, while the altar is a sign of atonement. The second saying is the <u>qal vehomer</u>, that as stones should not be injured because they bring atonement, so sons of Torah should all the more so be free of injury from harmful forces. The <u>qal vehomer</u> has nothing to do with Yohanan's observation, and need not be directly attributed to him, though it occurs in all formulations of this passage. It seems to be a later development.

By way of amplifying the same matter, let me give a further instance of invoking what I then imagined was a trait of Aqiban tradents to explain diverse versions of similarly connected materials:

> Rabban Yohanan ben Zakkai says, "Behold it says, <u>[With] whole stones [avanim shelemot] will you build the altar of the Lord your God</u> (Deut. 27:5) -- Stones which make peace [shalom], and behold it is a matter of <u>qal vehomer</u>: Stones which do not see and do not hear and do not speak, because they bring peace between Israel and their father in heaven, Scripture says <u>You shall not lift up</u>

iron over them (Deut. 27:6). A man who brings peace between a man and his wife, between one family and another, between one city and another, between one province and another, between one nation and another -- how much the more so that punishment should not come near him!"

I then commented:

>The exegesis is practically identical with I.ii.1. The Scriptures are different. There it is "why is iron prohibited" and here it concerns the play on words: "whole stones -- stones which make peace." <u>Atonement</u> becomes <u>peace, sons of Torah</u> become <u>peacemakers</u>. The structure is otherwise the same; the thought is the same ("Peacemakers or those who atone for the world should come to not harm"). The details are somewhat different. Yet the differences are not very considerable. I suspect that Yohanan would have said something about the altar/altar-stones in the form of a <u>qal vehomer</u>. The context was Deut. 27:5 and 27:6. The play on words concerning the "whole stones" was dropped in I.ii.1, the stress on "iron" of all metals was omitted here. Strikingly, the Ishmaelean version, I.i.2, follows I.ii.5; both versions elide the <u>whole stones</u> play on words and the <u>qal vehomer</u> involving an iron tool. I should thus suppose that I.i.2 = I.ii.5. I.ii.1 differs, as I said, in omitting "whole stones" and stressing "iron." Both schools preserved an account exhibiting formal parallels (I.i.2 + I.ii.5), but the Aqibans alone preserved the other (I.ii.1), probably because they invented it. Some anterior version was available to both schools, and that anterior version derived from circles close to Yohanan himself. In a period of less than a few decades between Yohanan's death and the formation of the schools of Ishmael and Aqiba, a group of Yohanan's disciples must have put into final form materials which were subsequently made use of by <u>both</u> schools. This supposition is likely to be valid if the following conditions are also valid: (1) if both documents actually come from the schools to which they are attributed; (2) if the present form was edited ca. 200, if not somewhat earlier; and most important (3) if they were <u>not</u> expanded since that time. Then the story stands in both by A.D. 200 and was known to teachers in both schools. The common source of the story would have come substantially earlier than the founding of the two schools, ca. 100-120. In that case, as I said, the story is certainly part of the corpus of Yohanan-sayings edited by the time of Yavneh. We may safely go a step further and designate as Yavnean, <u>all</u> materials occurring in substantially similar form in materials ascribed to the two schools; as Ishmaelean, materials unique to that school, hence not necessarily later than Yavneh but probably from a circle at Yavneh not known or acceptable to the Aqibans; as Aqiban, materials unique to that school, within the same limitation. It would be tempting to suppose that materials unique to one or the other school were

later than materials common to both, but the obvious imponderables prevent it. It is consequential, since we have no documents edited at Yavneh, to recognize that within documents edited later on are materials which probably did come from Yavneh. But it is equally noteworthy that even the materials in the earliest collections have already undergone substantial development. Primitive logia, in which stories or sayings about Yohanan are transcribed close to when they happened or were actually stated, are unavailable. In general, the closest we can come to the man himself is through secondary materials based on Yavnean traditions.

In conclusion I stated these results:

> The condemnation of war and reproaches in its aftermath may likewise have been acceptable in the school whose master did not encourage the holy war of Bar Kokhba, but in any event ought to have been quite obnoxious to the one whose master did. Service of the Lord in love would have preserved the prosperity of the people, and the implied condemnation of war is present in the Ishmaelean stories about the Israelite girl.

> In all I think it has been proven that no <u>tendenz</u> concerning Yohanan <u>himself</u> characterized either school. Both preserved favorable, and more important, authoritative sayings and precedents. His legal role is, if anything, slightly greater among the Aqibans than among the Ishmaeleans, but the data are too sparse for them to matter much. Most important: <u>where the two schools differ in the sorts of stories they preserve about Yohanan, the reason for the difference is certainly found in the interests of the schools themselves, and not in their attitudes to Yohanan.</u>

As I sadly look back on the exercise at hand, I take comfort that, despite the obvious fundamentalism throughout, I did have the presence of mind to specify the premises. Accordingly, I emphasize that, even then, I stated as a condition that both documents (1) had to come from the schools to which they were attributed and (2) represent matters in a final way as they emerged from those schools at that time. Of course, those conditions were not met and cannot be shown ever to have been met. So the whole in retrospect stands as what I believe to be a good example of method and a bad example of result. But at least I did not make things up as I went along. And the concluding, underlined judgment is one by which I should firmly stand today. Besides paying attention to the definitive traits of a document, we thus ask about how the context of documents explains, and is explained by, alterations in received versions of sayings and stories.

The results just now presented mark the age in which they were composed, just as much as I claim the same for the sources under discussion. The focus of interest -- the historical Yohanan ben Zakkai -- to begin with limited matters. More important, the things taken for granted as facts comprise a long and disheartening list. But even then I asked what if the Mekhilta of Ishmael does not in fact represent the historical Ishmael and his disciples? What if Simeon did not really study with Aqiba, and what if the Mekhilta of Simeon is not "Aqiban"? what if both Mekhiltas are made up in medieval times? Then every word I wrote is not wrong but beside the point.

And, of course, I now grasp the obvious fact that the entire exercise at hand in its original formulation rested on premises that I can now call mere fundamentalism. How so? At every point I took for granted that whatever is imputed to a sage really was said about him, with only one exception: Yohanan ben Zakkai. I further assumed that whatever story was told really represented the state of affairs in the time and place to which the story referred, except for the historical setting of Yohanan ben Zakkai himself. On those bases the study at hand rested. But the premises scarcely escape the simple criticism that, at each point, they share those traits of gullibility and credulity that then, as now, I have attempted to overcome. Asking how we know what Yohanan ben Zakkai really said and did, I failed to inquire into how we know that anything imputed to anyone claiming to know what Yohanan ben Zakkai really said and did also demands answers to exactly the same question. It took me a long time -- several more books -- to understand that simple fact and also to confront it and draw the consequences dictated by it. Others assuredly recognized the same problem. But I was the only one to try to solve it. And by redefining the foci of inquiry, I did solve it.

The reason that <u>Development of a Legend</u> made so little impression in its day, however, is not that it was insufficiently critical. By the standards not only of that day but also of the present age, a decade and a half and many books later, <u>Development</u> remains too radical in its methods, in its points of fundamental insistence, for the generality of scholars in the field to confront. If they respond to the book at all, it is by pointing out misprints or minor variant readings that do not affect meaning. This means they cannot take up the challenge of the book and all that followed it. Why the avoidance? Because if <u>Development of a Legend</u> points to what work must be done, then the sort of scholarly work people now do cannot be done. It is one thing to recognize the utter obsolescence of everything accomplished in the critical study of the history of the Jews and of Judaism in late antiquity, so far as the rabbinic canon constitutes the principal literary source. It is quite another to insist, as I did and do insist, that everything people now propose as a scholarly program rests on the same false premises.

The way lies open to inquiry into the relationship of text to context, of detail to main point of insistence. Results of the inquiry will tell us something about why a given set of ideas became self-evident and remained manifestly "right" for a very long time. Then we also may find a clue on why those same ideas, that same system of a world-view and a way of life characteristic of a single social group for a long span of history, lost the trait of self-evidence and became manifestly irrelevant. That is to say, at stake is how to interpret the history of Judaism: its formation and persistence, change and renewal. The first task is to describe, analyze, and interpret the facts in hand. Among these facts, the obvious ones concern how, to the naked eye, a story will change as it is told and retold, a saying will undergo revision when it is repeated.

Let me close by placing into the correct, appropriately large, context the humble facts that have occupied us for so long. Why, specifically, do I regard as indicative the persistence and transformation of sayings and stories? And what do I hope will be indicated? The answer lies in the three basic dimensions by which we take the measure of every document of the canon of Judaism, from the Mishnah through the Bavli.

Every book of the canon stands by itself. Each is <u>autonomous</u>.

Except for the Mishnah and Scripture, every book in the canon refers back to some other book. Some of the books relate as a whole to the Mishnah. They serve as exegeses and amplifications of the Mishnah. Others depend upon Scripture. So every book in the canon, except for the Mishnah and Scripture, is not only autonomous but also <u>connected</u> to some other book. The autonomy is limited by connection.

And, finally, all of the books together, Scripture and the Mishnah, Tosefta and the Talmuds, Sifra, the two Sifres, Genesis Rabbah, Leviticus Rabbah, and the rest of the compositions, viewed whole, all at once, and in their entirety, constitute the "one whole Torah of Moses, our rabbi." That continuity is not merely the <u>post facto</u> assertion of the believing community. It also constitutes a fact to be induced from evidence by detailed inquiry into the shared conceptions and values, alleged at the end of the process of the formation of the canon as a whole, to characterize all documents of the canon. Looking backward, I should not be prepared to make an exception, in that characterization, even of Scripture. That is so even though sages, in the manner of their age and all ages before and since, read into Scripture whatever they wished to see there. That qualification should not present an exception to this simple claim: the documents all together do constitute a canon. So they establish a <u>continuity</u> from one to the next and among them all.

Two of the three dimensions of the canon -- autonomy, connection, continuity -- obviously appear to the naked eye: autonomy and connection. How so? A document, by definition, stands alone and autonomous. The Tosefta, the Mishnah, the two Sifres, each will afford examination on its own. The connection of all of the compositions of the canon to either Scripture or the Mishnah comes to vivid expression in the fundamental redactional preferences of each document. The Tosefta is organized in accord with the order of passages of the Mishnah, the two Talmuds with the same structure, and all compilations of scriptural exegeses ("midrashim") follow the order of verses in the book of Scripture they allegedly explain. The variations in degree of explicit dependence, for redactional order and structure, on one or the other of the two base-documents make little difference.

But when we ask whether and how the documents form a continuity from one to the next and, among all of them together constitute a canon, where shall we look for relevant data? I see only two sources of facts for the assessment of where and how documents relate as a whole to one another, not only back to a single shared source of structure supplied by Scripture or the Mishnah. One source flows from shared conceptions, symbols, fundamental and everywhere-definitive values. The other source derives from shared sayings and stories. The contrast speaks for itself.

The former source -- shared symbols -- flows at random and aimlessly, much as at floodtide the sea overcomes the shore, and the river its banks. We never know the limits. We form impressions of where the boundaries lie, only to discover, as water recedes and advances, that, short of going out and wading around, we have missed the mark dividing dry shore from ocean or river. But if we wade out in the shifting tide, we may drown. So too if we aimlessly seize upon one ubiquitous value or another and allege that one congeries defines what is shared, uniform, continuous, and another does not, we shall drown in facts. We shall never have a clear criterion for knowing when we are right, and when we are wrong. One need not dismiss as impressionistic the great and valiant efforts of such exemplary scholars as George Foot Moore and Max Kadushin (let alone lesser figures) to recognize the failures they left behind. The field of learning in the nineteenth and twentieth century is strewn with the carcasses of abandoned definitions of "Judaism," including the system of Judaism revealed by the canon concluded in late antiquity.

But there endures that other source of information -- shared sayings and stories -- on what moves in continuity from one document to another. These constitute the hard facts of the matter. What in fact travels from the Mishnah to the Tosefta to the Yerushalmi to the Bavli, or from a Mekhilta to the Tosefta to the Fathers according to Rabbi Nathan, or hither and yon or here and there? The peripatetic saying and the thrice-told tale -- these alone constitute concrete, material proofs of the actualities of continuity. They define facts of whatever continuity there is among the documents of the cannon and so to begin with make possible the claim that autonomous documents relate not in general, in "values," but very particularly, in verbatim sayings. Then we may see, in the character of detail, that main point that we seek. The shape of the whole, the measure of the dimension of continuity -- these to begin with emerge from the simple fact that the same saying or story will be shared among two or more documents of the canon. That synoptic fact validates the claim of continuity, though obviously not exhausting what is meant by the claim. But, in the details of what is like and what is unlike in the traveling tale and the peripatetic saying we see clearly, without distortion, what is common to important components of the canon of Judaism. True, all we have at the moment is detail. But of canonical Judaism we cannot speak just now, except to say that, after all, God really does live in the details.

VI
CONTEMPORARY SCHOLARSHIP ON ANCIENT JUDAISM
THREE SCHOOLS
URBACH, HIMMELFARB, BOKSER

Ephraim E. Urbach, <u>The Law. Its Sources and its Development</u>. (Jerusalem, 1984: Masadah) 405 pp. In Hebrew.

Martha Himmelfarb, <u>Tours of Hell. An Apocalyptic Form in Jewish and Christian Literature.</u> (Philadelphia, 1983: University of Pennsylvania Press) x + 198 pp.

Baruch M. Bokser, <u>The Origins of the Seder. The Passover Rite and Early Rabbinic Judaism.</u> (Berkeley, Los Angeles, London, 1984: University of California Press) xix + 188 pp.

    While these three current scholarly books purport to study the same topic, Judaism, in the same period in its history, namely, late antiquity, that is all they have in common. Seeing them together throws strong light on the sharp contrasts in scholarly programs and methods currently in contention. Indeed, we have to wonder whether discourse in scholarly issues will ever proceed to the fruitful exchange of ideas and insight, when, as the present lot of books testifies, no one seems to want to talk about anything in particular to anyone else.

    To state matters simply, Urbach resonates with the echo of a distant age. Had his book appeared in 1884 instead of 1984, it would have astonished no one of that time. I.H. Weiss and Z. Frankel would not have learned much from Urbach. Urbach writes as though he does not want to talk <u>to</u> anyone of his own day (apart from those who to begin with know his message and agree with it).

    Himmelfarb, for her part, has nothing to say. Her book follows no program, makes no points, merely offers episodic observations on this and that. It is an exercise in scholarly nihilism. So she has nothing in particular <u>to say</u>.

    Bokser does wish to address contemporary issues. Much is at stake in his book. But the work proves so diffuse and padded that, from one chapter to the next, one wonders whether he proposes to talk about something <u>in particular</u>, though he has much to say about many things.

    So, as I said, among the three dominant schools of learning in ancient Judaism that flourish today -- the Israeli-historical, the literary-philological-textual, and the American-history-of-religions -- represented by Urbach, Himmelfarb, and Bokser, we see a single trait. People either mutter to themselves. Or they talk clearly but about nothing.

Or they talk about so many things that no one thing provides focus. As a result one would be hard put to define that subject that all purport to address, namely, the formative age of the history of Judaism (Urbach, Bokser) or of both Judaism and Christianity (Himmelfarb).

In defense of Urbach, we have to recognize that this newest book of his, while repeating the same methods he has long employed and producing entirely familiar results, provides the final, definitive account of his approach to the history of the law. It vastly improves not only on his earlier work, all the best ideas of which flow into the pages of this last, best book. It also draws to a close the entire scholarly tradition that he here brings to authoritative statement. Lavishly produced, with credit to no fewer than nine co-workers, Urbach's book reviews issues as they have been defined from the beginning of the <u>Wissenschaft des Judentums</u> to our own day. Urbach follows the sources with admirable care and the accustomed perspicacity. The bibliography is ample and catholic. No one can fairly accuse Urbach of not reading books with which he does not agree, although his knowledge of schools other than his own naturally proves somewhat limited.

As to the program of the book, Urbach goes over issues in the study of law as he has framed them in a systematic and logical way. He starts with definitions of terms, for instance, decrees and ordinances, the role of custom. He proceeds to the relationship of Jewish law to Scripture. He reviews court systems and procedures. He presents a striking account of the place of precedent, testimony, and theological exegesis in the foundations of the law. In these chapters and many like them -- the book encompasses sixteen chapters in all and rests upon nearly a hundred pages of notes for somewhat over two hundred pages of text, Urbach does what Jerusalem scholarship does best. He goes over the texts and the conventional canon of learning and organizes and repeats what he deems established information.

Urbach's book presents only one problem. So far as Urbach claims not to report what the sources say, but to present a history of the topic about which the sources speak, that is, an account of the development and history of Jewish law through the Babylonian Talmud, he alleges he has done what he has not even tried to do. That is, to conduct a critical inquiry into historical issues and problems of how we know about change and development. Why not? Because Urbach has not yet grasped the problem of critical scholarship as conducted in the West: how do you know that what the source says really happened? The premise of his book, beginning, middle, and end, remains the same hopeless one that characterized I.H. Weiss and Z. Frankel and the other nineteenth century giants of Talmudic history. If a story tells something that happened, we have a historical event. If a saying claims that a rabbi said something, that rabbi really said it. The entire corpus of Talmudic literature therefore serves as an encyclopaedia of facts. The task of the scholar is to accumulate those facts and to arrange them into intelligible compositions, as Urbach has done, in my view better than anyone else in his school has ever done. When Weiss and Frankel read the sources historically, they materially advanced learning. When they took for granted the facticity of everything the sources said, they applied the historical methods everyone else in their time used. But when

Urbach and his school do the same, they do not advance learning. They impede even their own progress toward their goals. In no other field of the study of the history of the Jews, even in Jerusalem, do the canons of nineteenth century historiography still prevail as they do in the area of Talmudic history. And no where else in the scholarly world do people believe so much and conduct such trivial and slight analyses.

So if Urbach's premise is sound, then his book works. But if, as is the fact, his premise is unproved and almost certainly unsound, then nothing in his book makes any sense. What we cannot show we do not know. Urbach has not shown that his literalist and fundamentalist approach to the sources of Judaism corresponds to the actual character of the sources at hand. His history of the law and its development stands upon exactly the same foundations as would a biblical history of ancient Israel that began with the creation of the world, the ten generations from Adam to Noah, then the ten from Noah to Abraham, then stories of the patriarchs, then Israel's descent into Egypt, then the exodus from Egypt, and on and on. The stigmata of critical scholarship would appear here and there. Urbach might, for instance, concede that Methusalah really did not live nine hundred years, only a hundred and fifty, like the yoghurt-eaters of Georgia and Armenia (with a footnote to a medical article in the Tblisi Medical Society journal to prove it).

If out of any academic center of learning such a history of ancient Israel were to emerge, resting on premises such as Urbach's, people would reach judgments not about the history of ancient Israel but about the curious form of religious expression in the guise of historical scholarship emerging from that academic center. That is the issue here: piety in University-Orthodox Jerusalem. Urbach's book presents us with pathetic and disheartening evidence not merely that he has not learned very much, but that the Jerusalem school in Talmudic history cannot do very much more than it has done. Most of its devotees do not publish books any more, except summaries, anthologies of sources, and encyclopaedia articles. The younger epigones print curious little articles that announce ever more subtle or fanciful guesses about sources to begin with never subjected to the established critical probes of the age. The pathos is not that the old men have run out of ideas. It is that their younger successors do not even know or care that the world at large has declared them in bankruptcy. That is, they have run out of scholarly credit.

Himmelfarb's book forms a natural extension of that same judgment, but for a different reason. Urbach and his school present the merit of a particular program of inquiry. They propose to answer questions. Tney pursue studies in which something substantial is at stake. Himmelfarb's survey of seventeen tours of hell leads nowhere. It is an aimless journey. It is not that she began with an inquiry that failed. An experiment bearing negative results may present remarkably valuable insight. The problem is that Himmelfarb began with nothing. Apart from collecting a lot of information and making episodic remarks about this and that, she proves nothing.

She claims that her goal was to reconstruct as far as possible "the history of the development of the tradition of tours of hell." But she produces no history whatsoever. The fault is not hers: "Unfortunately for the historian who turns from the prehistory to the development of the tradition, it is extremely difficult to date most of the tours of hell or to place them geographically or culturally. While several of the texts can be dated within certain limits on the basis of patristic references or similar evidence, for most the dating is guesswork." And again: "The vacuum surrounding most of the texts discussed here makes a truly historical account of their emergence and development, relating them to specific trends in Jewish and Christian thought and movements in Jewish and Christian history, impossible. At this stage any study of the tours of hell must be almost exclusively literary." Now what Himmelfarb means by a literary study is difficult to guess. She immediately states, "Significant similarities of language and imagery are thus the primary evidence for relationships between texts ...." But she does not then come up with significant similarities of language and imagery linking her seventeen texts or any sizable set of them. Some relate to some others, but none stands for the whole or even a substantial part of the whole.

What Himmelfarb gives us therefore is simply a survey of the texts, "a careful examination of the contents of the tours of hell." It is an extended book report of junior high school provenance. We never know where we are. We never can follow an argument meant to make a point. Once more, Himmelfarb reviews her results: "Sometimes the similarities are so vague that one can speak only of the influence of other tours in the most general way rather than of common sources." And again an honest review: "These short treatments by their very nature are fragmented, concerned not with the whole picture but with single texts." This judgment -- hers on the preceding studies of the subject (if this can be called a subject at all) -- applies equally to her work.

Himmelfarb moreover does not demonstrate the persistence of an apocalyptic form. I am not sure what she thought "form" meant. All she gives us is a collection of information about a common theme as it occurs in a variety of unrelated and barely coherent texts. As I said at the beginning, we witness a futile exercise, an empty and purposeless work of pure scholarly nihilism. Why someone would want to undertake such a hopeless task I cannot say. I believe more useful work awaits us all.

Bokser has undertaken a far more promising set of questions. In general his methods prove current and suggestive. In these two ways his book far outweighs the works of Himmelfarb and Urbach. But Bokser presents a faulty execution of what can be a good idea, because his book is padded and claims to offer more than it delivers. Let me briefly describe what Bokser actually does, then assess his statement of what he proposes to achieve.

Bokser describes the character of the Mishnah and asks his question by stating a thesis: "the history of the Passover celebration is not an isolated phenomenon but instead illustrates the general early rabbinic reinterpretation of cultic rites and legitimization of extratemple means of religious expression." He proceeds to "pre-rabbinic descriptions of the Passover eve ritual: the centrality of the passover sacrifice." This carries us through biblical accounts, non-biblical second temple sources, wisdom, Philo, Josephus, early Christian literature -- the familiar and conventional agendum. But what is to be done with all of this? And how do the tediously-surveyed sources relate to the question at hand? I cannot find the answers to those questions.

Three Schools of Contemporary Scholarship 109

Bokser proceeds to translate Mishnah and Tosefta to Pesahim 10, that is, the earliest rabbinic text on the subject. In the chapter at hand <u>all</u> he does is translate the sources. There is not a single comment on them. He proceeds in the next chapter to analyze the texts. The analysis rests on this stated thesis: "the Mishnah's effort to reinterpret and supplement the earlier heritage can be discerned in nine distinct ways." But Bokser has not shown that the Mishnah's authors "<u>reinterpret</u> and <u>supplement</u> the earlier heritage." All he has done is survey a lot of information. He never substantiates the claim that the Mishnah will want to "reinterpret and supplement." That is simply the premise of the chapter at hand. Then he plunges into a morass of more discrete observations about this and that.

What is wrong here? It is simple. In no way does Bokser tease his points out of the threads and sherds of the texts. He does undertake a considerable labor of text-review, making all sorts of interesting observations about this and that. But most of what he says comprises intelligent observations. Few points advance, or even relate to, the argument he purports to take up. For example, Bokser claims to show that "the choice of subjects, wording, and sequence of Mishnah Pesahim 10 as well as its location within the tractate can be effectively explained by a single proposition: the editor of the Mishnah desires to emphasize that the Passover celebration can and should continue even without the paschal lamb." But Bokser concedes that the evidence is "indirect." So, he claims, the proposition is to be demonstrated "by tracing the biblical precedents and the history of the Passover celebration as well as by examining the peculiarities of the text of the Mishnah."

But I do not see where and how Bokser has done either. I see no "tracing of biblical antecedents and history ...." I see only a repertoire of sources laid out as a kind of chronological scrapbook. I certainly do not find a systematic and well-argued examination of "the peculiarities of the text of the Mishnah." Indeed, if something is supposed to be peculiar, then what is regular has also to be defined. And the definition must be made to stick. Bokser does not define or rigorously argue. Bokser's frame of reference focuses so narrowly on a single text that I do not know what indicates where the text at hand is "peculiar" and how I know where it is ordinary.

In other words, we have an interesting thesis, continuously reiterated in the context of an erudite survey of sources. Then comes the claim, at the end, that the much repeated thesis and the impressive array of learnedly portrayed sources have linked up to prove something. Would that they did! The remainder of the book goes over these issues: "a Jewish symposium? the Passover rite and earlier prototypes of meal celebrations"; "the perspective of early rabbinic Judaism"; "from form to meaning: the significance of the Passover rite and its place in early rabbinic Judaism." There are two appendices, "roasted meat or sacrifices after 70," and "the Hebrew texts of Mishnah and Tosefta Pesahim."

I therefore see as the critical flaw the too rapid leap from text to context, and then the long jump from context to matrix. Things are just not that easy. That is in no way to suggest Bokser's book makes no contribution to its subject. It provides a nearly encyclopaedic treatment of the topic. The problem is that in the array of information Bokser really has not proved his point, and I am not sure exactly where and how he thought he has even tried to prove it. In his own behalf, Bokser may fairly argue that he <u>does</u> establish the correct context in which to interpret the seder. That is a valid claim and not a negligible one. He shows that the seder is not part of the phenomenon of the symposium, and that the seder did not take shape as a response to the advent of Christianity. Bokser therefore insists that he has placed the development of the seder within the context of the Temple's destruction and the formation of early rabbinic Judaism. Maybe so, but only by a process of elimination.

In insisting that the historical context is important, in systematically working out other theses on the context of the seder and its history, Bokser has shown the way forward. So, in the balance, his book is to be judged as a partial success. The fundamental premises in my view accord with those routine in all historical study of ancient religion and history. The flaw in the book thus appears at the interstices between text and context, in the allusion to texts in the assumption that merely portraying a set of texts makes some point that otherwise requires neither articulation not sustained argumentation. That is a flaw so substantial as to limit the work's usefulness.

Bokser has produced considerably more than a set of texts, joined to elaborate bibliography and careful refutation of other viewpoints than the author's. But he has written much less than a well-argued and rigorously sustained, analytical inquiry. The reason is that, like the practitioners of the <u>Wissenschaft des Judentums</u> (and they are not alone!), Bokser knew where he wanted to emerge before he began his work. The key to a well-argued exercise lies in the correct approach. The only approach to a successful journey is the simple one of taking one step at a time. An inductive sifting of evidence, a systematic argument beginning with the pertinent texts and working outward from them -- these define the only correct route. Anything else is hack-work, the familiar and discredited deductive reasoning from proposition to proof, familiar (in the present context) in the standard works of Talmudic history. That is to say, it is talmudism extended to the realm of historical inquiry, where it simply does not belong.

The three schools of learning -- Jerusalem positivist fundamentalism, international textual-philological nihilism, American history-of-religions -- exhibit striking flaws. In general, however, the virtues of the one joined to the strengths of the next bear rich promise for the field at hand. No one can proceed, after all, without the hunting and gathering of facts that, in Himmelfarb's hands, produces an aimless book. No one can hope to address important insight without engaging in that search for cogent conclusions that, in Urbach's rather limited frame of reference, yields a comic repertoire of theological propositions in historical guise. And no one can expect to gain sound insight without proposing large explanations that, in Bokser's book, produce repeated assertions of what is not rigorously argued and in detail drawn out of texts.

If Bokser undertakes to work from text, then to context, and only finally to matrix, rather than in the other direction, he may well deliver what he promises but does not provide: a theory of origins based on an inductive exercise of step-by-step inquiry, a vigorously argued proposal adducing what is relevant and bypassing what is not. If

Himmelfarb finds the wit to revise erudition into intelligible insight, she will lead us to an understanding and appreciation of large scale themes in Judaic and Christian imaginative writing. The talent and the will have only to find focus and purpose.

It is difficult along these same lines to propose what the Jerusalem school can do to contribute to contemporary discourse. In Urbach's case, of course, it is too late to expect much. In the case of others whose work begins where it should end and ends where it should begin, it may not matter much. Work in Jerusalem tends to ignore work everywhere else. The contrary also is the fact. Apart from some limited exegetical insights, the Israeli school in Talmudic studies, including historical and cultural ones, scarcely pretends to wish to address the world beyond and does not have an international audience. We may have to accept the fact that, between that school and the other schools of learning in the field at hand stands a brazen wall. What goes on inside that wall matters mainly to insiders. Still, on the outside of the wall the fields spread forth in abundance, and scholars rightly expect to reap rich harvests of learning and insight. Here everyone is welcome to partake and to participate.

VII
THE JUDAIC SIDE OF NEW TESTAMENT STUDIES
CHILTON AND McNAMARA

Bruce D. Chilton, <u>A Galilean Rabbi and His Bible: Jesus' Use of the Interpreted Scripture of His Time</u>. Good News Studies 8. (Wilmington, DE, 1984: Michael Glazier, Inc.) 213 pp. $7.95, paper.

Martin McNamara, <u>Palestinian Judaism and the New Testament</u>. Good News Studies 4. (Wilmington, DE, 1983: Michael Glazier, Inc.) 279 pp. Paper.

Chilton presents an admirable model of how data deriving from Judaism ought to serve to illuminate the problems of New Testament interpretation. The reason is that he has taken account of the entire critical program of contemporary study of the rabbinic canon and built his inquiry upon that program. Accordingly, he avoids all the commonplace errors and -- more important -- he invents quite novel and precise ways of moving forward. He does everything right. He does not treat the rabbinic canon as uniform and monolithic and unilinear. He respects its diversity. He does not read the rabbinic writings as historical accounts of things really said and done in the setting to which they refer. He understands the long process of formation prior to the writing of the sayings and stories as we have them. On the positive side he frames his queston with great care and critical acumen. To understand his intellectual accomplishment in this splendid book, let me begin with the problem facing Chilton and then show how he has solved it. My claim that his book defines the critical measure and the program for future studies will then find ample justification.

Chilton recognizes that "the Targum," that is, the corpus of translations into Aramaic of Hebrew Scriptures, covers a broad variety of writings. These came into existence over a long period of time. He therefore avoids the simple-minded claim that "the Targum" is a single composition of uniform materials and provenance. He moreover understands that "the Targum" as we now have it cannot be said to have come into existence prior to the period in which Jesus lived and taught. Therefore he does not open "the Targum" in search for the bases (proof-texts) of Jesus's understanding of verses of the Hebrew Scripture.

What does he <u>do</u>? He asks (p. 137), "The question for us was not ... whether Jesus used the Isaiah Targum, but whether interpretative traditions later incorporated in the Targum had a formative influence on the wording of some sayings attributed to Jesus. Since this influence was most likely exerted at an early stage in the formation of the sayings as we know them, coherence with Targumic diction was seen to be significant in deciding whether a saying reflected Jesus' position more than interpretative adaptations of his words." What follows is the issue of how we know what is coherent and what is not. Chilton lists "instances of dictional coherence with the Targum in dominical references to Isaiah," then "instances of thematic coherence," then "instances of dictional coherence with the Targum in other dominical sayings," then "instances of thematic coherence of the same sort in other sayings of Jesus." Chilton's claim is backed up by detailed and careful classification of data and analysis of them. He then restates, with the expected precision and care, what he claims to have demonstrated: "Jesus did not depend on the Targum as we know it, but he does seem to have been influenced and informed by traditions which the Targum preserves better than anything else." That in my view has attained the status of fact.

Chilton then addresses the life of Christian faith today (with sympathetic interest in the life of Judaic faith) with the results of his historical and analytical work. In discussing Jesus' style of preaching Scripture as fulfilled, he maintains that the Bible can be used "within the fulfillment style of Jesus. We can approximate this style by working back through its three characteristics as we have come to know them: analogical, critical, experiential." He argues, then, that a biblical passage may present an analogy to our own situation, and, through a critical assessment of such a passage, people may relate it to their own experience. The part of the book treating the contemporary uses of his excellent findings is somewhat more diffuse and less cogently argued. Chilton pays attention to many opinions but gains less success in the well-proportioned presentation of his own views. Nonetheless, this part cannot be dismissed as mere homiletics; it is astute and full of insight.

McNamara's book, based on his Tuohy Lectures at John Carroll University, serves as a more general introduction to all forms of Judaism in relationship to the New Testament. He covers Apocalyptic Literature, the Essenes, the Dead Sea Scrolls and the New Testament, Rabbinic Tradition and the New Testament, and Aramaic Targums and the New Testament. The book is rather elementary and unsophisticated. It stands somewhat earlier in the unfolding of the contemporary encounter between Judaic and Christian studies of the early centuries before and after the beginning of the Common Era. While Chilton moves deeply into the problems of tradition and literature in the use of what we find in the Targums and in the Rabbinic canon for New Testament studies, McNamara proposes to treat matters in a more schematic way. What makes McNamara's work interesting is only his self-consciousness about the subject itself, just as Chilton's strength lies in his methodological sophistication. McNamara begins with the subject of Christian scholarship and Judaism, treating as "the problem and the setting" the very question of when and how Christian scholars take an interest in Judaism. Accordingly, the program of the book as a whole is reviewed, in the opening statement, in terms of antecedents to the work McNamara has taken for himself.

Of the many topics covered by McNamara, the one of keenest interest here is his discussion of rabbinic tradition and the New Testament. I regret to have to pronounce it ignorant and incompetent, because McNamara's selection of scholarship in this area is biased and stunningly incomplete. He quotes whom he will and ignores the rest. His discussion of this topic consequently presents a distorted and foolish melange of inanities. He would have done better to have omitted all reference to the subject of rabbinic Judaism than to treat it in the way he does. But if he did, what could he have reported about "Palestinian Judaism and the New Testament"? So, in all, he has reached for too much and grasped nothing.

In many ways the contrast between the two works provides a striking indication of where we now stand. The days of a scholarship of good will, a scholarship based on ecumenism, have ended. Why so? Because McNamara shows by his astonishing ignorance of scholarship that what is needed is more than good will. What is demanded is serious learning. It is no longer a sensation for a New Testament scholar to argue, as McNamara does, that Judaism must make contributions to New Testament studies. Everyone has known that for three generations. It is now necessary for New Testament scholars to follow the excellect example of Chilton. He has stopped talking about Judaism and begun working within the diverse texts of the various Judaisms of the age. He no longer announces the need for scholarship. He provides the scholarship.

A further dimension now demands attention as well. It is the as-yet-unmeasured extent to which New Testament and Patristic literature have now to contribute to the study of the Judaisms of late antiquity, and particularly to rabbinic or talmudic Judaism. As is clear from my description of the two books at hand, New Testament scholars quite properly ask the rabbinic canon to contribute to their interests and illuminate their inquiry. So they frame matters as they do. But the rabbinic canon for its part derives at least as much pertinent information from the writings of Christianity of late antiquity as that canon contributes to the study of Christianity. What should we want to know, if our principal focus of interest were the history of the formation of Judaism in late antiquity, rather than the history of the formation of Christianity? Then a kind of counter-agendum, a mirror-image of the Christian study of Judaism, must be framed by proponents of this other approach, namely, the Judaic study of Christianity.

In my Aphrahat and Judaism (Leiden, 1970) I asked that estimable father of the Syriac-speaking Church to teach me something about the Judaism that he knew. While no one can allege the answer for Aphrahat was definitive, I believe I was able to learn valuable lessons from him. I cannot think of equivalent studies of any of the other formidable figures of formative Christianity. Rabbinic studies of the Church Fathers generally have produced catalogues of parallels or episodic bits and pieces of narrow philological or exegetical interest only. In the next age in the modern encounter of the ancient faiths of Christianity and Judaism, I like to think, a scholar such as Chilton will show us how to study about the ways other rabbis, besides the Galilean one about whom he writes, used the interpreted Scripture of their time. I hope that, when scholars of Judaism turn to the sources of Christianity in their study of the formation of Judaism, they will approach matters with greater respect for the scholarship of the age than McNamara has done.

So these two books will serve as models for a kind of learning as yet in its infancy, one for how to do things, the other for how not to do them. But both of them equally --

McNamara as much as Chilton -- will provide definitive examples of the spirit in which the work will have to be done: a spirit of respect for the other, an attitude of genuine interest in the other. I hope that Judaic scholars of early Christianity and the rabbinic canon, in the model of Christian scholars of Palestinian Judaism and the New Testament, will treat the other -- that is, Christianity -- with respect and esteem, if also without apology.

PART THREE

THE LITERARY STUDY OF FORMATIVE JUDAISM

VIII
FORM ANALYSIS AND EXEGESIS
THE CASE OF MISHNAH TOHOROT 2:2-8

Form-analysis is the identification of recurrent syntactic patterns in the formulaic language of the Mishnah and the use of those patterns for literary-critical and exegetical purposes. The earliest exegetes of the Mishnah recognized that the language of the document follows disciplined patterns. They knew full well that these patterns at times may serve to indicate the meaning to be assigned to given lemmas. What has been grasped only in current studies is that the formal and formulaic patterning of language in the Mishnah constitutes the first and most important sustained commentary to the Mishnah itself. Form-analysis is the guide to the original meaning of the framers of the document as we now know it.

One principal contribution of form-analysis is to indicate what issues do, and what issues do not, inhere in the fundamental structure of a pericope. Because of the long history of the use of the Mishnah as a source for law far beyond its clear and explicit language, excluding what does not belong is probably the more important of the two exercises. But when we recognize the care with which the framers of the Mishnah have constructed their lists, laid out their triplets culminating in disputes, set forth contrasts between one proposition and its linguistically and conceptually matched opposite, and otherwise expressed their ideas with exquisite care, we grasp the proposition at hand.

In this paper I have chosen one of the most difficult units in the entire Mishnah, Mishnah Tohorot 2:2-8. In this example of how I believe the document must be interpreted, I indicate how the Mishnah's linguistic and syntactic patterns supply the key to its primary meaning. For the present purpose, the Tosefta is mostly ignored, since at only one point is it essential for the interpretation of the corresponding pericope of the Mishnah. I begin with an overview of the entire text and then turn to an analysis of its components.

The Text

Mishnah Tohorot 2:2-8

M. 2:2   A.   R. Eliezer [C: Leazar] says, "(1) He who eats food unclean in the first remove is unclean in the first remove;

"(2) [he who eats] food unclean in the second remove is unclean in the second remove;

"(3) [he who eats] food unclean in the third remove is unclean in the third remove."

B. R. Joshua says, "(1) He who eats food unclean in the first remove and food unclean in the second remove is unclean in the second remove.

"(2) [He who eats food] unclean in the third remove is unclean in the second remove so far as Holy Things are concerned,

"(3) and is not unclean in the second remove so far as heave-offering is concerned.

C. "[We speak of] the case of [N, Pa, P, K, Katsh #117, C, Maimonides' text lack:] unconsecrated food

D. "which is prepared in conditions appropriate to heave-offering."

M. 2:3 A. Unconsecrated food:
in the first remove is unclean and renders unclean;

B. in the second remove is unfit, but does not convey uncleanness;

C. and in the third remove is eaten in the pottage of heave-offering.

M. 2:4 A. Heave-offering:
in the first and in the second remove is unclean and renders unclean;

B. in the third remove is unfit and does not convey uncleanness;

C. and in the fourth remove is eaten in a pottage of Holy Things.

M. 2:5 A. Holy Things:
in the first and the second and the third removes are susceptible to uncleanness and render unclean;

B. and in the fourth remove are unfit and do not convey uncleanness;

C. and in the fifth remove are eaten in a pottage of Holy Things.

M. 2:6 A. Unconsecrated food:
in the second remove renders unconsecrated liquid unclean and renders foods of heave-offering unfit.

B. Heave-offering:
in the third remove renders unclean [the] liquid of Holy Things, and renders foods of Holy Things unfit,

C. if it [the heave-offering] was prepared in the condition of cleanness pertaining to Holy Things.

D. But if it was prepared in conditions pertaining to heave-offering, it renders unclean at two removes and renders unfit at one remove in reference to Holy Things.

M. 2:7 A. R. Eleazar [Eliezer: GRA, Rosh, V, N, M; Eleazar (Leazar): MA, K, Katsh #117, C, Pa, P, PB] says, "The three of them are equal:

B. "Holy Things and heave-offering, and unconsecrated food: "Which are at the first remove of uncleanness render unclean at two removes and unfit at one [further] remove in respect to Holy Things;

"render unclean at one remove and spoil at one [further] remove in respect to heave-offering;

"and spoil unconsecrated food.

C. "That which is unclean in the second remove in all of them renders unclean at one remove and unfit at one [further] remove in respect to Holy Things;

"and renders liquid of unconsecrated food unclean;

"and spoils foods of heave-offering.

D. "The third remove of uncleanness in all of them renders liquids of Holy Things unclean,

"and spoils food of Holy Things."

M. 2:8 A. He who eats food unclean in the second remove should not work ($y^c\underline{sh}$; alternate reading: $y^c\underline{sm}$) in the olive press [since he will render the oil unclean].

B. And unconsecrated food which is prepared in accord with the rules pertaining to Holy Things -- lo, this is like unconsecrated food.

C. R. Eleazar b. R. Sadoq says, "Lo, it is like heave-offering,

D. "conveying uncleanness at two removes and rendering unfit at one [further] remove."

Overview

M. Tohorot 2:2-8 presupposes knowledge of the rabbinic system of ritual purity. A review of some of its essential elements is necessary for an understanding of the arguments and analyses that follow.

In the rabbinic system, ritual impurity is acquired by contact with either a primary or a secondary source of uncleanness, called a "Father" or a "Child" (or "Offspring") of uncleanness, respectively. In the first category are contact with a corpse, a person suffering flux, a leper, and the like. Objects made of metal, wood, leather, bone, cloth, or sacking become Fathers of uncleanness if they touch a corpse.

Foodstuffs and liquids are susceptible to uncleanness, but will not render other foodstuffs unclean in the same degree or remove of uncleanness that they themselves suffer. Foodstuffs furthermore will not make vessels or utensils unclean. But liquids made unclean by a Father of uncleanness will do so if they touch the inner side of the vessel. That is, if they fall into the contained space of an earthenware vessel, they make the whole vessel unclean.

Food or liquid that touches a Father of uncleanness becomes unclean in the <u>first</u> remove. If food touches a person or vessel made unclean by a primary cause of uncleanness, it is unclean in the <u>second</u> remove. Food that touches <u>second</u> grade uncleanness incurs <u>third</u> grade uncleanness, and food that touches <u>third</u> grade uncleanness incurs <u>fourth</u> grade uncleanness, and so on. But liquids touching either a primary source of uncleanness (Father) or something unclean in the first or second remove (Offspring) are regarded as unclean in the first remove. They are able to make something else unclean. If, for example, the outer side of a vessel is made unclean by a liquid -- thus unclean in the second remove -- and another liquid touches the outer side, the other liquid incurs not second, but first degree uncleanness.

Heave-offering (food raised up for priestly use only) unclean in the third remove of uncleanness, and Holy Things (that is, things belonging to the cult) unclean in the fourth remove, do not make other things, whether liquids or foods, unclean.

The difference among removes of uncleanness is important. First degree uncleanness in common food will convey uncleanness. But, although food unclean in the second remove will be unacceptable, it will not convey uncleanness, that is, third degree uncleanness. But it will render heave-offering <u>unfit.</u>

Further considerations apply to heave-offering and Holy Things. Heave-offering can be made unfit <u>and</u> unclean by a first, and unfit by a second, degree of uncleanness. If it touches something unclean in the third remove, it is made unfit, but itself will not impart fourth degree uncleanness. A Holy Thing that suffers uncleanness in the first, second, or third remove is unclean <u>and</u> conveys uncleanness. If it is unclean in the fourth remove, it is invalid for the cult but does not convey uncleanness. It is much more susceptible than are noncultic things. Thus, common food that suffers second degree uncleanness will render heave-offering invalid. We already know that it makes liquid unclean in the first remove. Likewise, heave-offering unclean in the third remove will make Holy Things invalid and put them into a fourth remove of uncleanness.

Complications in the system will arise if common food is prepared in conditions of cleanness appropriate for either heave-offering or Holy Things. In that case it will be necessary to determine the status of the food and its susceptibility to uncleanness. This matter is raised in the pericopae discussed below.

With these data firmly in had, let us turn to a general discussion of M. Toh. 2:2-8.

M. 2:2 introduces the removes of uncleanness. Our interest is in the contaminating affect, upon a person, of eating unclean food. Does the food make the person unclean in the same remove of uncleanness as is borne by the food itself? Thus if one eats food unclean in the first remove, is he unclean in that same remove? This is the view of Eliezar. Joshua says he is unclean in the second remove. The dispute, M. 2:2A-B, at M. 2:2C-D is significantly glossed. The further consideration is introduced as to the sort of food under discussion. Joshua is made to say that there is a difference between the contaminating affects upon the one who eats heave-offering, on the one side, and unconsecrated food prepared in conditions of heave-offering, on the other. This matter, the status of unconsecrated food prepared as if it were heave-offering, or as if it were Holy Things, and heave-offering prepared as if it were Holy Things, forms a substratum of our chapter, added to several primary items and complicating their exegesis. T. 2:1 confirms, however, that primary to the dispute between Eliezer and Joshua is simply the matter of the affects of food unclean in the first remove upon the person who eats such food. The gloss, M. 2:2C-D, forms a redactional-thematic link between Joshua's opinion and the large construction of M. 2:3-7.

M. 2:3-5, expanded and glossed by M. 2:6, follow a single and rather tight form. The sequence differentiates unconsecrated food, heave-offering, and Holy Things each at the several removes from the original source of uncleanness.

Eleazar, M. 2:7, insists that, at a given remove, all three are subject to the *same* rule. The contrary view, M. 2:3-6, is that unconsecrated food in the first remove makes heave-offering unclean and at the second remove spoils heave-offering; it does not enter a third remove and therefore has no affect upon Holy Things. Heave-offering at the first two removes may produce contaminating effects, and at the third remove spoils Holy Things, but is of no effect at the fourth. Holy Things in the first three removes produce uncleanness, and at the fourth impart unfitness to other Holy Things. M. 2:6 then goes over the ground of unconsecrated food at the second remove, and heave-offering at the third. The explanation of M. 2:6C is various; the simplest view is that the clause glosses M. 2:6B by insisting that the heave-offering to which we refer is prepared as if it were Holy Things, on which account, at the third remove, it can spoil Holy Things.

At M. 2:7, as I said, Eleazar restates matters, treating all three -- Holy Things, heave-offering, and unconsecrated food -- as equivalent to one another at the first, second, and third removes, with the necessary qualification for unconsecrated food that it is like the other, consecrated foods in producing effects at the second and even the third removes. Some commentators read *Eliezer*. They set the pericope up against Joshua's view at M. 2:2, assigning to Joshua M. 2:3ff. as well. My picture of the matter is significantly different from the established exegesis.

M. 2:8 is a singleton. First, we go over the matter on which Joshua and Eliezer agree at M. 2:2, which is that one who eats food unclean in the second remove is unclean in that same remove. Accordingly, he can make liquid unclean, and it is unclean in the first remove. Therefore he should not work in the olive press, since he will make the oil unclean. Then we raise the issue which never is wholly spelled out in one place as an integrated problem: What is the rule if we prepare unconsecrated food *as if* it were Holy Things? M. 2:8B says it remains in the status of unconsecrated food. Eleazar b. R. Sadoq ways it is like heave-offering. Our chapter does not contain the view that it indeed is like Holy Things. Yet one way of harmonizing M. 2:7 with M. 2:3-6 would be to assert that Eleazar holds that the unconsecrated food of which he speaks has, in fact, been prepared as if it were Holy Things, which accounts for the fact that it produces the same effects as do Holy Things.

Thus, one persistent exercise in our chapter is the introduction of the differentiation between unconsecrated food, on the one hand, and unconsecrated food prepared in accord with the rules of cleanness applicable to heave-offering, and, further, to Holy Things, on the other. The issue is intruded, in particular, at M. 2:2, 6, and 8. At M. 2:2, it is surely secondary to the dispute between Eliezer and Joshua, as shown both by form-critical considerations and by T.'s version of the problem under discussion. As to the former, Eliezer says that which is unclean in the first remove makes a person who eats it unclean in the first remove, and so with the second and third. Joshua's theory matches Eliezer's in formal articulation. If one eats something unclean in the first remove, he himself becomes unclean in the second. To be sure, he agrees that if one eats something unclean in the second remove, he too is unclean in the second remove. But, T. explains, that is because what is unclean in the second remove makes the spit in his mouth -- liquid -- unclean in the first remove, and that in turn makes him unclean in the second. Then comes the intrusion, "in respect to unconsecrated food prepared in accord with the rules of cleanness applicable to heave-offering." MSS variants give, further, "heave-offering prepared in accord, etc.," that is, omitting unconsecrated food. On the face of it, this formal issue is secondary, as I said, and T. knows nothing of it. But reading it as part of Joshua's saying, we have then to interpret the whole pericope to deal with two problems.

The second of these problems is the preparation of food in accord with rules of cleanness not applicable to it, unconsecrated food as heave-offering, M. 2:6; heave-offering prepared as Holy Things; and, M. 2:8, unconsecrated food prepared as Holy Things -- the three possibilities. The three are not assembled in a single pericope, rather, added as a layer to the several primary rulings and disputes.

Naturally, the further exegetical problem will be raised, in the Talmuds, about whether we regard the unconsecrated food prepared as it were heave-offering, or the heave-offering prepared as if it were Holy Things, as wholly subject to the rules applicable to the higher degree of sanctity, or as only partially subject to those rules.

It remains to ask, Is it possible that the issue of unconsecrated food prepared in conditions of cleanness required for heave-offering, and heave-offering prepared in conditions of cleanness required for Holy Things, has been intruded because of some sort of difficulty in the process of transmission of the primary pericopae to which it is attached?

A comparison of M. 2:2 and M. 2:6 makes this seem unlikely. The relationship between the segments is unmistakable, and each item means what it says. M. 2:2C-D speaks of unconsecrated food prepared under the conditions of cleanness required for heave-offering, and M. 2:6 clearly wishes to speak of heave-offering prepared under the rules of cleanness required for Holy Things. There is no repetition of the same words in the two pericopae, which might lead to the conclusion that they do not belong in one or the other unit. The issue is clearly secondary in both pericopae, but is formulated with precision.

To which stratum shall we assign the several pericopae of the chapter?

Let us begin with M. 2:2. Here Joshua and Eliezer debate a fundamental point, the affect of eating unclean food upon the person who eats the food. Is he in the same remove of uncleanness as is the food he eats? Shall we assign to that same stratum the issue of the rules for unconsecrated food prepared as if it were heave-offering? It is difficult to know. Since Eleazar b. R. Sadoq treats the parallel matter -- unconsecrated food prepared as if it were Holy Things -- it is hardly a matter whose status was settled before Ushan times.

Moreover, the issue is secondary to, and a logical development of, the matter under dispute between Joshua and Eliezer. Why? Once we ask about whether unclean food produces an equivalent, or a diminished, level of uncleanness upon the person who eats it, we have then to ask about the parallel question of unclean food that naturally belongs in one category (unconsecrated), but which has been placed into another, more sensitive category (heave-offering), by the owner's intent. Is this treated, for purposes of imparting contamination, as if it were in the category into which it has been raised? So we ask first about how ordinary food imparts uncleanness, and then about how extraordinary food imparts uncleanness. The logical connection to the former issue is tight.

What about the complex at M. 2:3-6+7, the removes of uncleanness applicable to unconsecrated food, heave-offering, and Holy Things? M. 2:3 allows two removes for unclean unconsecrated food, and M. 2:5 reenforces unconsecrated food, saying it affects Holy Things. ^CAqiva, in a quite separate pericope, is explicit on the matter. While we cannot be sure which Eleazar is before us, not knowing whether it is a Yavnean or an Ushan Eleazar or Eliezer (b. Hyrcanus, as at M. 2:2), ^CAqiva tells us that the issue is live at Yavneh. He takes up a position contrary to that of M. 2:3-6, and, it follows, the topic under dispute is to be assigned to Yavneh, in the theory that what we have are several opinions formed (if not formulated) at the time that the issue was current.

M. 2:2 is Yavnean; M. 2:3-7 concern rather basic questions about the removes of uncleanness for unconsecrated food, heave-offering, and Holy Things, evidently under discussion in the later Yavnean and Ushan circles. Overall, the impression left by the chapter is that the differentiation among the several removes of uncleanness, as these pertain to various sorts of food to which uncleanness is imparted, as well as the differentiation of the contaminating affects <u>upon</u> such foods of various <u>sources</u> of uncleanness, was accomplished primarily at Yavneh and Usha, upon the basis of remarkably little tradition from the period before 70.

Let us now turn to a closer reading of the chapter's components.

Analysis

M. 2:2

A. R. Eliezer [C: Leazar] says, "(1) He who eats food unclean in the first remove is unclean in the first remove;

"(2) [he who eats] food unclean in the second remove is unclean in the second remove;

"(3) [he who eats] food unclean in the third remove is unclean in this third remove."

B. R. Joshua says, "(1) He who eats food unclean in the first remove and food unclean in the second remove is unclean in the second remove.

"(2) [He who eats food] unclean in the third remove is unclean in the second remove so far as Holy Things are concerned,

"(3) and is not unclean in the second remove so far as heave-offering is concerned.

C. "[We speak of] the case of [N, Pa, P, K, Katsh #117, C Maimonides' text lack:] unconsecrated food

D. "which is prepared in conditions of cleanness appropriate to heave-offering."

The dispute formally is complete and balanced in A-B. C-D then introduce a complication to gloss the terms of the dispute. So far as Joshua and Eliezer are concerned, the issue is the affect, upon a person, of eating unclean food.

Eliezer's view is that the person enters the same remove of uncleanness as that of the food he has eaten. If he ate food unclean in the first remove, he too is unclean in the first remove and produces equivalent effects, so too second and third.

This simple ruling is rejected by Joshua. His view is that a person who eats food unclean in the first remove is not unclean in the same remove, but only in the second remove; he concurs as to eating food in the second remove. In both cases, the person makes heave-offering unfit if he touches it. Why not lower the person who eats unclean food in the second remove to the status of the third remove? Because, as Rosh and Sens say, following T. 2:1 = b. Hul. 33b, the food he eats makes the spit in his mouth unclean, and, as liquid, it is unclean in the first remove and makes him unclean in the second remove. Clearly, therefore, Joshua's ruling is based upon a somewhat more complex picture.

This further affects his view of a person who eats food unclean in the third remove. Will he make the liquid in his mouth unclean, which food then is unclean in the first remove and places him into the second remove? With respect to Holy Things, he will. With respect to heave-offering, he will not. Why? Because in the former, the man unclean in the third remove produces a fourth remove, and, accordingly, the liquid too is affected (GRA). But in the latter, there is no further remove of uncleanness, so the liquid too cannot be affected.

C-D form a problem because of the MS variants that omit unconsecrated food. If we read C-D as given here, the point is that the foregoing dispute (B) about food unclean in the third remove concerns not heave-offering but unconsecrated food prepared within the discipline applying to heave-offering. The point of the gloss then is that a third remove now applies to unconsecrated food. If we do not read unconsecrated food, then C-D refer back to B's "is not unclean in the second remove so far as heave-offering in concerned." The point is that the third remove applies to Holy Things but not to heave-offering prepared in conditions of cleanness that apply to heave-offering (and not to Holy Things). But if the heave-offering is prepared in conditions applying to Holy Things, it is subject to the rules of Holy Things, and he who eats food unclean in the third remove places it into the third or fourth remove, as specified.

In any event, on the surface C-D qualify only Joshua's saying. Since Eliezer makes reference neither to Holy Things nor to heave-offering, the qualification and the problem solved by it are not pertinent to his opinion.

A. Said R. Joshua to R. Eliezer, "Where do we find a form of uncleanness in the Torah which produces another uncleanness which is like it [at the same remove, and not at one remove of diminished virulence], that you say, 'It produces [uncleanness at] the first, remove'?"

B. He said to him, "Also you say, 'it [that which is unclean in the second remove] produces something unclean in the second remove'!"

C. He said to him, "We find that that which is unclean in the second remove renders liquid unclean to produce uncleanness at the first remove, and the liquid renders food unclean to produce uncleanness at the second remove.

D. "But we do not find something unclean in the first remove which makes something else unclean in the first remove in any instance."

T. Toh. 2:1

T. treats only M. 2:2A-B, omitting reference to the third and fourth removes and to the matter of Holy Things and heave-offering. This strongly suggests that the essential dispute is at M. 2:2A-B1-2. Eliezer does not answer Joshua's question. He simply points out that Joshua has to answer the same question. At C Joshua does, and it is in accord with T. that we interpreted M. D simply repeats Joshua's opinion in M., in more elaborate language.

M. 2:3-7

2:3 A. Unconsecrated food:
in the first remove is unclean and renders unclean;

B. in the second remove is unfit, but does not convey uncleanness;

C. and in the third remove is eaten in the pottage of heave-offering.

2:4 A. Heave-offering:
in the first and second remove is unclean and renders unclean;

B. in the third remove is unfit and does not convey uncleanness;

C. and in the fourth remove is eaten in a pottage of Holy Things.

2:5 A. Holy Things:
in the first and the second and the third removes are susceptible to uncleanness and render unclean;

B. and in the fourth removes are unfit and do not convey uncleanness;

C. and in the fifth remove are eaten in a pottage of Holy Things.

2:6 A. Unconsecrated food:
in the second remove renders unconsecrated liquid unclean, and renders foods of heave-offering unfit.

B. <u>Heave-offering</u>:
in the third remove renders unclean [the] liquid of Holy Things, and renders foods of Holy Things unfit,

C. if [the heave-offering] was prepared in the condition of cleanness pertaining to Holy Things.

D. But if it was prepared in conditions pertaining to heave-offering, it renders unclean at two removes and renders unfit at one remove in reference to Holy Things.

2:7 A. R. Eleazar [<u>Eliezer</u>: GRA, Rosh, V, N, M; <u>Eleazar</u> (Leazar): MA, K, Katsh #117, C, Pa, P, PB] says, "The three of them are equal:

B. "<u>Holy Things and heave-offering and unconsecrated food</u>:
"which are at the first remove of uncleanness render unclean at two removes are unfit at one [further] remove in respect to Holy Things,
"render unclean at one remove and spoil at one [further] remove in respect to heave-offering,
"and spoil unconsecrated food.

C. "That which is unclean in the second remove in all of them renders unclean at one remove and unfit at one [further] remove in respect to Holy Things,
"and renders liquid of unconsecrated food unclean,
"and spoils food of heave-offering.

D. "The third remove of uncleanness in all of them renders liquids of Holy Things unclean,
"and spoils food of Holy Things."

What is now to be done, before reviewing the interpretation of the pericope in the light of the great commentaries, is to ask, If we had no prepared agendum of questions and no preconceptions, formed on the basis of other rules, what should we understand by the present set of rules? The first, M. 2:3, tells us that unconsecrated food in the first remove from the original source of uncleanness is unclean and renders unclean. That language seems to me to mean exactly what it says, which is that unconsecrated food in the first remove is capable of a further affect of contamination, so that what touches unclean unconsecrated food in the first remove, thus in the second remove, is unfit but does not convey uncleanness. Does heave-offering appear? Obviously not. The simple meaning, therefore, is that unconsecrated food in the second remove is unfit for consumption, presumably by people who wish at home to keep the laws of cultic cleanness. Unconsecrated food in the third remove produces no contamination. The entire interest of the pericope, therefore, is in unconsecrated food. M. 2:4 then speaks of heave-offering and tells us that heave-offering in the first and second removes are unclean and impart uncleanness. To what do they impart uncleanness? To heave-offering, in the third remove. And that heave-offering is unfit, as we know. The same is to be said of Holy Things. They impart uncleanness at three removes. Accordingly, unconsecrated food produces not two further removes of contamination, but three.

The first remove at M. 2:3 makes something it touches unclean. What it touches should be that which is unclean -- in the second remove. But we are told, explicitly, that what is unclean in the second remove is <u>unfit</u>, but does not convey uncleanness. The difficult point, therefore, is the second remove. What we should want, for M. 2:3B, if dictated by M. 2:3A, should make provision for the uncleanness referred to at M. 2:3A, and so we should have:

Unconsecrated food which is unclean in the first remove is unclean
<u>and conveys uncleanness</u>
Unconsecrated food which is in the second remove is unclean
<u>but does not convey uncleanness</u>
That which is unclean in the third remove ...

What is somewhat confusing is replacing the <u>tm'</u> of M. 2:3A with <u>pswl</u> at M. 2:3B (and the same with the parallels of M. 2:4-5). Why has the model of M. 2:3A been abandoned at B? For the contrast clearly is between <u>unclean/renders unclean</u> and <u>unclean/does not render unclean</u>. Why substitute <u>unfit</u> for <u>unclean</u> at B and not at A? The question applies to M. 2:7, <u>render unclean</u> at two removes and <u>unfit</u> at one [third] remove. This bears the same redundancy. If we said only, <u>render unclean at two removes,</u> it would follow that what is at the third remove does not <u>render</u> unclean -- but it <u>is</u> unclean. In other words, at the foundation of the shift in language is the evident purpose of marking the end of a chain of contaminating contacts with <u>unfit</u>, rather than <u>unclean</u>, thus <u>mtm'... pswl ...</u>, rather than M. 2:3A's <u>tm'... mtm'</u>. Notice, moreover, that Maimonides uses both word choices (<u>Other Fathers of Uncleanness</u> 11:2B) "And whence do we learn that food stuff suffering <u>second grade uncleanness</u> is <u>invalid ...</u>?" I cannot imagine why, except for mnemonic reasons, someone should have shifted the usage, but it is done consistently.

Let us now ask a much more important question: Do M. 2:3-6 continue the opinion of Joshua at M. 2:2? He says that one who eats food unclean in the first and second remove is unclean in the second remove. Will he agree with M. 2:3, assuming we speak of unconsecrated food? Of course he will, because M. 2:3 is of the view that unconsecrated food at the second remove is unfit/unclean. But what do we gain -- for Eliezer, M. 2:2A2, says exactly the same thing. Only if we insist that Eleazar at M. 2:7 is Eliezer of M. 2:2 shall we assume that there is disagreement between Eliezer and Joshua on the issues of the present pericope. This brings us to the main point I here contribute. The disagreement is between M. 2:3-6 and M. 2:7, as follows:

M. 2:3	M. 2:7
Unconsecrated food unclean in the first remove:	Unconsecrated food unclean at the first remove:
Contact 1: Unclean, imparts uncleanness at	Contact 1: Unclean, imparts uncleanness at

Contact 2: Unfit (= unclean, but does not impart uncleanness; there is no contact 3)

Contact 2: Unclean, imparts uncleanness at

Contact 3: Unfit
in respect to Holy Things

Contact 1: Unclean, imparts uncleanness at

Contact 2: Unfit (= unclean, etc.!)
in respect to heave-offering

Contact 1: Spoils unconsecrated food
(= makes it unclean, but it does not impart uncleanness; there is no contact 2)

If we assume that M. 2:3-6 are talking, at M. 2:3, about the affects of unconsecrated food upon unconsecrated food, then the difference between M. 2:3 and M. 2:7 (Eleazar) is very clear. Eleazar is of the view that unconsecrated food in the first remove does not impart uncleanness at all. It may become unclean, but it has no affect upon other food.

What sort of food does have an impact upon other food? Only heave-offering and Holy Things. They indeed do produce the affect of uncleanness/unfitness, and may further produce the affect of such severe contamination that a further stage of contamination is possible.

If that indeed is Eleazar's view, then to whom will it be important to insist that, when unconsecrated food does have the capacity to impart uncleanness, it is in fact unconsecrated food which has been prepared under conditions of cleanness required for heave-offering -- to whom, if not to Eleazar! The gloss of M. 2:2C-D in fact brings Joshua into conformity with Eleazar's quite separate point, by making him say that, when he speaks of food in the first, second, and third removes producing uncleanness, it is specifically unconsecrated food prepared under conditions of cleanness required for heave-offering. But why should Joshua alone be made to say so? For Eliezer of M. 2:2 has told us that he who eats food unclean in the first remove in unclean in the first remove -- which is to say, unclean food imparts uncleanness. So C-D must in fact be read as (Eleazar's) glosses of both Eliezer's and Joshua's total and completed dispute.

What about the equivalent gloss at M. 2:6? There we are told that heave-offering prepared in conditions of cleanness required for Holy Things when in the third remove produces uncleanness -- that is, it makes fluids of Holy Things unclean and renders food of Holy Things unfit. (To put it otherwise, the liquid falls into the first remove and so has the capacity to render other things unclean, but the solid food does not, so is merely unclean itself, without further contaminating capacity.) What is Eleazar's view of the capacity of heave-offering to render something unclean? At M. 2:7D, he speaks of the third remove of "the three of them" (including heave-offering). What does it do? It renders unclean liquids of Holy Things and renders unfit food of Holy Things(!). Does Eleazar disagree with M. 2:6? Of course not -- that is, if we include the gloss of M. 2:6C:

heave-offering at the third remove renders liquid of Holy Things unclean and foods of Holy Things unfit.

What is it that the glosses accomplish?

First, they eliminate the dispute (?) between Eleazar and Joshua and Eliezer of M. 2:2, on the one side.

Second, they force M. 2:6 to concur with Eleazar.

And what is Eleazar's position in these matters? In his view, the unconsecrated food not prepared as if it were heave-offering and the heave-offering not prepared as if it were Holy Things has precisely the same contaminating power as if it were prepared in accord with the more strict set of rules, respectively.

At issue, then, is nothing other than the (unstated) agendum of our chapter, the capacity to raise food to a higher order of sensitivity to uncleanness by subjecting it to rules of cleanness not ordinarily required, unconsecrated food to heave-offering, heave-offering to Holy Things. That which is not essential at M. 2:2, 6, (and 8) in fact has shaped the articulation of the whole set, M. 2:2-8. If the fact is that M. 2:2C-D serve as a gloss, to bring that set into relationship to Eleazar's opinion, then what shall we isolate as the equivalent gloss to the set M. 2:3-6? The answer is obvious: the whole of M. 2:6 serves to gloss M. 2:3-5 in much the same way as M. 2:2C-D revise M. 2:2A-B.

Who is this Eleazar, who holds that it makes no difference whether we prepare unconsecrated food as unconsecrated food, or whether we prepare it as heave-offering, and whether we prepare heave-offering as such, or whether we prepare it as Holy Things? It is none other than the authority of M. 2:8B, who tells us that if we prepare unconsecrated food as if it were Holy Things, it has exactly the same capacity to impart uncleanness as other unconsecrated food. Eleazar b. R. Sadoq, who holds that unconsecrated food prepared as if it were Holy Things produces the contaminating affects of heave-offering, will differ. And we have, in fact, an Ushan construction, between Eleazar b. R. Sadoq and an Ushan Eleazar (or Eliezer, it hardly matters among Ushans) on exactly the same point.

And why is it that Eleazar takes this position? Because, so far as he is concerned, what is important is not the source of contamination -- the unclean foods -- but that which is contaminated, the unconsecrated food, heave-offering, and Holy Things.

He could not state matter more clearly than he does when he says that the three of them are exactly equivalent. And they are, because the differentiations will emerge in the food affected, or contaminated, by the three. So at the root of the dispute is whether we gauge the contamination in accord with the source -- unconsecrated food, or unconsecrated food prepared as if it were heave-offering, and so on -- or whether the criterion is the food which is contaminated. M. 2:3-5 are all wrong, Eleazar states explicitly at M. 2:7A, because they differentiate among uncleanness imparted by unclean unconsecrated food, unclean heave-offering, and unclean Holy Things, and do not differentiate among the three sorts of food to which contamination is imparted.

It is surely a logical position, for the three sorts of food to exhibit differentiated capacities to receive uncleanness; one sort is more contaminable than another. And so

132   The Literary Study of Formative Judaism

too is the contrary view logical: <u>what is more sensitive to uncleanness also will have a greater capacity to impart uncleanness</u>. The subtle debate before us clearly unknown to Eliezer and Joshua at M. 2:2. To them the operative categories are something unclean in the first, second, or third <u>removes</u>, without distinction as to the relative sensitivities of the several types of food which may be unclean.

The sequence thus begins with Eliezer and Joshua, who ask about the contaminating power of that which is unclean in the first and second removes, without regard to whether it is unconsecrated food, heave-offering, or Holy Things. To them, the distinction between the capacity to impart contamination, or to receive contamination, of the several sorts of food is unknown. Once, however, their question is raised -- in such general terms -- it will become natural to ask the next logical question, one which makes distinctions not only among the several removes of uncleanness, but also among the several sorts of food involved in the processes of contamination. That step is not before us. Only the still further, logical extension of the issue <u>is</u> before us, the third dimension in our three-dimensional construction: (1) removes, three; (2) types of food, three; and finally, (3) whether the important aspect of the types of food is its susceptibility to <u>receive</u> uncleanness or its capacity to <u>impart</u> uncleanness, three respectively. Each system -- Eleazar's and the authority of M. 2:3-5's -- bears twenty-seven possibilities, therefore, with the difference in the systems coming in at the 18th through 27th cases, so to speak. Our picture of the matter will intersect with the inherited one, but also come into conflict, for fairly obvious reasons.

M. 2:8

A. He who eats food unclean in the second remove should not work (y^csh; alt.: y^csm) in the olive press, [since he will render the oil unclean].
B. And unconsecrated food which is prepared in accord with the rules pertaining to Holy Things -- lo, this is like unconsecrated food.
C. R. Eleazar b. R. Sadoq says, "Lo, it is like heave-offering,
D. "conveying uncleanness at two removes and rendering unfit at one [further] remove."

A is separate from B-C. Why should a person who has eaten food unclean in the second remove not work in the olive press? Because the olive oil will emerge. The person is unclean in the second remove, as both Eliezer and Joshua will agree, and he will render the liquid unclean in the first remove. This will render the press unclean (T. 1:7C).

B now returns to the issue of M. 2:2C-D. There we are told that unconsecrated food which is prepared in accord with the rules of the cleanness of heave-offering produces a third remove, just as does heave-offering. B now adds that unconsecrated food prepared in accord with the rules pertaining to the cleanness of Holy Things is unchanged and remains adjudged in accord with the rules, for the cleanness and removes from uncleanness, of unconsecrated food, and with those alone. That matter is not raised at M. 2:2C-D, nor does it occur at M. 2:6. The former tells us about unconsecrated food prepared as if it were heave-offering. The later speaks of heave-offering prepared as if it were Holy Things. So we can raise each level by one: (1) unconsecrated food to heave-offering; (2) heave-offering to Holy Things. But (3) we cannot raise the first to the third level.

Eleazar b. R. Sadoq says that if we treat unconsecrated food as if it were Holy Things, to be sure it does not fall into the category of Holy Things. But it does fall into the category of heave-offering and becomes subject to its rules of contamination, the other possible position. What is curious is that these matters are not put together into a single pericope but scattered among the several as glosses.

IX
REDACTION AND FORMULATION
THE TALMUD OF THE LAND OF ISRAEL AND THE MISHNAH

i. Seeing the Whole Whole

Grasping whole and complete documents produced by the rabbis of late antiquity is not easy because of the sheer size of the texts. Perhaps that is why people limit their perspectives to exegesis of bits and pieces of the whole. They take as the exegetical task the comparison of one bit of one document with a slice of a different document. In doing so, they obliterate all lines of historical, hence also social, demarcation. For, failing to see any document whole and complete, they cannot take a sighting on its context in history and society, its distinguishing and characteristic traits of style and substance. Accordingly, situating a document in its own time and place is never attempted. It follows that no one attempts to describe the distinctive viewpoint of a document as a whole and to ask about why the people behind the document chose to say what they do rather than something else, to express themselves in one way rather than another. Everything is read in one enveloping context, established by such circumlocutions as "the rabbis," or "Talmudic Judaism," or just "Judaism," or "the Midrash" or "the Talmud." Indeed, since medieval and even early modern writers and compilers followed established literary conventions and produced compilations of exegeses of Scripture (midrashim), it has now become possible to treat as a single, continuous, essentially non-historical and non-contextual corpus of midrashic materials, writings extending over nearly fifteen hundred years and three continents.

Seeing the whole in a whole way defines the first step in differentiation of one document from another. It allows us for the first time to ask about the viewpoint expressed by one group of compilers or redactors in making up or selecting and then putting things together as they did, as distinct from the viewpoint expressed by some other group in dealing with materials whether of a parallel or a different sort. Rather than assuming there is a single, "rabbinic" or "midrashic" viewpoint on anything and everything including aesthetics, we may then investigate the parts of Judaism of the rabbinic sort, prior to asking whether and how they fit together and why they have reached their present condition as a whole. In the absence of historical differentiation and description, literary criticism of rhetoric and other aesthetic conventions of expression seems unlikely to make much progress beyond the mere guess-work and free-association that now prevail. But the ancient and medieval rabbis did not make things up as they went along. They labored within constraints of convention and tradition, at the same time vastly expanding and enriching the inherited corpus through their own imagination and theological and rhetorical inventiveness. Contemporary literary criticism can do no less than deal with a document in its context of both continuity and creativity, rather than as an undifferentiated mess of proof-texts.

If we wish to see a document as a whole, the first thing we must look for is regularities, rules of formulation everywhere present. From such simple and external things, and only from them, we may then proceed to posit recurrent principles or ideas: the things the document's author(s) or compiler(s) wished to say. The former procedure is not subjective, the latter may be. In the former case we look for such things as recurrent particles or word-groupings, syntactic patterns, word-choices and how they work -- facts of rhetoric and expression. These either are there, or they are not there. No one can tell us that he does not see them -- or (as is common in theological and literary-critical fields) he does not "agree." If, by contrast, we start our work with an account of what we think the text wishes to tell us, the fundamental and generative problematic the document takes up, we may be right, but in the charged contemporary context of discourse, it may not matter very much. For everyone's opinion is as good as everyone else's, concerning a text no one has studied beginning to end anyhow. Once more the sheer volume of any significant document presents formidable obstacles to rational and informed discourse. If, as in the present case, one proposes to make judgments never before attempted, it is therefore best to begin at the beginning.

ii. The Talmud of the Land of Israel

The Talmud of the Land of Israel (also: the Palestinian Talmud, Yerushalmi, or the Jerusalem Talmud), ca. A.D. 400, consists of thirty-nine tractates, each one devoted to a corresponding tractate of the Mishnah, concluded in ca. A.D. 200. The Mishnah, for its part, is divided into sixty-two tractates (excluding reference to Abot) and stands behind not only the Palestinian Talmud but also the Babylonian one. The two Talmuds, then, took shape around a single prior document. Each takes up its own selection of Mishnah-tractates.

The first translation into English of the Talmud under discussion is accomplished. I have completed twenty-nine of the thirty-nine tractates, in twenty-four volumes, and others, mainly my students, are working on the rest, under the title, The Talmud of the Land of Israel. A Preliminary Translation and Explanation (Chicago, 1982ff.: The University of Chicago Press). Volume 35 serves as an introduction.

It seems to me essential to translate into our own language any text subject to sustained and systematic study. First of all, we thereby make available for all to see precisely what is subject to discussion. Second, we make a commitment to the meaning of the text at every point, thereby exposing the numerous points at which matters really are not very clear. If the translation retains a close relationship to the original, as mine does, and constitutes more than a mere paraphrase (unlike that of Moise Schwab, Le Talmud de Jérusalem. Traduit pour la première fois en français [Paris, 1871-1890]), then the literary-critical labor will be shown to rest not on guess-work or subjective impressions. Nor will it depend on random selection of odd and interesting things. Rather it will take up the entire text, its gross and prevailing traits. If and when systematic historical and literary work on the Talmud of the Land of Israel gets under way in the State of Israel, colleagues there, for their part, will find they have to translate the entire document into

Israeli Hebrew. The alternative is a text never subject to minute analysis, results never available for testing and replication.

The translation I have made is called preliminary, and I wish briefly to digress to explain why. The tentative character of the translation governs the status of all results based upon it.

My translation into English of the Talmud of the Land of Israel ("Palestinian Talmud," Yerushalmi") is provisional, even though it is not apt to be replaced for some time. It is preliminary, first, because a modern commentary of a philological and halakic character is not yet available; second, because the available dictionary is not up-to-date; and, third, because even the lower criticism of the text has yet to be undertaken. Consequently, the meanings imputed to the Hebrew and Aramaic words and the sense ascribed to them in this translation at best are merely a first step. When a systematic effort at the lower criticism of the extant text has been completed, a complete philological study and modern dictionary along comparative lines made available, and a commentary based on both accomplished, then the present work will fall away, having served for the interim. Unhappily, as I said, that interim is likely to be protracted. Text-critics, lexicographers, and exegetes are not apt to complete their work on Yerushalmi within this century or even the next.

The purpose of my preliminary translation is to make possible a set of historical and religious-historical studies on the formation of Judaism in the Land of Israel from the closure of the Mishnah to the completion of the Talmud of the Land of Israel and the time of the composition of the first midrashic compilations. Clearly, no historical, let alone religious-historical, work can be contemplated without a theory of the principal document and source for the study, the Palestinian Talmud. No theory can be attempted, however tentative and provisional, without a complete, prior statement of what the document appears to wish to say and how its materials seem to have come to closure. It follows that the natural next steps, beyond my now-finished history of Mishnaic law and account of the Judaism revealed in that history, carry us to the present project. Even those steps, when they are taken, will have to be charted with all due regard to the pitfalls of a translation that is preliminary, based upon a text that as yet has not been subjected even to the clarifying exercises of lower criticism. Questions will have to be shaped appropriate to the parlous state of the evidence. No one can proceed without a systematic account of the evidence and a theory of how the evidence may, and may not, be utilized.

Let us now turn to the question with which we began: how to see the whole whole. It must be emphasized that the sole acceptable method is inductive inquiry. Everything that follows assumes we know nothing a priori about the Talmud under study. We must reason about its character without prior information of any kind, even concerning the presence of a completed document, the Mishnah, around which the (nascent) compilation of the Palestinian Talmud is arranged and shaped.

iii. The Starting Point

To describe the Talmud we first take up the whole and proceed to ask about its principal components. Looking at the Talmud whole, we notice two totally distinct sorts of materials: statements of law, then discussions of and excurses on those statements. We bring no substantial presuppositions to the text, if we declare these two sorts of materials to be, respectively, primary and constitutive, secondary and derivative. Calling the former, the declaration of laws, the Mishnah-passage, and the latter, the exegesis of these laws, the Talmud proper, imposes no a priori judgment formed independently of the literary evidence in hand. We might as well call the two "the code" and "the commentary." The result would be no different.

In fact, as we see everywhere, the Talmud is made up of two elements, each with its own literary traits and program of discussion. Since the Mishnah-passage at the head of each set of Talmudic units of discourse defines the limits and determines the theme and, generally, the problematic of the whole, our attention is drawn to the traits of the Mishnah-passages as a group. Here, of course, a certain measure of descriptive work has been done. But even if we for the first time saw these types of pericopes of the Mishnah (embedded as they are in the Talmud and separated from one another), we should discern that they adhere to a separate and quite distinctive set of literary and conceptual canons from what follows and surrounds them. Hence at the outset, with no appreciable attention to anything beyond the text, we should distinguish two "layers" of the Talmud and recognize that one "layer" is formed in one way, the other in another way. (I use "layer" for convenience only; it is not an apt metaphor.)

As I just said, if then we were to join together all the Mishnah-pericopes, we should notice that they are stylistically and formally coherent and also different from everything else in the compilation before us. Accordingly, for stylistic reasons alone we are on firm ground in designating the "layer" before us as the base-point for all further inquiry. For the Mishnah-"layer" has been shown to be uniform, while the Talmud-"layer" is not demonstrably so. Hence, itself undifferentiated, the former -- the Mishnah-"layer" -- provides the point of differentiation. The latter -- the Talmud-"layer" -- presents the diverse materials subject to differentiation. In the first stage in the work of making sense of the Talmud and describing it whole, what is the initial criterion through which the Talmud's diverse types of units of discourse are differentiated? It is the varied relationships, to the Mishnah's rule, exhibited by the Talmud's several, diverse units of discourse. Let me now expand on and qualify this point, for it is the principle of the opening initiative in this exercise of taxonomy and typology.

To amplify what I have said: since the Palestinian Talmud carries forward and depends upon the Mishnah, to describe that Talmud we have to begin with its relationship to the Mishnah, which is the Talmud's own starting point. While the Mishnah admits to no antecedents and neither alludes to nor cites anything prior to its own materials, a passage of the Talmud is often incomprehensible without knowledge of the passage of the Mishnah around which the Talmud's discourse centers. Yet in describing and defining the Talmud, we should grossly err if we were to say it is only, or mainly, a step-by-step commentary on the Mishnah, defined solely by the Mishnah's interests. We may not even say -- though it is a step closer to the truth -- that the Talmud before us is a commentary on or secondary development of, the Mishnah and important passages of the Tosefta. Units of discourse which serve these sorts of materials stand side by side with many which in an immediate sense do not. Accordingly, while a description of the Talmud requires attention to the interplay between the Talmud and the Mishnah and Tosefta, the diverse relationships between the Talmud and one or the other of those two documents constitute only one point of description and differentiation. For the Talmud is in full command of its own program of thought and inquiry. Its framers, responsible for the units of discourse, chose what in the Mishnah will be analyzed and what ignored. True, there could be no Talmud without the Mishnah and Tosefta. But knowing only those two works, we could never have predicted in a systematic way the character of the Talmud's discourse at any point.

The Mishnah nonetheless permits us at the outset to gain perspective on the character of Yerushalmi. For the Mishnah does exhibit a remarkable unity of literary and redactional traits. By that standard our Talmud presents none. Accordingly, while whatever materials reached the framers of the Mishnah -- ca. 175-200 -- were revised by them in line with a single and simple literary and redactional program, the same is not the case for the Talmud of the Land of Israel. Whatever the stages of redaction of the document as a whole, let alone of its components, we may say with certainty that the people ultimately responsible for the document as we have it did not do to the materials in their hands what the framers of the Mishnah did to theirs. The ultimate redactors did not participate in the work of formulation. Units of discourse framed in some prior setting have been preserved as is (though we do not know to what extent as to detail). They were drawn together whole and complete with other such essentially fixed and final units of discourse. That is the principal result of what follows in this chapter.

It might be wise to present charts to prove the present proposition about the fundamental difference between the literary and redactional condition of the Mishnah and that of the Talmud. But the reader need only open to any passage of the Mishnah and set it side by side with any passage of the Talmud of the Land of Israel. Later we shall do just that. The contrast then will be clear. The former is constructed out of a severely limited repertoire of syntactic and rhetorical forms. The latter is diffuse and stylistically promiscuous. The former is tight, the latter loose; the former amply articulated, the latter remarkably elliptical; the former uniform and stylistically coherent, the latter, diverse and formally incoherent. The former speaks in whole sentences, the latter in short-hand, abbreviated, notes toward discourse never amply articulated. Accordingly, it suffices to state as fact that what the Mishnah's redactors did to the Mishnah, Yerushalmi's redactors did not do to Talmud Yerushalmi. Our first task is to attempt to describe what they did do. But before proceeding, let us review the principal traits of the composition of the Mishnah. That exercise permits us to gain perspective as we proceed to the work of describing the literary traits of the Talmud of the Land of Israel.

iv. Redaction and Formulation: Yerushalmi Contrasted with Mishnah

We now ask about the formulation and redaction of the Talmud of the Land of Israel as we know it -- the end-product in our hands -- and not the formation, in earlier times, of ideas or whole discussions now contained within the document. The nature of the antecedent materials can only be determined when we have described what must be deemed the work of ultimate redaction. We shall first determine whether the process also included systematic formulation, or reformulation, of units of discourse already completed.

When I undertook to ask about the role of redaction in the formulation of the Mishnah, working on the division of Purities as my sample (roughly 25% of the entire Mishnah), I began from the outside and worked my way in. To review the process and its principal results: I began by asking this question: if all we had were a mass of words, how should we know where one thing stops and another starts? The first question is easy to answer definitively. We know that the mass of words is broken up (for Mishnah's division of Purities), into twelve principal divisions (tractates), uneven in length, because the subject of one long sequence of undifferentiated words ends, and a new subject begins. There are, accordingly, lines of demarcation clearly drawn by the shift in theme or primary topic of discussion. What is blocked out, moreover, is consistent in its devotion to that given theme or primary topic, rarely dealing with a subject wholly irrelevant to the theme. It follows that the principal mode of organization is thematic. As is clear, the principal lines of division will be into tractates devoted to their respective, diverse topics. What is important is that that fact is shown on the basis of the internal character of the document, not merely of the post facto way in which exegetes, copyists, and printers organized matters.

Having proved that the Mishnah is organized, in its principal divisions, in accord with the unfolding of thematic and logical principles, I proceeded to ask about the delineation of the Mishnah's intermediate divisions. I avoided the word, "chapters," because it can only yield confusion with the extant chapters, which are the work of copyists and printers, perhaps even of the earliest exegetes. These tell us nothing whatsoever about the original intent of the people who come before and stand behind the document, but only about the exegetical perceptions of the people who come afterward. How on the basis of internal evidence are intermediate divisions to be discerned? Having shown that the redactors not only organize their materials topically but also lay out the discussion of each topic in accord with its logically sequential parts, I am on firm ground in maintaining that one criterion for a demarcation-line of undifferentiated columns of words of a Mishnah-tractate, or principal division, will be a shift in topic or theme. What applies to, and emerges from, the whole surely must be asked to serve as criterion for what pertains also to the parts. There is, moreover, a second important criterion of delineation, and that is, recurrent grammatical patterns or arrangements of words. This entails inquiry into the large-scale interplay between theme and form, between what is said and how it is said.

The first thing we notice when we study a Mishnah-tractate from its opening sentence onward is that, when the subject changes, the formulary pattern shifts too. A given subtopic of a topical unit -- a principal division -- will be expressed in a distinctive pattern of syntax. These syntactical patterns, moreover, are divisible into two broad categories, tight and loose. The tight syntactical pattern will govern the layout of words for each concept, thought, or rule devoted to a given subtopic. The loose pattern will not. Rather, it emerges chiefly at the commencement of every conceptual unit. The former is therefore called an internally-unitary formulary pattern, in that the paramount formulary pattern everywhere governs the internal construction and wording of what is expressed. The latter is named an externally-unitary formulary pattern, in that the formulary pattern is external to what is expressed, being imposed primarily upon the opening clauses of a conceptual unit, not on the later wording. The remainder of the unit then will proceed in unpatterned sentences or clauses. To put matters more descriptively, we are unable to discern, in sentences which follow the commencement of the matter, any systematic pattern at all.

These results impose the requirement of further definition, differentiation, and analysis of the recurrent patterns by which sentences are constructed. The reason is that, once we recognize intermediate divisions because of the congruence of form and theme within a group of sentences, we come to the stage of the analysis of form. The appropriate framework for form-analysis is the redactionally sizable, intermediate unit. For it is within the setting of the intermediate unit that the patterning and formalization of language become self-evident. It ceases to be a subjective observation that things seem to be stereotyped, only when we see that, within circumscribed but sizable sequences of sentences, things indeed are not random but recurrent. Within that same framework we discern precisely what patterning of language is undertaken, how thought is reduced not merely to words, but to words laid out in distinctive, recurrent syntactical structures.

It is at this point that we must define the smallest unit of formal analysis, which for the Mishnah I call "the cognitive unit." A cognitive unit is the formal (and formalized) result of a single cogent process of cognition, that is, analysis of a situation and statement of a rule pertaining to it, or some other, similar intellectual process. The Mishnah's smallest whole and irreducible literary-conceptual units are the end-result of a single sequence, or process, of thought. Formal or formulary traits of such a unit commonly occur at the outset or in the first element of the result of cognition to be set into words and given linguistically formal character. After that point in the unit, what follows commonly exhibits no equivalent formalization. The remainder of the cognitive unit will generally consist of simple declarative sentences exhibiting no recurrent pattern and lacking all syntactical distinctiveness. The cognitive unit rarely stands by itself but is grouped together with other such units, devoted to a single principle or theme and exhibiting a single, distinctive syntactical trait or preference. Accordingly, the form-analytical work yields the result that the cognitive unit is shaped within the processes of organization of the intermediate (and principal) divisions of the Mishnah.

This means that the work of giving formalized verbal expression to cognitive units and the work of organizing them into groups go together and reciprocally govern one another's results.

To state the historical result simply: The Mishnah's formulation and its organization are the result of the work of a single generation of tradent-redactors -- tradents, who formulate units of thought, and redactors, who organize aggregations of these units. The Mishnah is not the product of tradents <u>succeeded</u> by redactors. It is not possible upon the basis of objective, internal literary evidence revealed by the Mishnah itself to specify much in formulation which derives from the period before that of redaction itself.

We may now rapidly relate these results to the document at hand. In the case of the Palestinian Talmud, the principle of organization is provided by the Mishnah itself. Tractates begin and end where the Mishnah does. Accordingly, if all we had were a mass of words, we should know the beginning and end of a tractate of our Talmud precisely as we do in the case of the Mishnah, because the point of demarcation is identical.

When it comes to the unfolding of intermediate divisions -- "units of discourse" in my earlier paragraphs -- we are in a different situation entirely. A glance at any volume of the translation will show that, in nearly all cases, the Talmud's discussion attached to a given pericope of the Mishnah runs through two or more completed units of discourse. In general, therefore, the principle of organizing a discussion is not supplied solely and completely by the logical, or other exegetical, requirements of a passage of the Mishnah. The principle by which a discussion is inaugurated, worked out, and concluded, is different from that of the Mishnah in general. It also differs from that supplied by a given intermediate unit of the Mishnah in particular cases. Since the intermediate divisions of the Yerushalmi are not demarcated by the requirements of the Mishnah, we cannot attempt to relate the delineation of those units to formal traits of the Mishnah. Formal considerations do not come into play in the Talmud before us in so rigid and disciplined a way as they govern the formulation of the Mishnah's ideas. It must follow that the work of ultimate redaction of the Palestinian Talmud is wholly separate from the work of formulation of individual units of discourse.

The upshot is that while the framers of the Talmud of the Land of Israel refer constantly to the Mishnah, they do not see themselves as bound by its patterns of formulation or even of redaction, let alone by its program and problems. They have in hand, or have created, diverse sorts of units of discourse, some of them essentially exegetical and tied to the Mishnah, others doing the same for Tosefta, still others of a quite separate literary character and substantive purpose. That is why, to describe the Talmud as a whole, we have to develop a taxonomy of its several types of units of discourse, in comparison and contrast to those of the Mishnah.

v. Yerushalmi's Redactional Program

To develop a taxonomy of the units of discourse contained within the Talmud of the Land of Israel, we begin by describing gross redactional traits. These are visible to the naked eye. The question then is simple: What kinds of units of discourse does the document exhibit and how are they arranged? The answer to this question should yield a first glimpse of the redactional program of the ultimate framers of the Talmud. Once we differentiate by type among the materials in the hands of the arrangers of the whole, we also may observe what principles, if any, guide their work of arrangement. For the present purpose, seeking the most general traits of the whole, a modest probe suffices. I review five tractates, a small one (Niddah), a very large one (Sanhedrin), an egregious one (Baba Mesia), and two medium ones (Nedarim and Sukkah).

By unit of discourse, as I said earlier, I mean simply a discussion on a single topic, beginning either at a pericope of the Mishnah or at the point at which that topic is raised, ending either at the next pericope of the Mishnah or at the point at which some other topic is introduced, respectively. These have been designated in my translation of the Talmud by Roman numerals. While the divisions are in some measure subjective, or may occasionally appear arbitrary, the relationship of a given set of materials ("unit of discourse") to the Mishnah will remain constant. I do not propose that quantitative numbers of units of discourse materially change matters, and, accordingly, the indications of units of discourse will not greatly affect the argument.

What is more important from the redactional perspective is the sequence of these units. As we shall see in a moment, where there is direct analysis of the Mishnah, or, at the very least, inquiry into the Scriptural foundations of the pericope at hand, the unit of discourse presenting such analysis or inquiry normally is the opening one in a sequence, designated as I. Among 335 Mishnah-pericopes enumerated in my probe, the results of which I summarize here, only 26 units of discourse pertinent to the Mishnah-rule at hand commence discussion of that rule other than as unit I, less than 8% of the whole. (I exclude reference to the handful of Mishnah-pericopes in which there is no analysis of the Mishnah-law at all; I also exclude reference to the passages in which Tosefta's complement to the Mishnah's rule stands at the commencement of the discussion.) Accordingly, it will become clear that the usual redactional practice was to take a unit of discourse closely pertinent to the Mishnah and to place it at the commencement of discourse on the passage of the Mishnah at hand.

There is a further tendency to include in that opening unit, or in the one(s) immediately following, materials now found in Tosefta pertinent to the Mishnah. These Toseftan passages are cited either to amplify and extend the Mishnah's rule or otherwise to facilitate discourse about (or around) it. If not part of unit I, these tend to bear the unit-numbers II or III; in Baba Mesia, that is invariably the case.

I differentiate among six possible relationships to the Mishnah-pericope at hand, hence six types of units of discourse in the Yerushalmi.

1. <u>Mishnah-Exegesis</u>: There is reason, of course, to differentiate among types of treatments of the Mishnah, e.g., citation and gloss, inquiry into Scriptural foundations for the Mishnah's rule, rephrasing or restatement of the rule, and so on. All we want to know is whether those units of discourse that take up the systematic and direct exegesis of the Mishnah-pericopes exhibit a redactional pattern. The answer, as I said, is that they do -- all the time, and, normally, at the very starting-point of the Talmud's discussion.

2. **Tosefta: Citation and Exegesis**: The Palestinian Talmud frequently cites verbatim, or nearly verbatim, statements which also are found in the Tosefta. Moreover, where there are differences in wording between what we find in the Talmud and what we find in the Tosefta as we now have it, time and again we discover that the Talmud's discussion presupposes the text now found in Tosefta, rather than that now found in the Talmud. For that reason I do not think I claim too much in regarding this sort of material as the Tosefta's contribution. (I hasten to add the qualification that much more work has to be done on the matter than, for my purposes, I have thought necessary.) When Tosefta does appear, it tends to appear fairly early in the unfolding of the Talmud's discourse. In a fair number of instances where there is no clearcut discourse on the Mishnah-passage itself, the Talmud will cite the Tosefta and discuss that. The Talmud's contribution to the exegesis of the Mishnah consists in the elucidation of the Tosefta's complement to the Mishnah, an orderly procedure indeed. This is a tendency, not a fixed rule.

3. **Legal Speculation and Reflection Primary to the Mishnah**: A unit of discourse may well carry forward a discussion superficially separate from the Mishnah. Yet upon close inspection, we notice that the discussion at hand speculates on principles introduced, to begin with, in the Mishnah's rule or in Tosefta's complement to that rule. Here the entries tend to be more complex in structure, commonly, also, a good bit longer, than the units of discourse catalogued on the first two lists. There is a marked tendency for this type of unit to be included only in sequence after the first and second types.

4. **Harmonization of Distinct Laws of the Mishnah**: One of the more interesting kinds of units of discourse is that in which principles are abstracted from utterly unrelated rules of the Mishnah (less commonly, of the Tosefta). These are then shown to intersect and to conflict; or opinions and principles of a given authority on one such matter will be shown to differ from those of that same authority on another, intersecting matter. These units tend to occur at several different tractates verbatim, since they serve equally well (or poorly) each Mishnah-pericope cited therein. Items on this list stand side by side with those on the foregoing. Both sorts of units of discourse relate to the Mishnah in essentially the same way. They vastly amplify the principles of the Mishnah. But they do not serve for a close exegesis of its wording or specific rule. These are few, but always substantial and difficult. The reason is that several different kinds of law have to be mastered, then the underlying principles made explicit and brought into juxtaposition with those of other laws on other topics.

5. **Legal Speculation and Reflection Independent of the Passage of the Mishnah at Hand**: There are units of discourse essentially independent of the Mishnah-pericope with which they are associated. These pursue questions not even indirectly generated by the law in hand. From time to time we may guess at why the redactor thought the discourse belonged where he placed it. While there are not a great many of these, as in the foregoing instance, they are long and involved, and always difficult and unusually interesting. They tend to occur not at the initial stages of a Talmudic passage attached to a pericope of the Mishnah, but rather late in the sequence of types of units of discourse. At Baba Mesia, for example, with its rather brief units of discourse, dominated

by (mere) citation of Tosefta, they invariably occur in the second of two units. In Sanhedrin we find them at the higher end of the scale of numbers of units of discourse, III, IV, and beyond, and the same is so, in general, at Niddah and Sukkah. But this is only a tendency, by no means a rule so fixed as the one governing placement of units of discourse devoted to Mishnah-exegesis.

6. Anthology, Relevant to the Mishnah only in Theme: There are sizable units of discourse joined together only by a common theme, and joined to the Mishnah-pericope at which they occur only because, in some rather general way, someone supposed their themes to intersect with those of the Mishnah-passage at hand. This type of unit of discourse is especially common in tractate Sanhedrin. In particular, it predominates in those chapters where the Mishnah's statements, for their part, pertain not to law but to lore. Most such anthologies are rich in citation of, and comment upon, verses of Scripture. But the present category includes by no means the bulk of the Talmud's Scriptural exegeses and comments in the tractates at hand. There is a tendency for this type of unit of discourse to occur later in the unfolding of a Talmudic passage assigned to a given Mishnah-pericope, just as is the case in the foregoing.

Let me proceed to generalization. The redactional program of the men responsible for laying out the materials of Yerushalmi may now be described in simple terms. Most important, we see that there was such a program. There is nothing random. That is clear because, within the differentiation of units of discourse I have defined, diverse types of units of discourse are not mixed together promiscuously. There is a pronounced tendency to move from close reading of the Mishnah and then Tosefta to more general inquiry into the principles of a Mishnah-passage and their interplay with those of some other, superficially unrelated passage, and, finally, to more general reflections on law not self-evidently related to the Mishnah-passage at hand or to anthologies intersecting only at a general topic. Now while that program may appear self-evident and logical, we must not assume there were no choices in how to lay things out. The program I have described exhibits sufficient variation to rule out the possibility that our Talmud's way is the better way of doing things. The case of Baba Mesia, moreover, different in program as is that tractate from the others we probed, leaves no doubt about the matter. <u>Things are the way they are because people wanted them to be this way and not some other way.</u> We know this because the paramount traits of several hundred Talmudic passages devoted to units of the Mishnah, are, if not everywhere uniform, then fairly constant and consistent.

It therefore follows that the redactors of our five tractates knew precisely how they wished to lay out the materials that they drew together into the Talmud. Accordingly, the work of redaction was active and followed a program. Whether or not that work was done in a single generation is unclear. Perhaps there was a shared program among the various schools, along these lines: "Since we are studying the Mishnah and Tosefta as our principal texts, we shall now lay out some permanent guidelines on how to read these texts and interpret and apply them." The one thing that is clear is that the redactors took full charge of the layout of whatever materials came to hand. They made significant decisions about the order in which diverse types of discourse were to be carried on: this, then that.

If therefore we now take as fact that the Talmud before us is the result of a generation, or several generations, of redaction, it is because we see the evidence of active participation in the formation of the document: a plan, a program. The contrary possibility, that this is just how things happened to come to hand, seems unlikely, given the disproportionate replication of a single logical, self-evident pattern. The second question flows from the first. If the redactors participated in the organization of units of discourse, did they also place their mark upon the formulation of those same units of discourse? It is to this question that we must now turn.

vi. <u>From Redaction to Formulation?</u>

The lists of facts we have reviewed point to a general uniformity, from one tractate to the next, in redactional processes. Accordingly, we are on firm ground in maintaining that we may speak of the Talmud as a whole, even though our sample is only five tractates. Since the present book stands at the end of a complete translation, moreover, the reader may spot-check the generalizations offered here. We must always allow for variation here and there. But uniform work on the whole Talmud clearly was done and done systematically, since, as we have seen, the fundamental policy governing organization of materials is uniform for the tractates at hand.

It follows that we may turn from redaction to formulation. Once more, with all due respect for variation and diversity, we seek gross and general traits, affecting the whole of the Talmud under study.

Since the close interplay between redaction and formulation constitutes the sole firm result of our study of the Mishnah, we ask about the same matter for our Talmud. The issue is whether we can find evidence of systematic attention to formulating units of discourse in such a way as formally or syntactically to relate one to the next within a single redactional program or process. If there is such evidence, we must conclude that even in the ultimate redactional stages of the formation of the Talmud, work went on not merely in minor correction, revision, or glossing of a passage. Such work pertained even to the very formulation of the statement of its main points, in the structure and wording by which those points would be expressed. It would then follow that, prior to the redaction of the whole, we are unable to posit the existence of units of discourse as we know them. If we find no points of correlation between redactional policies and problems of formulation of units of discourse, on the other hand, it must follow that, separate from (perhaps then, prior to) the redactional stages (though we do not know how long before) a process of formulation of units of discourse was underway.

Our question thus is, did the redactors work with essentially finished units of discourse? Or did they themselves participate in the formation of the completed units of discourse which they also organized and juxtaposed? The criterion for positive evidence for the second proposition -- hence, also, negative evidence for the first -- derives from comparison with the Mishnah. What we compare are units of discourse of our Talmud and the formulary traits of Mishnah-pericopes. The latter indicate the hand of redaction and organization within the very phrasing of individual units of law of the Mishnah. Absence of equivalent traits then will signify for the Talmud a different relationship of redaction to formulation from that prevalent in the Mishnah. For the Mishnah, essential to the organization and layout of completed units of discourse is the very pattern of formulating those same units of discourse. The result is proof, for the Mishnah, that redaction is prior and critical to formulation. In the Mishnah, redaction is not solely a process of joining together statements bearing no formal relationship to one another, hence existing before (we do not know how long before) the process of organization and layout we call redaction. A clear grasp of how the Mishnah works is then essential to a comparative inquiry into the Talmud's traits.

Now to spell out the interplay of formulation and redaction in the Mishnah. The principal result of my inquiry was to show constant and close relationship between the one and the other. Specifically, I found that when the Mishnah's redactors wished to indicate the formation of a unit of discourse (which I called, in that setting, "intermediate unit"), they would take up a distinctive formulary pattern or form, different from that which they had used beforehand and also from that which they would use in the following unit. They would carefully group their smallest whole statements ("smallest units of cognition") so that each one would repeat the same syntactic pattern, setting up (in general) groups of three or multiples of three, or groups of five or multiples of five, with such internally patterned statements of a single principle being applied to a single theme. This seemed to me definitive evidence that the whole could not have been formulated prior to the work of redaction, at which point -- and not before -- the larger program of arrangement of topics and principles expressed in connection with those topics was in hand. Only when the whole was fully in view was it possible to form the parts in the uniform way in which they were formed. There is no other economical way of explaining the facts I have discovered, since, as is clear, the whole was planned before the parts were laid out in their matching and distinctive syntactic patterns and in their little sets of three or five repetitions of such patterns.

The issue when we turn to the Talmud cannot of course be framed in the same way. But to begin with, we must ask ourselves whether we discern any formulary patterns at all, not merely those of a redactional type. When we speak of formulary patterns -- to review -- we mean recurrent arrangements of words in a given syntactic formula. Whether or not we may relate the use of such a pattern to a redactional plan is only second in line of inquiry. To present this matter as clearly as I can, I wish first of all to show, in three units selected at random, the Mishnah's formal traits. Then, for those same chapters, we shall look at the Talmud's formal or patterned language, if any. The former will be seen to exhibit patterned language at a gross and recurrent level. The latter will not.

I do not seek evidence from the recurrence of particles or rhetoric lacking more than merely conventional status in the formation of thought. That is, in context, syntactic structures matter, rhetorical patterns do not. The reason is that rhetorical patterns are not distinctive to the document at hand; they not only occur elsewhere but may well tell us merely how people said things. Consistent resort to a few, fixed syntactic structures, by contrast, tells us choices made by the framers of the document at hand. These choices furthermore may be shown to be deliberate, because of their recurrence in fixed patterns, and also particular to the document. Accordingly, the fact that the speech of the document contains fixed rhetorical patterns signifies something quite separate from the presence of patterns at the deep syntax of the document. The presence or absence of these other patterns of language, as distinct from mere rhetoric, alone testifies to the issue at hand. The fact, for example, that a Mishnah-passage cited by the Talmud will ordinarily be introduced with a rhetorical pattern, "We have learned there...," does not seem to me to contain implications about the formulation of the construction in which such particles or rhetorical usages occur. They testify rather to the overall rhetorical conventions, independent of all redactional or formulary context. In the nature of our inquiry, it is distinctive context which concerns us.

It is easier to prove than to disprove the proposition that a unit of discourse is framed to follow a syntactic pattern. In the former case (for the Mishnah), I simply point out the traits of the pattern and then list all of the examples of that pattern. If I maintain, as I do, that the whole of the document is patterned, I further distinguish that pattern from some other and indicate the interrelationships and proportions of each in the whole. Should there be (to my eye) unpatterned units, I so indicate. I also am able to point to the limits of the formalization of syntax and formulation. This I do by showing those parts of a unit of discourse -- as distinct from those whole units of discourse -- in which I discern no distinctive formulations or recurrent patterns at all. All of this is done for the Mishnah. But wishing to show the independence of formulation from redaction, how am I to prove that a unit of discourse follows no syntactic pattern? A catalogue of non-patterned instances must include all possible examples. That is hardly worth the effort; it fills the antecedent thirty-four volumes.

Accordingly, the simplest way to make the basic point at hand is to present instances in which redaction plays a role in the patterned formulation of a sizable unit of discourse, then to present the Talmud's contribution to the same unit of discourse. This allows us to contrast the Mishnah's gross literary traits with those of the Talmud's. By seeing what a passage looks like when redaction controls formulation -- selection of recurrent forms and formulary syntactic patterns -- we shall recognize what a passage looks like when it does not. While three examples, however striking, hardly prove anything, the reader will then be able to make a survey of any number of Mishnah-passages, chapters or even whole tractates. The same result will be replicated at all points. While, in due course, in our Talmud we may find forms of consequence, we shall invariably discover them wholly irrelevant to any large-scale redactional purpose discernible to us.

We proceed to deal with two units of Y. Baba Mesia (B.M.), because here the Talmud is brief and highly disciplined. Then we consider one of Y. Sanhedrin (San.). If we are going to find formalization of the Talmud's units of discourse, it is more likely to be in the context of a Caesarean tractate than a later one. Hence it is advisable to use both an earlier and a later tractate. The later tractates bear heavy accretions of all sorts, beyond the modest limits of Mishnah-exegesis and Tosefta-citation and exegesis. Accordingly, we look first to the most likely source of examples of some sort of patterning based on redactional considerations -- agglomeration of units -- of the formulation of the language of the Talmud.

The fact is that I cannot find a single instance, in the twenty-nine tractates I have translated, where the unit of discourse is so formulated as to indicate an intention to relate what is formulated to its redactional context or to the larger needs of combining two or more completed units of thought into a principal redactional unit (a complete discussion of a Mishnah-pericope, for instance).

Let us now briefly review our passages. First we deal with the Mishnah-pericope, then with the accompanying Talmudic discussion. While the division of the Talmud breaks up what in fact are formal units, that fact need not concern us, since it is not primary to the text but the work of copyists and even printers. A brief comment at the end of the Mishnah-passage is intended to highlight the formal traits, unifying several distinct statements into a single, patterned whole. This is done without regard to the time in which authorities cited in the passage were believed to have flourished, let alone traits of speech characteristic of individual authorities. Then the Talmudic discussion of that Mishnah-passage, viewed as a whole, is reproduced. Where the Talmud breaks up a Mishnah-unit into two (or more) parts, I have preserved my original unit-numbering system, so indicated here; this facilitates reference to the translation. A Roman numeral at the side of a Mishnah-unit signifies one component of a whole intermediate unit of Mishnah, matched in its patterned language, as I explain, with other such components. The final number then indicates the number of examples of each formal entry in the whole construction. As in the translation-volumes, the Mishnah-passage is given in italics, and that shared with Tosefta in bold face type.

Mishnah Baba Mesia 1:1

I   A.   *Two [in court] lay hold of a cloak* --
     B.   *this one says, "I found it!"* --
     C.   *And that one says, "I found it!"* --
     D.   *This one says, "It's all mine!"* --
     E.   *And that one says, "It's all mine!"* --
     F.   *This one takes an oath that he has no less a share of it than half,*
     G.   *and that one takes an oath that he has no less a share of it than half.*
     H.   *And they divide it up.*

II I.   *This one says, "It's all mine!"*
     J.   *And that one says, "Half of it is mine!"*
     K.   *The one who says, "It's all mine" takes an oath that he has no less a share of it than three parts.*
     L.   *And the one who says, "Half of it is mine," takes an oath that he has no less a share of it than a fourth part.*
     M.   *This one then takes three shares, and that one takes the fourth.*

Mishnah Baba Mesia 1:2

III A.   *Two were riding on a beast,*
     B.   *or one was riding and one was leading it* --

C. this one says, "It's all mine!" --
D. and that one says, "It's all mine!" --
E. this one takes an oath that he has no less a share of it than half,
F. and that one takes an oath that he has no less a share of it than half.
G. And they divide it.
H. But when they concede [that they found it together] or have witnesses to prove it, they divide it without taking an oath.

The recurrent triplicate pattern is not in the first clause of the apocopated sentence, that is, M. 1:1A, 1:2A, B, but rather in the second, that is M. 1:1B-E, I-J, M. 1:2C-D. The repeated triplicate pattern, in the apodosis of the same sentence, M. 1:1F-G, H, M. 1:1K-M, and M. 1:2E-G, is not to be missed. So what we have are three individual statements, all of them constructed in extreme apocopation, illustrative of three aspects of the same point. The several statements may or may not represent diverse authorities' views. They may or may not have existed in some prior and different form. We only know that, in order to put together the several ideas before us, expressive of several aspects of the same general conception, the framer of the whole also participated in the formulation of the individual components. Hence redaction plays a principal role governing the character of the pericope, and that is without regard to what is stated in the laws themselves. We proceed now to the Talmud, which treats M. 1:1 separately from M. 1:2. For the reader's convenience in making sense of what is before us, I reproduce here my brief explanation of the passage.

I A. [The following is a paraphrase of T. Shebu. 5:3, which is as follows: **If the plaintiff was claiming a maneh in the presence of a court, and the defendant denied it, and two witnesses came and gave testimony that he owes him fifty zuz, lo, this one pays (fifty zuz) and is exempt from the requirement of taking an oath. But if there was only a single witness who was giving evidence against him, lo, this one takes an oath covering the whole amount.**] It was taught: A man who said to his fellow, "Give me the maneh which you owe me!"
B. The other said to him, "It never happened!"
C. The lender went and brought witnesses that he owes him fifty zuz....
D. [Concerning the foregoing case,] R. Hiyya the Elder said, "The statement by witnesses [that the man owes the money] is tantamount to his own admission [that he owes part of the debt, namely, the fifty zuz which the witnesses say has been lent out of the hundred claimed by the creditor],
E. "and consequently, the borrower must take an oath covering the remainder [of what has been claimed by the creditor]."
F. R. Yohanan said, "The statement by witnesses is by no means tantamount to his own admission which would produce the consequence that the borrower must take an oath covering the remainder [and he need not do so]."
G. Said R. La, "The position of R. Hiyya the Elder derives from Two in court lay hold of a cloak [M. B.M. 1:1A-H]. Since the man is holding on to half of [the cloak], it is as if he brought witnesses to court that half of it belongs to him.

Redaction and Formulation 151

And you then rule that he takes an oath [as at M. 1:1F, G] and retains possession of the half in his hand.

H. Now this case before us is similar to that case. [Possession of the cloak is deemed parallel to having witnesses to ownership thereof.]"

II A. Rabbah bar Mamal and R. Amram introduced the following issue of Rab into [the present discussion]:

B. [Rab] said to [R. Hiyya], "Do they then not hand over an oath [for swearing by] someone suspect of lying? [For the debtor of T. Shebu. 5:3, cited above, has alleged that he owes nothing. The witnesses prove that he is a liar. How then can he take an oath covering the remainder since he is a known perjurer?]"

C. He said to him, "Even a statement using the language of an oath [but omitting the operative clauses] they do not hand over to him."

III A. [With reference to M. 1:1F, G: <u>This one takes an oath that he has no less a share of it than half...</u>,] how does he then swear? [What sort of language is used here? For the claim is that the man owns not less than half of the cloak. Even if the man owns none of the cloak, he can make that statement without in fact lying under oath, since, indeed, he does not own less than half, for he owns none of it.]

B. R. Huna said, "'By an oath! I have a right to it, and I own no less of it than part worth a <u>perutah</u>.' [By using this language, the problem of A is avoided. These are meaningful statements.]"

IV A. [Reverting to I G,] said R. Yohanan, "If from this matter [that the parallel to M. B.M. 1:1 is decisive], [you prove that an oath is required], then it is an oath [at M. B.M. 1:1] which has been ordained as a remedy [by the rabbis]. [Each party may take the same oath, and further the two parties could divide the claimed cloak without taking any oath at all inasmuch as their actual possession is the equivalent of witnesses to their claim. Accordingly, the case of M. B.M. 1:1 is not pertinent to the matter under discussion at T. Shebu. 5:3 at all, with the consequence that the claim of Rabbi La is not valid.]"

V A. It was taught: **Two who were laying hold of a document [bond] --**

B. **This one says, "It is mine, and I lost it!"**

C. **And that one says, "It was in my possession, and I already paid you for it!" --**

D. **"Let the document be confirmed through the signatures of the witnesses that it bears," the words of Rabbi.**

E. **And (Rabban Simeon b.) Gamaliel says, "Let them divide it [the money] between them"** [T. B.M. 1:15]. [Rabbi's position is that the former admits that he has written the bond and it is necessary to confirm the bond. If the creditor is able to do so, he has a valid claim and divides up the money covered by the bond. If not, the creditor has no share in the proceeds of the bond. Simeon b. Gamaliel's position is that it is not necessary even to confirm the bond; in any event the claimants divide the funds at issue.]

F. R. Eleazar said, "All depends upon which one of the claimants holds the part on which the witnesses have signed their names. [The party holding the part of the bond containing the confirmation by witnesses is the one who wins the case.]"

G. Said R. Hisda, "If you accept this view, you accord with the position of R. Simeon [b. Gamaliel]. [But Rabbi will want the witnesses to confirm the bond in court.]"

VI A. **This one says, "It's all mine!"**

B. **And that one says, "A third of it is mine!"**

C. The one who says, "It's all mine" takes an oath that he has no less of a share of it than five parts.

D. And the one who says, "A third of it is mine!" takes an oath that he has no less of a share of it than a sixth [part].

E. **The governing principle of the matter: One is subjected to an oath only up to one-half of his claimed share alone** [T. B.M. 1:2].

Now to explain: If each claims the whole thing, then it is divided. But the one who claims only half concedes to the other party the other half, in which case we divide only the half under dispute. So the claimant of the half takes a fourth, and the claimant of the whole takes the half conceded by the other as well as the quarter he gains in the compromise. The Talmud presents a sustained and varied discussion of M.'s pericope. The obvious question to someone who knows the Mishnah will be the relationship between the oath of which M. B.M. 1:1 speaks and the larger theory of oaths at tractate Shebuot. This is what is accomplished at units I, II, and IV, interrupted by the brief interpolation at unit III. This discussion is formally disjointed but substantively coherent. Units V and VI then move on, quite systematically, to important ideas of Tosefta. This now brings us to the Talmud's unit for M. B.M. 1:2.

<u>Y. B.M. 1:2</u>

I A. Said R. Huna, "There it is taught:

B. "A woman who was riding along on a beast, with two men leading it,

C. "[and she comes to court and claims,] 'These are my slaves and the ass and its burden belong to me,'

D. "while this one says, 'This is my wife, and the other man is my slave, and the ass and its burden are mine,'

E. "and the other party claims, 'this is my wife, and the other man is my slave, and the ass and its burden are mine' --

F. "she requires a writ of divorce from each of the men, and she must also declare both of them free men.

G. "And both of them issue writs of emancipation to one another.

H. "And as to the ass and its burden, all three of them lay an equal claim [and divide it up]."

The inescapable conclusion is that the considerations important in the formulation of the Mishnah-passage play no role whatsoever in the framing of the Talmud's units of discourse, jointly or severally. As a group, of course, they have not a single stylistic trait in common. Individually, the units appear discrete from one another. Unit I provides a set of declarative sentences, in which several rabbis comment on a case supplied, essentially, out of Tosefta. Unit II follows the same pattern, a kind of artificial debate-discourse, in which the sole recurrent formulation consists in the attributive particle (said, or, he said to him). This adds up to nothing, since the substance of what is said is unaffected. Units III and IV have in common an uncited allusion to a phrase of the Mishnah. Beyond that point there is no trace of formalized syntax. The same pattern we see at unit I -- an allusion to, or citation of, Tosefta -- recurs at the end. All is consistent in relating to the Mishnah. The organization clearly is dictated by the sequence of clauses -- details -- of the Mishnah-passage. But there is not the slightest indication that the formulation of the patterns aimed at formalized patterning of the language for any purpose whatever. The Talmud serving M. B.M. 1:2 consists simply of a statement of Huna, citing some antecedent corpus. The Talmud's case is simply a variation on the Mishnah's. One may see at Y. B.M. 1:2C, D, E, and F, G, H, some sort of imitation of the speech-patterns of the Mishnah. For our purposes that fact changes nothing. We turn now to a second instance in the same tractate.

Mishnah Baba Mesia 2:3

I
- A. [If] behind a fence or a hedge one found pigeons tied together,
- B. or on paths in fields,
- C. lo, this one should not touch them.
- D. [If] he found a utensil in a dung-heap,
- E. if it is covered up, he should not touch it.
- F. If it is uncovered, he takes but must proclaim [that he has found it].

II
- G. [If] he found it in a pile of debris or in an old wall, lo, these belong to him.
- H. [If] he found it in a new wall,
- I. if it is located from its mid-point and outward, it is his.
- J. If it is located from its midpoint and inward, it belongs to the householder.
- K. If he had rented [the house] to others,
- L. even [if he found it] in the house,
- M. lo, these are his.

Mishnah Baba Mesia 2:4

III
- A. [If] he found [utensils] in a store, lo, these are his.
- B. [If a utensil was located] between the counter and the storekeeper, it belongs to the storekeeper.

IV
- C. [If he found them] in front of the money-changer, lo, they are his.
- D. [If he found them] between the stool [of the money-changer] and the money-changer, lo, these belong to the money-changer.

V
- E. He who purchases produce from his fellow,
- F. or sent produce to his fellow,
- G. [if] he found coins among his produce, lo, these are his.
- H. If there they were bound together, he takes [the money] but proclaims [that he has found it].

The definitive formal trait here appears to be the two-part apodosis, if..., if.... This occurs, then, at the five units I have indicated. Then M. 2:3K-M function as a complement to their unit. M. 2:3G introduces that same unit, a somewhat more developed item than we should expect. M. 2:4A-B, C-D, and E, G-H, show us the simplest version of the form. The opening unit, M. 2:3A-C, happens to supply the point of the whole and therefore should not be seen as a prefixed interpolation. If there is locational evidence that an object belongs to someone, that evidence suffices. All the rest then serve to exemplify locations which, all by themselves, indicate that someone has put aside and expects to retrieve what is located there. But, as is clear, there are Mishnah's expected complications, and spelling these out is the purpose of the five-part set. If the object is covered in the dung-heap, someone has deliberately hidden it. If an object is in a new wall, someone may recently have put it there for safe-keeping. If an object is at a point at which a store-keeper or a money-changer can have dropped it, then it is not deemed lost, and so on. The Talmud for M. B.M. 2:3 is as follows.

I   A. [As to the pigeons tied together at M. B.M. 2:3A,] R. Judah said, "That is on condition that the pigeons are tied together at their wing-tips. [This is the ordinary sort of tying them together. Any other bond would be deemed a special mark, and the rule will not apply.]"

    B. R. Ba bar Zabeda found an ass with its burden [of a leather skin], and he took it. He went and asked Rab. He said to him, "You did not do right."

    C. He said to him, "Shall I return it?"

    D. He said to him, "No. For I rule that the owner came and looked for it, but, not finding it, despaired of getting it back [and so gave up ownership, which you now enjoy]."

II A. It was taught: [If] **one found an object on a dung-heap,**

    B. **he is required to make proclamation.**

    C. **For it is usual for a dung-heap to be cleared away** [T. B.M. 2:11].

    D. [If] one found an object in a pile or in an old wall,

    E. lo, these things which he finds are his [M. 2:3G],

    F. **For he can say to [any claimant], "They come from the time of the Amorites"** [T. B.M. 2:12].

    G. It was taught: [If] he found [an object] between the boards [at the threshold of the doorway to the house],

    H. [if the object was located] from the door-jamb and outward, it belongs to [the finder]. If it was located from the door-jamb and inward, it belongs to the householder.

    I. As to M. 2:4 H-J: ([If] one found an object in a hole or new wall, if [the object] was located from the mid-point and outward, it belongs to [the finder]. [If the object was located] from the mid-point and inward [toward the inside of the house], it belongs to the householder (M. 2:4H-J).) [If **the wall or hole] was open wholly outward, even if the object was located from the mid-point toward the inside of the house, it belongs to the finder.**

Redaction and Formulation 155

J. [If the wall or hole] was open wholly inward, even if the object was located from the mid-point toward the outside of the house, it belongs to the householder [T. B.M. 2:13].

K. If he had rented the house to others, even if he found it in the house, lo, these are his [M. 2:4K-M].

III A. [With reference to the following statements of Simeon b. Eleazar at T. B.M. 2:1, 2: R. Simeon b. Eleazar concedes in the case of new merchandise which has been used [that] one is required to make a proclamation [that he has found it and will return it upon proper identification] (M. 2:1G). And so did R. Simeon b. Eleazar say, "He who rescues something from the mouth of a lion, a wolf, or a bear, or from a rip-tide in the sea or a sudden surge of a river -- and he who finds something in a large plaza or parade ground -- lo, these are deemed forthwith to be his, for the owner despairs [of ever getting it back,"] R. Jeremiah said, "There is a dispute concerning what is found in an inn. [In such a case, Simeon will take the position conceded by him. There will then be a dispute in the public piazza, such as T. indicates.] But as to what is found in a courtyard, all parties concur that one is required to make proclamation."

B. Said R. Yose, "In a case involving a courtyard they are in disagreement. But as to an inn all parties concur that the object belongs to the one who finds it."

Now to explain: If the object is covered in the dung-heap, someone has deliberately hidden it. If an object is in a new wall, someone may recently have put it there for safekeeping. If, we see at M. 2:5, an object is at a point at which a storekeeper or a money-changer can have dropped it, then it is not deemed lost. Unit I clarifies M.'s opening rule, as indicated. Unit II then introduces a substantial entry of T., which directly cites or at least completely depends upon M. for meaning. Unit III reverts to earlier materials and is out of place here.

Y. B.M. 2:5 [serving M. 2:4, 5]

I A. Said R. Eleazar, "[When the Mishnah states that if the money is found between the stool of the moneychanger and the person, the money belongs to the moneychanger, it means also to state that if the money is found] on the stool itself, it belongs to him;

B. "if it is found on the counter, it belongs to the storekeeper."

II A. Simeon b. Shetah was employed in flax [to support himself]. His disciples said to him, "Rabbi, remove [this work] from yourself, and we shall buy you an ass, and you will not have to work so much."

B. They went and bought him an ass from a Saracen. Hanging on it was a pearl.

C. They came to him and told him "From now on you do not have to work any more."

D. He said to them, "Why?"

E. They told him, "We bought you an ass from a Saracen, and hanging on it was a pearl."

F. He said to them, "Did its master know about it?"

G. They said to him, "No."

H. He said to them, "Go, and return it...."

The rest of unit II has no bearing on the present passage or on our problem. We note that the statement assigned to Eleazar simply glosses the Mishnah's rule. It exhibits a common rhetorical pattern, that is, a contrast of A to B. But there is no redactional function served in the rhetoric, so far as I can see.

Since it may fairly be claimed that Baba Mesia bears special traits and is unrepresentative of the generality of the Talmud of the Land of Israel, we turn, for our third exercise, to tractate Sanhedrin. Here, I choose a Mish- nah-passage in which the pattern of formalized syntax is simpler and more directly accessible: five instances of a single kind of declarative-sentence, followed by a separate but related rule, breaking the formal pattern.

M. Sanhedrin 1:3

I   A. They judge a tribe, a false prophet [Deut. 18:20], and a high priest, only on the instructions of a court of seventy-one members.

II   B. They bring forth [the army] to wage an optional war only on the instructions of a court of seventy-one.

III   C. They make additions to the city [of Jerusalem] and to the courtyards [of the Temple] only on the instructions of a court of seventy-one.

IV   D. They set up sanhedrins for the tribes only on the instructions of a court of seventy-one.

V   E. They declare a city to be "an apostate city" [Deut. 3:12ff.] only on the instructions of a court of seventy-one.

     F. And they do not declare a city to be "an apostate city" on the frontier,

     G. [nor do they declare] three [in one locale] to be apostate cities],

     H. but they do so in the case of one or two.

I   A. One should take note of the following: two individuals [namely, the false prophet and the high priest] are not judged [by an ordinary court]. Is it not an argument *a fortiori* that an entire tribe [should not be judged by an ordinary court, but only by one of seventy-one members]?

     B. Said R. Mattenaiah, "The Mishnah-pericope refers to the patriarch of a tribe [and not a whole tribe, for that is an obvious fact]. [The point is that the patriarch of a tribe is judged only by a sanhedrin with seventy-one members.]"

     C. Said R. Eliezer, "The Mishnah speaks of a tract of forest between the territory of two tribes [and makes the point that, if there is a suit involving such territory, then even though it is a property case, it is settled by a court of seventy-one, just as, to begin with, the Land was divided up in accord with the instructions of such a court]."

II   A. Said R. Zira, "'Presumptuously' ["The man who acts presumptuously, by not obeying the priest... shall die" (Deut. 17:12)] is stated in one context, and 'presumptuously' ["But the prophet who presumes to speak a word in my name which I have not commanded him to speak,... the prophet has spoken it presumptuously..." (Deut. 18:20, 22) is stated in another context.

Redaction and Formulation 157

B. "Just as in the reference to presumptuousness in the latter passage Scripture speaks of a false prophet, so in the reference to presumptuousness in the former passage, Scripture speaks of a false prophet."

C. Said R. Hezekiah, "'Speaking' is mentioned in the one context ["According to the instructions which they give you, and according to the decision which they pronounce to you, you shall do" (Deut. 17:11), and later on it is stated, '...when a prophet speaks in the name of the Lord...' (Deut. 18:22)].

D. "Just as in the latter usage Scripture speaks of a false prophet, so in the former instance, the same usage indicates that Scripture speaks of a false prophet."

III A. They bring forth the army to wage an optional war only on the instructions of a court of seventy-one [M. San. 1:3B]. [They make additions to the city... only on the instruction of a court of seventy-one (M. San. 1:3C).] [The following serves M. Shebu. 2:2B-F: They add to the city and courtyards only on the instructions of the king and prophet, the Urim and Thummim, and the Sanhedrin of seventy-one members, with two thank offerings and singing. The court goes along with the two thank offerings behind them, and all the Israelites after them. The one offered inside is eaten, and the one offered outside is burned. And any area which is not treated wholly in this way (with the proper rites) -- he who enters that area -- they are not liable on that account.]

B. R. Judah says, "At the outset [of designating the holy ground of Jerusalem], 'So David went up at Gad's word' (II Sam. 24:19) -- thus the king and prophet [of M. Shebu. 2:2].

C. "'Then Solomon began to build the house of the Lord in Jerusalem on Mount Moriah, where the Lord had appeared [to David his father]' (II Chr. 3:1) -- thus the Urim and Thummim.

D. "'To David, his father' -- this refers to the Sanhedrin.

E. "'Ask your father, and he will show you, your elders, and they will tell you' (Deut. 32:7) -- [this refers to consecrating the new territory] with song.

F. "'And after them went Hoshaiah and half of the princes of Judah' (Neh. 12:32) -- [this refers to the requirement of bringing] thank offerings."

G. "And I appointed two great companies which gave thanks and went in procession. One went to the right upon the wall to the Dung Gate" (Neh. 12:31).

H. Said R. Samuel bar Yudan, "Why is it written, 'moved in procession' (MHLKWT), not 'walked in procession' (THLWKWT)? The meaning is that the thank offerings were carried by another person [and did not go on foot]."

I. R. Huna bar Hiyya in the name of Rab derived from the Torah itself [proof that the king, prophet, Urim and Thummim, and Sanhedrin, are required to add to the city]: "According to all that I show you concerning the pattern of the tabernacle, and of all its furniture, so you shall make it" (Ex. 25:9).

J. "Thus you shall make it" — for generations to come.
K. "Moses stands for the king and prophet.
L. "And Aaron stands for the Urim and Thummim.
M. "'And the Lord said to Moses, Gather for me seventy men of the elders of Israel' (Num. 11:16) -- this refers to the Sanhedrin.
N. "'Ask your father and he will show you, your elders, and they will tell you' (Deut. 32:7) -- [this refers to consecrating the new territory] with song.
O. "'And after them went Hoshaiah and half of the princes of Judah' (Neh. 12:32) -- [this refers to the requirement of bringing] thank offerings.
P. "'And I appointed two great companies which gave thanks and went in procession. One went to the right upon the wall to the Dung Gate' (Neh. 12:31)."
Q. Said R. Samuel bar Yudan, "Why is it written, 'moved in procession' and not, 'walked in procession'? The meaning is that the thank offerings were carried by another person [and did not go on foot]."
R. How were they borne?
S. R. Hiyya the Great and R. Simeon bar Rabbi -- one said, "One opposite the other," and the other said, "One behind another."
T. Both of them interpret biblical verse: "The other company of those who gave thanks went to the left, and I followed them" (Neh. 12:38).
U. The one who says they came opposite another [cites as evidence]: "They are dwelling opposite me" (Num. 22:5).
V. The one who says they came one after another [cites as evidence]: "He shall wring its head from behind its neck" (Lev. 5:8).
W. The one who says that they came toward one another maintains that it so happened that every place was atoned for with a single thank offering.
X. The one who said they came one after the other maintains that it turned out that every place was atoned for through two thank offerings.
Y. The one who maintains that they came one after the other finds no difficulty in that which we have learned: **The inner one [nearest the court] is eaten, and the outer one is burned** [T. San. 3:4E].
Z. But the one maintains that they came toward one another -- which of the two thank offerings will be the inner one?
AA. It is the one which is the nearer to the house [the Temple].
BB. R. Yosa in the name of R. Yohanan: "At the instruction of a prophet is the thank offering [offered on the occasion of the consecration of the city] to be eaten.
CC. Said R. Zira, "There we learn: 'If the prophet is here, then what need have I for the Urim and Thummim?'
DD. He found it taught: R. Judah says, "There is need for Urim and Thummim."
IV A. Said R. Abbahu, "R. Yohanan and R. Simeon b. Laqish differed.
B. "One said, 'First they build, then they consecrate.'

	C.	"The other said, 'First they consecrate, then they build.'"
	D.	As to the view of him who said, "First they build and then they consecrate" -- do they not regard the walls [of the Temple] as if they were burnt offerings [so how will it be possible to continue the building process once the Temple has been consecrated]?"
V	A.	[If] they wished to add to the courtyards, with what [offerings] do they [commemorate] the additions?
	B.	With two loaves of [leavened] bread.
	C.	And do they consecrate [Temple-space] on a festival day? [Where will they get leavened bread?]
	D.	But: it is done with the show bread [after it is removed from the altar].
	E.	And do they consecrate on the Sabbath [when that bread is put out]?
	F.	But: it is done by night.
	G.	But do they consecrate by night?
	H.	Said R. Yose b. R. Bun, "[They consecrate] with a meal offering which is baked in the oven [which may be eaten in the courtyard]."
	I.	This view is suitable for the case in which they came up from the Exile, in which case they made an offering, and afterward they consecrated the Temple.
	J.	But when they entered the Land, how did they consecrate?
	K.	Said R. Yose b. R. Bun, "With two thank offerings which come from Nob and Gibeon."
VI	A.	**Abba Saul says, "There were two valleys in Jerusalem, a lower one and an upper one.**
	B.	**"The lower one was sanctified with all these procedures, but the upper one was not sanctified.**
	C.	**"And when the Exiles came up, without a king, without Urim, without Thummim, in the lower one, which had been consecrated completely, the people of the land would eat Lesser Holy Things and second tithe, and associates would eat Lesser Holy Things but not second tithe.**
	D.	**"And in the upper one, which had not been consecrated completely, the people of the land would eat Lesser Holy Things and not second tithe, while the associates [would eat] neither Lesser Holy Things nor second tithe.**
	E.	**"And on what account did they not sanctify it? Because it was a weak point in Jerusalem, and it was easily conquered"** [T. San. 3:4].
VII	A.	<u>They set up sanhedrins for the tribes only [on the instructions of a court of seventy-one]</u> (M. San. 1:3D).
	B.	Scripture says, "[You shall appoint judges and officers in all your towns which the Lord your God gives you, according] to your tribes; and they shall judge the people" (Deut. 16:18).
VIII	A.	<u>They declare a city to be an apostate city</u>, etc. (M. San. 1:3E-H).
	B.	R. Yohanan in the name of R. Hoshaiah: "There are three authorities [who differ in this regard].

C. "One said, 'One they do declare to be apostate, two they do not declare to be apostate' (cf. M. San. 1:3F-H).
D. "Another said, 'Those that are contiguous they declare apostate cities, those that are scattered about they do not declare apostate cities.'
E. "And the third said, 'Those that are scattered they do not declare apostate cities at all, lest gentiles break in and enter the Land of Israel.'"
F. And there is he who proposes to state, "Lest the enemy break in and come upon totally unsettled areas [meeting no resistance because of the absence of populations]."

Following two rather routine exercises, units I, II, the Talmud concentrates its attention on M. 1:3C. But here too the point of interest is not the pericope before us, but rather M. Shebu. 2:2, as cited. Clearly, III E-H, N-Q, require attention. It seems to me that S carries forward N-Q, E-H break into the discourse established by A-D, I-M, so it is the former appearance which must be deleted. Units IV, V, and VI enrich the discussion of consecrating Jerusalem and the Temple area; here too the appropriate pericope is at M. Shebuot. So we are left with I, II, and, at the end, VII, VIII, all of them brief and essentially descriptive pericopae.

The antecedent comment makes clear that before us is a miscellany. No one was concerned to formalize language or to establish any sort of encompassing structural, let alone syntactic, patterns at all. There are conventions operative in the formation of some materials (sometimes awkwardly translated by me, e.g., I.A., "One should take note..."). Once more we notice ample use of the attributive particle, which proves nothing. There is a form of a dispute at III.S: "Name I, Name II, one said..., and the other said...." Such a construction bears no redactional implications that I can discern. The formalization that follows, "Both of them..., the one who says..., the one who says..., the one who said..., the one who said..., and so on," is striking, and the whole may be important. But it is unrelated to the larger arrangement of the materials of which it is part. We may say, therefore that III.S-AA exhibits important formalized traits affecting its own formulation -- that is, the way that sub-unit itself is expressed. But these formal traits have no bearing upon its location among other, distinct sub-units of discourse. That is clear when we reach unit IV, and find the same formal construction. There is no way that one can argue unit IV has been placed where it is, or formulated the way it is, because of its proximity or other relationship to III.S-AA. The other units or parts of units seem to me lacking in any striking evidence of patterning of language or recurrent syntactic patterns of any sort.

vii. Conclusion

These exercises suffice to illustrate a simple proposition. If the traits of the Mishnah indicate that central to the process of organizing materials was the work of formulating them, then the absence of the same traits in the Talmud indicates the opposite. The work of redaction of units of discourse in the Talmud therefore was distinct from, and later than, the work of formulation. There was a distinct stage of redaction, in which already available materials were laid out in accord with a few simple rules, governed by the relationship to the Mishnah exhibited by a given unit of discourse.

We now have a notion of what the two documents look like when seen whole and complete, hence also in contrast to one another. It is banal to note that much more work needs to be done. To begin to describe the Talmud of the Land of Israel as a whole, I have investigated its gross redactional traits, on the one side, and ask about the impact, if any, of redaction upon the formulation of the several units of discourse of which the Talmud is composed, on the other. We can now describe how the redactors did their work and what they proposed to accomplish. We also know that they worked with essentially finished units of discourse. These they shaped into extended discussions focused upon the passages of the Mishnah, in sequence. So the Talmud is made to appear to carry forward and amplify what is in the Mishnah.

In point of fact the Talmud viewed at the end does considerably more than that. For the system of thought revealed by Yerushalmi and that constructed by the Mishnah, despite the interplay of superficial detail, are essentially different from one another. The Mishnah's system presents issues important to the surviving priesthood of the second century in rhetoric precious to the surviving scribes of that same time. It knows nothing of rabbis and their authority, exegesis of Torah as the basis of law, schools as the foci of Jewish authority, and all of the other distinctive and characteristic traits of Judaism as expressed by the Talmud of the Land of Israel (all the more so, the other Talmud as well). So the substance of the Talmud bears witness against its redactional form. But that is a separate question, to be investigated in its own framework.

X
STUDYING SYNOPTIC TEXTS SYNOPTICALLY
THE CASE OF LEVITICUS RABBAH

i. "Studying Synoptic Texts Synoptically"

When two or more documents share the same saying or story, those documents at the points of their intersection simultaneously say the same thing in the same words and so may be regarded as synoptic. How so? Synoptic texts are documents of a single canon that share sayings or stories in common. Studying such synoptic texts "synoptically" focuses upon the character of the shared materials and upon the diverse modes of utilization, in two or more documents, of sayings or stories held in common. In the classic work, Tannaitic Parallels to the Gospels, Morton Smith first made the observation that the relationship existing between books comes under analysis in the comparison of what he calls "Tannaite Literature" and the Gospels:

> Every literature consisting of several books -- such as the Gospels or T[annaitic] L[iterature] -- makes possible the discussion of the relationship which exists between the books, and in the comparison of literatures it is possible to compare the relationship which exists between the books of one literature with the relationship which exists between the books of a second literature [Smith, p. 142].

Smith further observes that all four gospels are "very close to each other" and alleges that that is the case also in Tannaitic Literature:

> The striking fact is the large numbers of complete parallels to be found between its various books, especially between the Mishnah and Tosefta, Mekilta of R. Simon and Sifre on Deut., Sifre Zutta and Sifra, Mekilta and Sifre on Numbers. But apart from these pairs, there are to be found many passages common to all the midrashim [Smith, p. 142].

In his enthusiasm for the proposition at hand Smith goes on even to allege:

> I cannot recall even a word by any Jewish scholar remarking ... that the problem of the relationship between Tosefta and the Mishnah is similar to the synoptic problem, and this in spite of the fact that they are so similar as to be practically inseparable, and that any theory begun from a study of the one literature should have immediate application in the study of the other [Smith, p. 143].

A footnote to Smith's framing of the matter derives from S.J.D. Cohen, who states, "Synoptic texts must always be studied synoptically, even if one text is 'later' than another" [Cohen, p. 56].

Let us turn to Smith's allegation that the relationships between certain rabbinic compositions are such that a theory begun in the study of the Gospels should have immediate application in the study of any document of the rabbinic canon of late antiquity. In order to do so, we rapidly review the premises of synoptic study of the gospels. These are, first, that the Gospels go over verbatim or nearly so the same materials, e.g., sharing the same sayings and stories, and, second, that some of the Gospels drew upon an available source of such sayings and stories ("Q"). Smith himself goes further than the stated premises in claiming, in regard to all four Gospels:

> As a matter of fact all of the four are very close to each other, and the more they are studied the more superficial their differences and the more important their similarities are seen to be [Smith, p. 142].

We may accordingly introduce a third premise in assessing the allegation of "parallels of parallelism" (in Smith's phrase). It is that given documents are "very close to each other," so differences among them are vastly outweighed by similarities.

Now the obvious strategy for examining the allegation at hand demands that we turn to compositions attributed to Tannaite authorship, since Smith makes explicit reference, in his catalogue, to those writings. But when Smith wrote, people took for granted that if a document's authors imputed sayings only to first and second century authorities ("Tannas"), then that document derived from, or formed part of, "Tannaitic Literature," of that period. In a formal sense, of course, that is so. In a concrete historical sense it is unlikely. The reason is that documents assigned to Tannaite authorship, e.g., Mekhilta, Sifra, Tosefta, now are known to have reached closure long after the second century. Since, in his treatment of the subject, Smith points toward Mishnah-Tosefta relationships, it is worth noting that the Tosefta has now been shown [Neusner, 1974] to stand as a secondary expansion and commentary to the Mishnah. So the Tosefta is not only not "Tannaitic" but probably fourth century or later [Herr]. The framers of the Tosefta, for instance, very often cite verbatim and then gloss or rework statements of the Mishnah. Much of the Tosefta is incomprehensible out of relationship to the Mishnah, but one can intelligibly read Matthew without reading Mark.

Accordingly, it is easy to show that the problem of the relationship between Tosefta and the Mishnah is in no way similar to the Synoptic problem. Why not? For the Synoptic Gospels to present us with a parallel to the actual relationship between the Mishnah and the Tosefta, Luke would have to be incomprehensible except in relationship (e.g., juxtaposition) to Mark, or Luke and Mark to "Q," just as vast tracts of the Tosefta prove incomprehensible except in juxtaposition to passages of the Mishnah. In point of fact the relationship between the Mishnah and the Tosefta bears no parallel of any consequence but one to the relationship between two Gospels or among all four of them.

That one exception is simple. It is the fact that, just as the Gospels share sayings and stories, the Mishnah and the Tosefta, among most rabbinic compositions, share sayings and stories. But very often when the Tosefta shares materials with the Mishnah, the Tosefta cites those materials briefly and not completely, and then expands upon the allusion. Where does an author of a Gospel cite another Gospel briefly, by way of allusion, and then expand upon what is clearly material quoted from another document? The answer is, no where. So the relationships in no way are parallel, even where materials are shared.

Let me state matters in somewhat more general terms. Just as Gospels, e.g., Luke and Matthew, know sayings and stories unknown to one or more of the others, so rabbinic writings, e.g., the two Talmuds (the one of the Land of Israel, ca. A.D. 400, the other of Babylonia, ca. A.D. 600) know sayings and stories unknown to other writings within the same canon. Stated in this way, the exception turns out to be trivial. Why so? The relationship among two or more documents based upon the appearance, in all of them, of the same sayings or stories turns out to be altogether general. What do we know about those documents and the relationships among them because they share a given saying or story? In my judgment the answer is that we know only that they share a given saying or story. Beyond that fact everything remains as before. We do not grasp, solely out of the self-evident but trivial relationship of materials held in common, any further facts about the documents at hand. For example, we do not know about their common access to a prior source ("Q"), let alone the viewpoint and contents of that prior source, the disposition of the authors of the several documents of what they chose to utilize out of that prior source, and the like.

That is to say, the discovery of parallel relationships between the books of one canon and those of another canon can produce consequential results only when results of two types emerge.

First, if the parallel relationships point to a common source, then the growth of the materials in the synoptic documents, out of the common source, will present important insight into the character of the documents at hand.

Second, if the parallel relationships permit description of the contents of the common source, then the pre-history of the documents, that is, the intellectual history of the authors, becomes accessible. In my view one of the great achievements of Gospels' scholarship is the discovery of "Q." Knowing only that the Gospels go over shared materials, without the recognition of "Q," we should not have that great edifice of learning comprised by Gospels' scholarship in the past and present centuries. All we should have is the Diatesseron. So "Q" is at the center. To state matters more generally, the critical issue is the nature and character of the shared materials.

ii. Framing the "Synoptic Problem" in the Context of Rabbinic Canon

The point of entry into the problem is this: does a document serve merely as a convenient utensil for the collection and composition of diverse sayings widely available for use anywhere and for any purpose? Or does a document define its own patterns of expression, thought, and composition? The issue as I frame it demands a different analogy from "Q." I draw an analogy from the issue of the relationship between Samuel and Kings, on the one side, and Chronicles on the other. Do the books of Chronicles and those of Samuel and Kings share a common source? Do the books of Chronicles draw upon and rework only the available materials of Samuel and Kings? Framing the issue in terms of a set of rabbinic compositions, we ask whether a given book draws upon sources common to it and to other books, or whether a given composition defines and frames its interests and materials essentially independently of those books with which there admittedly are points of intersection and even concurrence.

When I frame matters in terms of the problem of the rabbinic document, I thus ask what defines a document as such, the text-ness, the textuality, of a text. How do we know that a given book in the canon of Judaism is something other than a scrap book? The choices are clear. One theory is that a document serves solely as a convenient repository of prior sayings and stories, available materials that will have served equally well (or poorly) wherever they took up their final location. The other theory is that a composition exhibits a viewpoint, a purpose of authorship distinctive to its framers or collectors and arrangers. Such a characteristic literary purpose -- by this other theory -- is so powerfully particular to one authorship that nearly everything at hand can be shown to have been (re)shaped for the ultimate purpose of the authorship at hand, that is, collectors and arrangers, who demand the title of authors. To resort again to a less than felicitous neologism, I thus ask what signifies or defines the "document-ness" of a document and what makes a book a book. I therefore wonder whether there are specific texts in the canonical context of Judaism or whether all texts are merely contextual.

In asking the question as I have, I of course lay forth the mode of answering it, one book at a time. We need to define the integrity of texts one by one. We have to confront a single rabbinic composition, and ask about its sources. By "sources" I mean simply passages in a given book that occur, also, in some other rabbinic book. Such sources -- prior to the books in which they appear -- fall into the classification of materials general to two or more compositions and by definition not distinctive and particular to any one of them. The word "source" therefore serves as an analogy to convey the notion that two or more sets of authors have made use of a single, available item. About whether or not the shared item is prior to them both or borrowed by one from the other at this stage we cannot speculate.

To summarize: once we know what is unique to a document, we can investigate the traits that characterize all the unique and so definitive materials in that document.

We ask about whether the materials unique to a document also cohere, or whether they prove merely miscellaneous. If they do cohere, we may conclude that the framers of the document have followed a single plan and a program. That would in my view justify the claim that the framers carried out a labor not only of conglomeration, arrangement and selection, but also of genuine authorship or composition in the narrow and strict sense of the word. The document emerges from authors, not merely arrangers and compositors.

We take up and analyze in exactly the same way and for the same purpose the items shared between that document and some other or among several documents. We ask about the traits of those items, one by one and all in the aggregate, following the same program.

In these stages for the case at hand we may solve the problem of the rabbinic document: do we deal with a scrapbook or a cogent composition? A text or merely a literary expression, random and essentially promiscuous, of a larger theological context? That is the choice.

iii. The Problem and Its Solution

I propose to demonstrate in the case of Leviticus Rabbah that a rabbinic document constitutes a text, not merely a scrapbook or a random compilation of episodic materials.

A text is a document with a purpose, one that exhibits the traits of the integrity of the parts to the whole and the fundamental autonomy of the whole from other texts. I shall show that the document at hand therefore falls into the classification of a cogent composition, put together with purpose and intended as a whole and in the aggregate to bear a meaning and state a message. I shall therefore disprove the claim, for the case before us, that a rabbinic document serves merely as an anthology or miscellany or is to be compared only to a scrapbook, made up of this and that. In the present, exemplary instance I shall point to the improbability that a document has been brought together merely to join discrete and ready-made bits and pieces of episodic discourse. A document in the canon of Judaism thus does not merely define a context for the aggregation of such already completed and mutually distinct materials. Rather, I claim, a document constitutes a text. So in method at issue then is what makes a text a text, that is, the textuality of a document. At stake is how we may know when a document constitutes a text and when it is merely an anthology or a scrapbook. Once that question is settled, the further issue of a "synoptic" study of the particular text at hand will work itself out.

I choose for the test-case Leviticus Rabbah, because I already have made my own translation of it and have also completed certain studies of its rhetoric, modes of argument, and essential message. I could as well have chosen the Mishnah, the Tosefta, Sifra, the Yerushalmi, the Bavli, or other documents on which I have worked at length. Each of these, as well as every other document of the canon of Judaism completed in late antiquity, demands equivalent inquiry. Leviticus Rabbah forms no more promising, nor less promising, an arena for study than any other as to the synoptic side of rabbinic texts. Still, it is more difficult than the Mishnah, which is a far more cogent formal construction. It also appears to be less difficult (so I have the impression) than Genesis Rabbah, on the one side, and the Fathers according to Rabbi Nathan, on the other. As an outsider to those texts, I do have the impression that they fall more readily into the category of scrapbooks or anthologies than cogent compositions. But only further study will tell. A long series of detailed analyses of each rabbinic composition of late antiquity therefore will flow from the present one. So, to conclude, I hope here to inaugurate a useful method of inquiry into a long-standing and much debated, if little-studied, question: whether and how rabbinic documents on their own constitute complete and autonomous statements, addresses exhibiting integrity and those traits of proportion and composition that we associate with well-crafted literature.

Let me spell out the method I shall follow. First, I have to prove that the document at hand rests upon clearcut choices of formal and rhetorical preference, so it is, from the viewpoint of form and mode of expression, cogent. If one taxonomy serves all and encompasses the bulk of the units of discourse at hand, I may fairly claim that Leviticus Rabbah does constitute a cogent formal structure, based upon patterns of rhetoric uniform and characteristic throughout.

Second, I isolate those passages in the document at hand that in fact are not unique to it but are shared with one or more other documents of the same larger canon. These ("synoptic") passages will not only link one document to the next. As I said, they also will call into question the claim that any document stands essentially on its own, exhibiting an integrity that distinguishes that document from all others. What is shared and not unique by definition challenges any claim to integrity and autonomy. If, therefore, what is not particular proves to form an important component of the whole, or if it bears a substantial part of the burden of the message of the whole, then the document as a whole cannot be characterized as autonomous. It would appear, rather, that the document under study must constitute yet another, scarcely differentiated utensil for containing a message indifferent to its bearers. Then, as I said, one document cannot demand differentiation from others. The claim that a given document bears its own message and viewpoint and constitutes a statement of integrity will have to give way to the opposite one. We should then have to claim (with Judaic theologians) that all documents equally bear the message of the whole. Then any one of them indifferently may supply a context for the expression of what is common to them all. Hence, documents will turn out to constitute not texts but merely contexts. So at issue in the analysis of what is shared is the critical claim at hand.

Third, I have to return to the materials unique to the document at hand and bring them into relationship with materials shared among two or more documents. The compositions particular to the document along with shared materials have to be reexamined and described. These now become the criteria: which sort of materials -- unique or common -- bear the main formal components of the formal construction of the whole? Are the unique or are the shared materials episodic? If materials unique to Leviticus Rabbah, those that conform to its recurrent literary structures, prove to form the principal parts, then we may say that we deal with a document made up by a distinct set of authors. This authorship has agreed on the formal and rhetorical preferences and has executed them consistently, time and again. If, again, the literary structures unique to the document as a whole cohere and present a cogent composition, then we may claim to know what is primary to the document, what expresses its topical and logical message. More than that, on formal grounds of rhetoric and pattern we again may allege that the document does present its own rhetorical and logical program. I have also to go back to the materials not particular to the document at hand and undertake to describe them. Do shared materials form a large or a negligible proportion? Do they cohere in formal or aesthetic or rhetorical ways? Or do they constitute a miscellany?

If they constitute a miscellany, one might wish to ask whether, in some documents other than the one at hand, the several shared items fit more suitably into an established formal and rhetorical setting than they do in the document under study. If it turns out that what is shared between the document under study and some other document exhibits the characteristic literary traits of that other document, on formal and rhetorical grounds one may claim that that other document, and not the one under study, bears the principal burden of the particular unit of discourse at hand. To state matters simply, it will turn out that in the case of shared items the document under study uses what is not native and natural to it. Rather, the document before us has borrowed from some other document, which then demands study on its terms and in its own analytical context.

It will follow that we can answer the question, for the document under study, of whether or not we deal with a text, exhibiting traits of composition, deliberation, proportion, and so delivering a message on its own. If we do not, then we shall turn out to affirm the now-broadly-held opinion that all of the documents in the canon of Judaism speak pretty much at random to a single common program. All contribute to Judaism equally and without differentiation. To describe Judaism -- a theological or legal point -- one may equally cite what is found in one document alongside what is located in some other. We then do not have to pay much attention to the locus of a given passage. We may ignore its relationship to what stands fore and aft. We may assume that all things are part of one thing, whether we call it "the one whole Torah of Moses, our rabbi," or merely "Judaism," "the halakhah," or "theology of Judaism" not making much difference. So, in all, the stakes are very high, and the work at hand will be protracted, so far as facts make a difference.

iv. Recurrent Literary Structures of Leviticus Rabbah

A literary structure is a composition that adheres to conventions of expression, organization, or proportion, extrinsic to the message of the author. Such a structure conforms to rules that impose upon the individual writer a limited set of choices about how he will convey whatever message he has in mind. Or it will limit an editor or redactor to an equally circumscribed set of alternatives about how to arrange received materials. We obviously cannot allege on the basis of what merely appears to us to be patterned or needless formal that we have a structure in hand. Nor shall we benefit from bringing to the text at hand structures shown in other texts to define conventions for communicating ideas in those other texts. A text has to define its own structures for us. This its authors do simply by repeatedly resorting to a given set of literary conventions. It follows that the adjective "recurrent" constitutes a redundancy when joined to the noun "structure." That is to say, we cannot know that we have a structure if the text under analysis does not repeatedly resort to the presentation of its message through that disciplined structure.

Leviticus Rabbah comprises large-scale literary structures. How do we know that fact? It is because when we divide up the undifferentiated columns of words and sentences and point to the boundaries that separate one completed unit of thought or discourse from the next such completed composition, we produce rather sizable statements conforming to a single set of patterns. While in the Mishnah, for example, we can distinguish a few sentences as a paragraph, and a few paragraphs as a concluded statement, a completed unit of discourse, in Leviticus Rabbah we cannot. Rather, our divisions encompass many more sentences, a great many more words, than is the case in the Mishnah. On the other hand, in comparing the dimensions of completed units of discourse in Leviticus Rabbah to those in the Yerushalmi or the Bavli, we find in the former less sustained, less protracted discourse than in the latter. That is to say, a unit of thought or analysis in one of the two Talmuds in the average will be made up of a great many more subunits or components. On the other hand, these components of large-scale analytical units of discourse will appear autonomous of the larger composition in which they occur. They will not prove cogent within that composition. By contrast, units of discourse in Leviticus Rabbah tend not to run on as do those of the two Talmuds. But the components do prove more cogent with the larger discourse which they serve. In all, what I mean when I claim that Leviticus Rabbah is made up of large-scale literary structures is simple. When we divide a given parashah, or chapter, of Leviticus Rabbah into its sub-divisions, we find these sub-divisions sustained and on occasion protracted, but also stylistically cogent and well-composed.

What these facts mean is that, in Leviticus Rabbah, the repeated patterns follow protracted orbits, covering a sizable volume of material. The patterns are large in scale. We deal not with small-scale syntactic formalization, such as the Mishnah's authors use to good effect, for example three or five sentences made up of parts of the speech arranged in exactly the same way. But we do deal with a stylized mode of discourse, unlike the Tosefta's rather miscellaneous style in conveying its authors' ideas. Were we to be guided by either the Yerushalmi's or the Bavli's writers, further, we should look for rigid but abbreviated rhetorical patterns, signals conveyed by little more than parts of speech so set forth as to convey the purpose and sense of sizable discussion. We should be disappointed were we to ask the authors at hand in Leviticus Rabbah to demonstrate their equivalent skill at the use of rhetoric to lend structure and impart sense to otherwise unformed sentences. Where those authors excel, it is at holding in the balance a rather substantial composite of seemingly diverse materials, systematically and patiently working their way from point to appparently miscellaneous observation, and only at the end drawing the whole to an elegant and satisfying conclusion. So we look for large-scale patterns and point to such unusually sizable compositions as characteristic because they recur and define discourse, parashah by parashah. Indeed, as we shall now see, a given parashah is made up of a large-scale literary structure, which I shall define in a moment, followed by further, somewhat smaller, fairly formalized constructions.

How shall we proceed to identify the structures that define the document before us? It seems to me we had best move first to the analysis of a single parashah. We seek, within that parashah, to identify what holds the whole together. The second step then is to see whether we have identified something exemplary, or what is no example but in fact a phenomenon that occurs in fact only once or at random. For the first exercise, we take up Parashah Five. As we proceed, of course, we shall then provide statistics covering all thirty-seven of the parashiyyot and see the extent to which the patterns exhibited in one parashah in fact characterize the entire lot.

v. Leviticus Rabbah Parashah 5

Let us begin with the parashah as a whole and then proceed to the work of classifying its units of discourse and explaining the order in which units of each classification are presented.

Parashah Five

V:I

1. A. "If it is the anointed priest who sins, [thus bringing guilt on the people, then let him offer to the Lord for the sin which he has committed a young bull without blemish]" (Lev. 4:3).
   B. "When he is quiet, who can condemn? When he hides his face, who can set him right [RSV: behold him] [whether it be a nation or a man? that a godless man should not reign, that he should not ensnare the people]" (Job 34:29-30).
   C. R. Meir interpreted [the matter] [Gen. R. 36:1], "'When he is quiet' -- in his world, 'when he hides his face' -- in his world.
   D. "The matter may be compared to the case of a judge who draws a veil inside and so does not see what goes on outside.
   E. "So the people of the generation of the flood thought: 'The thick clouds cover him, so he will not see [what we do]' (Job 22:14)."
   F. They said to him, "That's enough from you, Meir."

2. A. Another interpretation: "When he is quiet, who can condemn? When he hides his face, who can set him right?" (Job 34:29)
   B. When he gave tranquility to the generation of the flood, who could come and condemn them?
   C. What sort of tranquility did he give them? "Their children are established in their presence, and their offspring before their eyes. [Their houses are safe from fear, and no rod of God is upon them]" (Job 21:8).
   D. R. Levi and rabbis:
   E. R. Levi said, "A woman would get pregnant and give birth in three days. [How do we know it?] Here, the word, 'established,' is used, and elsewhere: 'Be establshed in three days' (Ex. 19:15). Just as the word, 'established,' used there involves a span of three days, so the word, 'established,' used here means three days."
   F. Rabbis say, "In a single day a woman would get pregnant and give birth.
   G. "Here, the word, 'established,' is used, and elsewhere: 'And be established in the morning' (Ex. 34:2). Just as the word 'established' stated there involves a single day, so the word 'established' used here involves a single day."

3. A. "And their offspring before their eyes" -- for they saw children and grandchildren.
   B. "They send forth their little ones like a flock, [and their children dance]" (Job 21:11).
   C. [The word for "children" means] "their young."
   D. Said R. Levi, "In Arabia for children they use the word 'the young.'"

4. A. "And their children dance" (Job 21:11) --
   B. ["they dance"] like devils.
   C. That is in line with the following verse of Scripture: "And satyrs will dance there" (Is. 13:21).

5. A. They say: When one of them would give birth by day, she would say to her son, "Go and bring me a flint, so I can cut your umbilical cord."
   B. If she gave birth by night, she would say to her son, "Go and light a lamp for me, so I can cut your umbilical cord."
   C. M^{C}SH B: A woman gave birth by night and said to her son, "Go and light a lamp for me, so I can cut your umbilical cord."
   D. [In Aramaic:] When he went out to fetch it, a devil, Ashmadon [Asmodeus], head of the spirits, met him. While the two were wrestling with one another, the cock crowed. [Ashmadon] said to him, "Go, boast to your mother that my time has run out, for if my time had not run out, I could have killed you."
   E. He said to him, "Go, boast to your mother's mother that my mother had not cut my umbilical cord, for if my mother had cut my umbilical cord, I would have beaten you."
   F. This illustrates that which is said: "Their houses are safe from fear" (Job 21:9) -- from destroying spirits.

6. A. "And no rod of God is upon them" -- [for their houses are free from suffering.
   B. [And this further] illustrates that which is said: "[When he is quiet, who can condemn,] when he hides his face, who can put him right" (Job 34:30).
   C. When [God] hides his face from them, who can come and say to him, "You have not done right."
   D. And how, indeed, did he hide his face from them? When he brought the flood on them.
   E. That is in line with the following verse of Scripture: "And he blotted out every living substance which was upon the face of the earth" (Gen. 7:23).

7. A. "Whether it be to a nation [or a man together]" (Job 34:29) -- this refers to the generation of the flood.
   B. "Or to a man" -- this refers to Noah.
   C. "Together" -- he had to rebuild his world from one man, he had to rebuild his world from one nation.

On the surface, the sole point of contact between the base-verse and the intersecting verse, Lev. 4:3 and Job 34:29-30, is in the uncited part of the passage of Job, "that he should not ensnare the people." The anointed priest has sinned and in so doing has brought guilt on the entire people. If, however, that is why the entire assembly of exegeses of Job has been inserted here, that theme plays no rule in making the collection of materials on Job. For at no point in the present unit (or in the next one) does the important segment of the passage of Job come under discussion. The interpretation of Job 34:29 in light of the story of the flood predominates here. No. 1 has Meir's view that the entire passage refers to God's failure to intervene, with special reference to the flood. No. 2 pursues the same line of thought. No. 3 illustrates the notion that their children "are established in their presence," and Nos. 3-4 continue to spell out the phrase-by-phrase exegesis of the same verse. No. 5 pursues the same line of thought. No. 6 shifts the ground of interpretation. Now God is "quiet," but later, in "hiding his face," he brings punishment on them. No. 7 completes the exegesis of the cited passage of Job in line with the view that Job was a contemporary of Noah and spoke of his ties. Noah might then serve as the counterpart and opposite of the priest who brings guilt on the people. But that is by no means the clear intent of the passage at hand.

V:II

1. A. Another interpretation: "When he is quiet, who can condemn" (Job 34:29).
   B. When he gave tranquility to the Sodomites, who could come and condemn them?
   C. What sort of tranquility did he give them?
   D. "As for the earth, out of it comes bread, but underneath it is turned up as by fire. Its stones are the place of sapphires, and it has dust of gold" (Job 28:5-6).
2. A. "That path no bird of prey knows, and the falcon's eye has not seen it" (Job 28:7).
   B. R. Levi in the name of R. Yohanan bar Shahina: "The falcon [bar haday-ya-bird] spots its prey at a distance of eighteen mils."
   C. And how much is its portion [of food]?
   D. R. Meir said, "[A mere] two handbreadths."
   E. R. Judah said, "One handbreadth."
   F. R. Yose said, "Two or three fingerbreadths."
   G. [In Aramaic:] And when it stood on the trees of Sodom, it could not see the ground because of the density of [the foliage of] the trees.
3. A. "When he hides his face, who can put him right?" --
   B. When he hid his face from them, who comes to say to him, "You did not do rightly"?
   C. And when did he hide his face from them?
   D. When he made brimstone and fire rain down on them.
   E. That is in line with the following verse of Scripture: "Then the Lord made brimstone and fire rain on Sodom and Gomorrah" (Gen. 19:24).

The second unit simply carries forward the exercise of reading Job 28:5ff., now in line with the story of Sodom and Gomorrah, rather than the Generation of the Flood.

V:III

1. A. Another interpretation of "When he is quiet, who can condemn? When he hides his face, who can set him right?" (Job 34:29).
   B. When he gave tranquility to the ten tribes, who could come and condemn them?
   C. What sort of tranquility did he give them? "Woe to those who are at ease in Zion, and to those who feel secure on the mountain of Samaria, the notable men of the first of the nations, to whom the house of Israel to come" (Amos 6:1).
2. A. "Woe to those who are at ease in Zion" refers to the tribe of Judah and Benjamin.
   B. "Those who feel secure on the mountain of Samaria" refers to the ten tribes.

C. "The notable men of the first of the nations" who derive from the two noteworthy names, Shem and Eber.

D. When the nations of the world eat and drink, they pass the time in nonsense-talk, saying, "Who is a sage, like Balaam! Who is a hero, like Goliath! Who is rich, like Haman!"

E. And the Israelites come after them and say to them, "Was not Ahitophel a sage, Samson a hero, Korah rich?"

3. A. "Pass over to Calneh and see, [and thence go to Hamath the great, then go down to Gath of the Philistines. Are they better than these kingdoms? Or is their territory greater than your territory?]" (Amos 6:2).

B. [Calneh] refers to Ctesiphon.

C. "Hamath the great" refers to Hamath of Antioch.

D. "And go down to Gath of the Philistines" refers to the mounds of the Philistines.

E. "Are they better than these kingdoms? Or is their territory greater than your territory?"

F. "O you who put far away the evil day" (Amos 6:3) [refers to] the day on which they would go into exile.

4. A. "And bring near the seat of violence?" (Amos 6:3). This refers to Esau.

B. "Did you bring yourselves near to sit next to violence" -- this refers to Esau.

C. That is in line with the following verse of Scripture: "For the violence done to your brother Jacob, [shame shall cover you]" (Obad. 1:40).

5. A. "[Woe to] those who lie upon beds of ivory" (Amos 6:4) -- on beds made of the elephant's tusk.

B. "And stink on their couches" (Amos 6:4) -- who do stinking transgressions on their beds.

C. "Who eat lambs from the flock [and calves from the midst of the stall]" (Amos 6:4).

D. They say: When one of them wanted to eat a kid of the flock, he would have the whole flock brought before him, and he would stand over it and slaughter it.

E. When he wanted to eat a calf, he would bring the entire herd of calves before him and stand over it and slaughter it.

6. A. "Who sing idle songs to the sound of the harp [and like David invent for themselves instruments of music]" (Amos 6:5).

B. [They would say that] David provided them with musical instruments.

7. A. "Who drink wine in bowls" (Amos 6:6).

B. Rab, R. Yohanan, and rabbis:

C. Rab said, "It is a very large bowl" [using the Greek].

D. R. Yohanan said, "It was in small cups."

E. Rabbis say, "It was in cups with saucers attached."

F. Whence did the wine they drink come?

	G.	R. Aibu in the name of R. Hanina said, "It was wine from Pelugta, for the wine would entice (PTH) the body."
	H.	And rabbis in the name of R. Hanina said, "It was from Pelugta' [separation], since, because of their wine-drinking, the ten tribes were enticed [from God] and consequently sent into exile."
8.	A.	"And anoint themselves with the finest oils" (Amos 6:6).
	B.	R. Judah b. R. Ezekial said, "This refers to oil of unripe olives, which removes hair and smooths the body."
	C.	R. Haninah said, "This refers to oil of myrrh and cinnamon."
9.	A.	And [in spite of] all this glory: "They are not grieved over the ruin of Joseph" (Amos 6:6).
	B.	"Therefore they shall now be the first of those to go into exile, [and the revelry of those who stretch themselves shall pass away]" (Amos 6:7).
	C.	What is the meaning of "the revelry of those who stretch themselves"?
	D.	Said R. Aibu, "They had thirteen public baths, one for each of the tribes, and one additional one for all of them together.
	E.	"And all of them were destroyed, and only this one [that had served all of them] survived.
	F.	"This shows how much lewdness was done with them."
10.	A.	"When he hides his face, who can set him right?" (Job 34:29).
	B.	When he hid his face from them, who then could come and say to him, "You did not do right"?
	C.	How did he hide his face from them? By bringing against them Sennacherib, the king of Assyria.
	D.	That is in line with the following verse of Scripture: "In the fourteenth year of King Hezekiah, Sennacherib, king of Assyria, came up [against all the fortified cities of Judah and took them]" (Is. 36:1).
11.	A.	What is the meaning of, "and took them"?
	B.	Said R. Abba b. R. Kahana, "Three divine decrees were sealed on that day.
	C.	"The decree against the ten tribes was sealed, for them to fall into the hand of Sennacherib; the decree against Sennacherib was sealed, for him to fall into the hand of Hezekiah; and the decree of Shebna was sealed, to be smitten with leprosy.
12.	A.	"Whether it be a nation [or a man]" (Job 34:29) -- this refers to Sennacherib, as it is said, "For a nation has come up upon my land" (Joel 1:6).
	B.	"...or a man" (Job 34:29) -- this refers to Israel: "For you, my sheep, the sheep of my pasture, are a man" (Ez. 34:31).
	C.	"Together" (Job 34:29) -- this refers to King Uzziah, who was smitten with leprosy.
	D.	That is in line with the following verse of Scripture: "And Uzziah the King was a leper until the day he died" (2 Chr. 26:21).

13. A. [Margulies: What follows treats "...whether it be a nation or a man together" (Job 34:29):] Now the justice of the Holy One, blessed be he, is not like man's justice.
    B. A mortal judge may show favor to a community, but he will never show favor to an individual.
    C. But the Holy One, blessed be he, is not so. Rather: "If it is the anointed priest who sins, [thus bringing guilt on the people,] then let him offer [for the sin which he has committed] a young bull [without blemish to the Lord as a sin-offering]" (Lev. 4:3-4).
    D. "[If the whole congregation of Israel commits a sin unwittingly, and the thing is hidden from the eyes of the assembly, and they do any one of the things which the Lord has commanded not to be done and are guilty, when the sin which they have committed becomes known,] the assembly shall offer a young bull for a sin-offering" (Lev. 4:13-14). [God exacts the same penalty from an individual and from the community and does not distinguish the one from the other. The anointed priest and the community both become subject to liability for the same offering, a young bull.]

Finally, at No. 13, we come to the verse with which we began. And we find a clear point of contact between the base-verse and the intersecting one, Job 34:29, as Margulies explains. Still, there is no clear reason for including a sustained exegesis of Amos 6:3ff. No. 1 completes the original exegesis by applying the cited verse to the ten tribes, first tranquil, then punished, as at V:I, II. 1.C then links Amos 6:1 to the present context. Once Amos 6:1 makes its appearance, we work through the elements of Amos 6:1-7. That massive interpolation encompasses Nos. 2-9. No. 10 resumes where No. 1 left off. No. 11 is tacked on to 10.D, and then Nos. 12, 13 continue the exegesis in terms of Israelite history of Job 34:29. Then, as I said, No. 13 stands completely separate from all that has gone before in V:I-III.12.

What then is the primary intent of the exegete? It is to emphasize the equality of anointed priest and ordinary Israelites. The expiation demanded of the one is no greater than that of the other. Considering the importance of the anointed priest, the ceremony by which he attains office, the sanctity attached to his labor, we cannot miss the polemic. What the anointed priest does unwittingly will usually involve some aspect of the cult. When the community commits a sin unwittingly, it will not involve the cult but some aspect of the collective life of the people. The one is no more consequential than the other; the same penalty pertains to both. So the people and the priest stand on the same plane before God. And the further meaning of the verse of Job then cannot be missed. When God hides his face, in consequence of which the people suffer, it is for a just cause. No one can complain; he is long-suffering but in the end exacts his penalties. And these will cover not unwitting sin, such as Leviticus knows, but deliberate sin, as with the Generation of the Flood, Sodom, and the Ten Tribes. There would then appear to be several layers of meaning in the exegetical construction, which we must regard as a sustained and unified one, a truly amazing achievement.

V:IV
1. A. Said R. Abbahu, "It is written, 'Take heed that you do not forsake the Levite [as long as you live in your land]' (Deut. 12:19). What follows thereafter? 'When the Lord your God enlarges your territory [as he has promised you]' (Deut. 12:20).
   B. "What has one thing got to do with the other?
   C. "Said the Holy One, blessed be he, 'In accord with your gifts will they enlarge your [place].'"
   D. R. Huna in the name of R. Aha, "If a slave brings as his offering a young bull, while his master brings a lamb, the slave takes precedence over his master.
   E. "This is in accord with what we have learned in the Mishnah: <u>'If the young bull of the anointed priest and the young bull of the community are waiting [sacrifice], the young bull of the anointed priest takes precedence over the young bull of the community in all aspects of the sacrificial rite'</u> (M. Hor. 3:6)."
2. A. "A man's gift makes room for him and brings him before great men" (Prov. 18:16).
   B. M^CSH B: R. Eliezer, R. Joshua, and R. Aqiba went to the harborside of Antioch to collect funds for the support of sages.
   C. [In Aramaic:] A certain Abba Yudan lived there.
   D. He would carry out his religious duty [of philanthropy] in a liberal spirit, but had lost his money. When he saw our masters, he went home with a sad face. His wife said to him, "What's wrong with you, that you look so sad?"
   E. He repeated the tale to her: "Our masters are here, and I don't know what I shall be able to do for them."
   F. His wife, who was a truly philanthropic woman -- what did she say to him? "You only have one field left. Go, sell half of it and give them the proceeds."
   G. He went and did just that. When he was giving them the money, they said to him, "May the Omnipresent make up all your losses."
   H. Our masters went their way.
   I. He went out to plough. While he was ploughing the half of the field that he had left, the Holy One, blessed be he, opened his eyes. The earth broke open before him, and his cow fell in and broke her leg. He went down to raise her up, and found a treasure beneath her. He said, "It was for my gain that my cow broke her leg."
   J. When our masters came back, [in Aramaic:] they asked about a certain Abba Yudan and how he was doing. They said, "Who can gaze on the face of Abba Yudan [which glows with prosperity] -- Abba Yudan, the owner of flocks of goats, Abba Yudan, the owner of herds of asses, Abba Yudan, the owner of herds of camels."
   K. He came to them and said to them, "Your prayer in my favor has produced returns and returns on the returns."

L. They said to him, "Even though someone else gave more than you did, we wrote your name at the head of the list."

M. Then they took him and sat him next to themselves and recited in his regard the following verse of Scripture: "A man's gift makes room for him and brings him before great men" (Prov. 18:16).

3. A. R. Hiyya bar Abba called for charity contributions in support of a school in Tiberias. A member of the household of Siloni got up and pledged a litra of gold.

B. R. Hiyya bar Abba took him and sat him next to himself and recited in his regard the following verse of Scripture: "A man's gift makes room for him and brings him before great men" (Prov. 18:16).

4. A. [In Aramaic:] R. Simeon b. Laqish went to Bosrah. A certain Abba [Lieberman deletes: Yudan], "the Deceiver," lived there. It was not -- Heaven forfend -- that he really was a deceiver. Rather, he would practice [holy] deception in doing the religious duty [of philanthropy].

B. [In Aramaic:] He would see what the rest of the community would pledge, and he would then pledge to take upon himself [a gift equivalent to that of the rest of the] community.

C. R. Simeon b. Laqish took him and sat him next to himself and recited in his regard the following verse of Scripture: "A man's gift makes room for him and brings him before great men" (Prov. 18:16).

We find neither a base-verse nor an intersecting one. Rather, what will be the secondary verse -- Prov. 18:16 -- comes in the distant wake of a problem presented by the information of Lev. 4. Specifically, we find reference to the sacrifice of the young bulls of the high priest, of the community, and of the ruler. The issue then naturally arises, which one comes first? The Mishnah answers that question, at M. Hor. 3:6. Reflection upon that answer generates the observation that the anointed priest comes first, as in Scripture's order, in particular when the offerings are of the same value. But if one offering is more valuable than the other, the more valuable offering takes precedence. Then comes secondary reflection on the fact that a person's gift establishes his rank even if it is on other grounds lower than what he otherwise would attain. No. 1 does not pursue that secondary reflection, but invites it at 1.C. The invocation of Prov. 18:16 then is not on account of Lev. 4 at all. It must follow that Nos. 2-4 would better serve a compilation of materials on Deut. 12:19-20 than the present passage. What follows No. 1 serves a purpose in no way closely connected either to the sense or to the syntax of our passage. The entire complex, Nos. 2-4, occurs at Y. Hor. 3:4. It is lifted whole, attached because of the obvious relevance to No. 1. We find no pretense, then, that these stories relate in any way to Lev. 4.

For the story teller at No. 2, the climax comes at L-M, the sages' recognition that their placing of Abba Yudan at the head of the list had made possible the serendipitous accident. Nos. 3 and 4 omit the miraculous aspect entirely.

V:V
1. A. Reverting to the base-text (GWPH): "If it is the anointed priest who sins" (Lev. 4:3).
   B. This refers to Shebna.
2. A. "[Thus says the Lord, God of hosts,] 'Come, go to this steward (SKN), to Shebna, who is over the household, [and say to him, 'What have you to do here and whom have you here, that you have hewn here a tomb for yourself, you who hew a tomb on the height and carve a habitation for yourself in the rock? Behold, the Lord will hurl you away violently, O you strong young man! He will seize firm hold on you, and whirl you round and round and throw you like a ball into a wide land; there you shall die, and there shall be your splendid chariots, you shame of your master's house. I will thrust you from your office and you will be cast down from your station]'" (Is. 22:15-19).
   B. R. Eliezer said, "He was a high priest."
   C. R. Judah b. Rabbi said, "He was steward."
   D. In the view of R. Eliezer, who said he was a high priest, [we may bring evidence from Scripture,] for it is written, "And I will clothe him with your robe [and will bind your girdle on him and will commit your authority into his hand]" (Is. 22:21).
   E. In the view of R. Judah b. Rabbi, who said he was steward, [we may bring evidence from Scripture,] for it is written, "And I will commit your authority to his hand" (Is. 22:21).
   F. R. Berekiah said, "What is a 'steward' (SWKN)? It is one who comes from Sikhni.
3. A. And he went up and was appointed <u>komes opsarion</u> [the Greek for chief cook] in Jerusalem.
   B. That is in line with the prophet's condemnation, saying to him, "What have you to do here, and whom have you here" (Is. 22:16).
   C. "You exile, son of an exile! What wall have you built here, what pillar have you put up here, and what nail have you hammered in here?!"
   D. R. Eleazar said, "A person has to have a nail or a peg firmly set in a synagogue so as to have the right to be buried in that place [in which he is living]."
   E. "And have you hewn here a tomb for yourself?" (Is. 22:16). He made himself a kind of a dovecot and put his tomb on top of it.
   F. "You who hew a tomb on the height" (Is. 22:16) --
   G. R. Ishmael in the name of Mar Uqba, "On the height the decree was hewn out concerning him, indicating that he should not have a burial place in the land of Israel."
   H. "You who carve a habitation for yourself in the rock" (Is. 22:16) -- a stone coffin.
   I. "Behold, the Lord will hurl you away violently" (Is. 22:17) -- one rejection after another.

J. "...hurl away violently (GBR)" -- [since the word GBR also means cock:] said R. Samuel b. R. Nahman, "[In Aramaic:], it may be compared to a cock which is driven and goes from place to place."

K. "He will seize a firm hold on you" (Is. 22:17), [since the words for "firm hold" may also be translated, "wrap around," thus: "And he will wrap you around"] the meaning is that he was smitten with sara^{c}at, in line with that which you find in Scripture, "And he will wrap his lip around" (Lev. 13:45).

L. "And whirl you round and round [and throw you like a ball]" (Is. 22:18) -- exile after exile.

M. "Like a ball" -- just as a ball is caught from hand to hand and does not fall to the ground, so [will it be for him].

N. "Into a wide land" -- this means Casiphia (Ezra 8:17).

O. "There you shall die and there shall be your splendid chariots" (Is. 22:18) --

4. A. In accord with the position of R. Eliezer, who said that Shebna had been a high priest, [the reference to the splendid chariots implies] that he had been deriving personal benefit from the offerings.

B. In accord with the view of R. Judah b. Rabbi, who said that he had been steward, [the reference to the splendid chariots implies] that he had derived personal benefit from things that had been consecrated for use in the upkeep of the sanctuary.

C. "You shame of your master's house" (Is. 22:18).

D. In accord with the position of R. Eliezer, who said that Shebna had been a high priest, [the shame was] that he had treated the offerings in a disgraceful way.

E. In accord with the view of R. Judah b. Rabbi, who said that he had been steward, [the shame was] that he had treated both of his masters disgracefully, that is Hezekiah, on the one side, Isaiah on the other.

5. A. R. Berekhiah in the name of R. Abba b. R. Kahana: "What did Shebna and Joahaz [2 Kngs. 18:18] do? They wrote a message and attached it to an arrow and shot it to Sennacherib through the window. In the message was written the following: "We and everyone in Jerusalem want you, but Hezekiah and Isaiah don't want you."

B. Now this is just what David had said [would happen]: "For lo, the wicked bend the bow, they have fitted their arrow to the string" (Ps. 11:2).

C. "For lo, the wicked bend the bow" -- this refers to Shebna and Joahaz.

D. "They have fitted their arrow to the string" -- on the bowstring.

E. "To shoot in the dark at the upright in heart" (Ps. 11:2) -- at two upright in heart, Hezekiah and Isaiah.

What the exegete contributes to the explanation of Lev. 4:3 is simply the example of how an anointed priest may sin. The rest of the passage is a systematic exposition of the verses about Shebna. But the entire matter of Shebna belongs here only within Eliezer's opinion that he was a high priest. That is a rather remote connection to the present passage of Leviticus. So because of the allegation that Shebna was high priest, the entire passage -- fully worked out on its own -- was inserted here. The redactor then appeals to theme, not to content, in drawing together the cited verses of Leviticus and Isaiah. Nos. 2, 4 are continuous with one another. No. 3 inserts a systematic, phrase by phrase exegesis of Is. 22:15ff. No. 5 then complements the foregoing with yet further relevant material. So the construction, apart from No. 1, is cogent and well-conceived. Only linkage to Lev. 4:3 is farfetched.

V:VI

1. A. "If it is the anointed priest who sins" (Lev. 4:3).
   B. [What follows occurs at T. Hor. 2:4, explaining M. Hor. 3:4, cited above at V:IV.1.E:] [If] the anointed high priest must atone [for a sin] and the community [SBWR for SRYK] must be atoned for [in line with Lev. 4:13], it is better that the one who [has the power to] make atonement take precedence over the one for whom atonement is made,
   C. as it is written, "And he will atone for himself and for his house" (Lev. 16:17).
   D. ["His house"] refers to his wife.
2. A. "If it is the anointed priest who sins" (Lev. 4:3) --
   B. Will an anointed priest commit a sin!
   C. Said R. Levi, "Pity the town whose physician has gout [and cannot walk to visit the sick], whose governor has one eye, and whose public defender plays the prosecutor in capital cases."
3. A. "[If it is the anointed priest who sins,] thus bringing guilt (L'SMT) [on the people, then let him offer for the sin which he has committed a young bull...]" (Lev. 4:3).
   B. Said R. Isaac, "It is a case of death (MWT) by burning ('S) [inflicted on one who commits sacrilege by consuming offerings from the altar]."
   C. "The matter may be compared to the keeper of a bear, who ate up the rations of the bear. The king said, 'Since he went and ate up the bear's rations, let the bear eat him.'
   D. "So does the Holy One, blessed be he, say, 'Since Shebna enjoyed benefit from things that had been consecrated to the altar [for burning], let fire consume him.'"
4. A. Said R. Aibu [Y. Ter. 8:3, A.Z. 2:3], "M^{C}SH B: Once there was a butcher in Sepphoris, who fed Israelites carrion and torn-meat. On the eve of the Day of Atonement he went out drinking and got drunk. He climbed up to the roof of his house and fell off and died. The dogs began to lick him.
   B. "[In Aramaic:] They came and asked R. Hanina the law about moving his corpse away from the dogs [on the Day of Atonement].
   C. "He said to him, '"You will be holy people to me, therefore you shall not eat any meat that is torn of beasts in the field, you shall cast it to the dogs" (Ex. 22:30).
   D. "'This man robbed from the dogs and fed carrion and torn-meat to Israelites. Leave him to them. They are eating what belongs to them.'"

5. A. "He shall bring the bull to the door of the tent of meeting before the Lord, [and lay his hand on the head of the bull and kill the bull before the Lord]" (Lev. 4:4).

B. Said R. Isaac, "The matter may be compared to the case of a king, one of whose admirers paid him honor by giving him a handsome gift and by offering him lovely words of praise. The king then said, 'Set this gift at the gate of the palace, so that everyone who comes and goes may see [and admire] it,'

C. "as it is said, 'And he shall bring the bull [to the door of the tent of meeting].'"

The opening units, Nos. 1-4, form a kind of appendix of miscellanies to what has gone before. No. 1 reaches back to V:IV, explaining the passage of the Mishnah cited there. No. 2 is joined to No. 3, which relates to the cited passage to Shebna. So Nos. 2-3 complete the discussion of V:V. It seems to me that No. 4 is attached to No. 3 as an illustration of the case of a public official who abuses his responsibility.

No. 5 provides a fresh point, moving on to a new verse. There is no intersecting verse; the exegesis is accomplished solely through a parable.

V:VII

1. A. "[If the whole congregation of Israel commits a sin unwittingly and the thing is hidden from the eyes of the assembly, and they do any one of the things which the Lord has commanded not to be done and are guilty, when the sin which they have committed becomes known, the assembly shall offer a young bull for a sin-offering and bring it before the tent of meeting;] and the elders of the congregation shall lay their hands [upon the head of the bull before the Lord]" (Lev. 4:13-15).

B. [Since, in laying their hands (SMK) on the head of the bull, the elders sustain (SMK) the community by adding to it the merit they enjoy,] said R. Isaac, "The nations of the world have none to sustain them, for it is written, 'And those who sustain Egypt will fall" (Ez. 30:6).

C. "But Israel has those who sustain it, as it is written: 'And the elders of the congregation shall lay their hands [and so sustain Israel] (Lev. 4:15).'"

2. A. Said R. Eleazar, "The nations of the world are called a congregation, and Israel is called a congregation.

B. "The nations of the world are called a congregation: 'For the congregation of the godless shall be desolate' (Job 15:34).

C. "And Israel is called a congregation: 'And the elders of the congregation shall lay their hands' (Lev. 4:15).

D. "The nations of the world are called sturdy bulls and Israel is called sturdy bulls.

E. "The nations of the world are called sturdy bulls: 'The congregation of [sturdy] bulls with the calves of the peoples' (Ps. 68:31).

F. "Israel is called sturdy bulls, as it is said, 'Listen to me, you sturdy [bullish] of heart' (Is. 46:13).

G. "The nations of the world are called excellent, and Israel is called excellent.

Studying Synoptic Texts Synoptically   183

H. "The nations of the world are called excellent: 'You and the daughters of excellent nations' (Ex. 32:18).

I. "Israel is called excellent: 'They are the excellent, in whom is all my delight' (Ps. 16:4).

J. "The nations of the world are called sages, and Israel is called sages.

K. "The nations of the world are called sages: 'And I shall wipe out sages from Edom' (Ob. 1:8).

L. "And Israel is called sages: 'Sages store up knowledge' (Prov. 10:14).

M. "The nations of the world are called unblemished, and Israel is called unblemished.

N. "The nations of the world are called unblemished: 'Unblemished as are those that go down to the pit' (Prov. 1:12).

O. "And Israel is called unblemished: 'The unblemished will inherit goodness' (Prov. 28:10).

P. "The nations of the world are called men, and Israel is called men.

Q. "The nations of the world are called men: 'And you men who work iniquity' (Ps. 141:4).

R. "And Israel is called men: 'To you who are men I call' (Prov. 8:4).

S. "The nations of the world are called righteous, and Israel is called righteous.

T. "The nations of the world are called righteous: 'And righteous men shall judge them' (Ez. 23:45).

U. "And Israel is called righteous: 'And your people -- all of them are righteous' (Is. 60:21).

V. "The nations of the world are called mighty, and Israel is called mighty.

W. "The nations of the world are called mighty: 'Why do you boast of evil, O mighty man' (Ps. 52:3).

X. "And Israel is called mighty: 'Mighty in power, those who do his word' (Ps. 103:20).

We see two distinct types of exegeses, one to which the base-passage is central, the other to which it is peripheral. Yet the two passages belong together, and we have every reason to suppose that they were made up as a single cogent statement. No. 1 focuses upon the double meaning of the word SMK, one, lay hands, the other, sustain, drawing the contrast stated by Isaac. Once such a contrast is drawn, a catalogue of eight further contrasts will be laid out. Since the opening set, 2.A-B, depends upon the passage at hand, we must accept the possibility that Eleazar's statement has been constructed to work its way through the contrast established by Isaac. For both authorities make the same point. Even though the nations of the word are subject to the same language as is applied to Israel, they still do not fall into the same classification. For language is dual. When a word applies to Israel, it serves to praise, and when the same word applies to the nations, it underlines their negative character. Both are called congregation, but the nations' congregation is desolate, and so throughout, as the context of the passage cited concerning the nations repeatedly indicates. The nations' sages are wiped out; the unblemished nations go down to the pit; the nations, called men, only work iniquity. Now that is precisely the contrast drawn in Isaac's saying, so, as I said, the whole should be deemed a masterpiece of unitary composition. Then the two types of exegesis -- direct, peripheral -- turn out to complement one another, each making its own point.

V:VIII

1.   A.   R. Simeon b. Yohai taught, "How masterful are the Israelites, for they know how to find favor with their creator."

      B.   Said R. Yudan, [in Aramaic:], "It is like the case of Samaritan [beggars]. The Samaritan [beggars] are clever at begging. One of them goes to a housewife, saying to her, 'Do you have an onion? Give it to me.' After she gives it to him, he says to her, 'Is there such a thing as an onion without bread?' After she gives him [bread], he says to her, 'Is there such a thing as food without drink?' So, all in all, he gets to eat and drink."

      C.   Said R. Aha [in Aramaic:], "There is a woman who knows how to borrow things, and there is a woman who does not. The one who knows how to borrow goes over to her neighbor. The door is open, but she knocks [anyhow]. Then she says to her neighbor, 'Greetings, good neighbor. How're you doing? How's your husband doing? How're your kids doing? Can I come in? [By the way], would you have such-and-such a utensil? Would you lend it to me? [The neighboring housewife] says to her, 'Yes, of course.'

      D.   "But the one who does not know how to borrow goes over to her neighbor. The door is closed, so she just opens it. She says [to the neighboring housewife], 'Do you have such-and-such a utensil? Would you lend it to me?' [The neighboring housewife] says to her, 'No.'"

      E.   Said R. Hunia [in Aramaic:], "There is a tenant-farmer who knows how to borrow things, and there is a tenant-farmer who does not know how to borrow. The one who knows how to borrow combs his hair, brushes off his clothes, puts on a good face, and then goes over to the overseer of his work to borrow from him. [The overseer] says to him, 'How's the land doing?' He says to him, 'May you have the merit of being fully satisfied with its [wonderful] produce.' 'How are the oxen doing?' He says to him, 'May you have the merit of being fully satisfied with their fat.' 'How are the goats doing?' 'May you have the merit of being fully satisfied with their young.' 'And what would you like?' Then he says, 'Now if you might have an extra ten <u>denars</u>, would you give them to me?' The overseer replies, 'If you want, take twenty.'

      F.   "But the one who does not know how to borrow leaves his hair a mess, his clothes filthy, his face gloomy. He too goes over to the overseer to borrow from him. The overseer says to him, 'How's the land doing?' He replies, 'I hope it will produce at least what [in seed] we put into it.' 'How are the oxen doing?' 'They're scrawny.' 'How are the goats doing?' 'They're scrawny too.' 'And what do you want?' 'Now if you might have an extra ten <u>denars</u>, would you give them to me?' The overseer replies, 'Go, pay me back what you already owe me!'"

G. Said R. Hunia, "David was one of the good tenant-farmers. To begin with, he starts a psalm with praise [of God], saying, 'The heavens declare the glory of God, and the firmament shows his handiwork' (Ps. 19:2). The Heaven says to him, 'Perhaps you need something?' 'The firmament shows his handiwork.' The firmament says to him, 'Perhaps you need something?'

H. "And so he would continue to sing: 'Day unto day utters speech, and night to night reveals knowledge' (Ps. 19:3).

I. "Said to him the Holy One, blessed be he, 'What do you want?'

J. "He said before him, 'Who can discern errors?' (Ps. 19:13).

K. "'What sort of unwitting sin have I done before you?'

L. "[God] said to him, 'Lo, this one is remitted, and that one is forgiven you.'

M. "'And cleanse me of hidden sins' (Ps. 19:13). '...from the secret sins that I have done before you.'

N. "He said to him, 'Lo, this one is remitted, and that one is forgiven to you.'

O. "'Keep back your servant also from deliberate ones.' This refers to transgressions done in full knowledge.

P. "'That they may not have dominion over me. Then I shall be faultless' (Ps. 19:14). This refers to the most powerful of transgressions.

Q. "'And I shall be clear of great transgression' (Ps. 19:14)."

R. Said R. Levi, "David said before the Holy One, blessed be he, 'Lord of the age[s], you are a great God, and, as for me, my sins are great too. It will take a great God to remit and forgive great sins: "For your name's sake, O Lord, pardon my sin, for [your name] is great" (Ps. 25:11).'"

Once more the construction appears from beginning to end to aim at a single goal. The opening statement, I.A, makes the point, and the closing construction, Gff., illustrates it. In the middle come three apt narratives serving as similes, all told in Aramaic, and all following exactly the same pattern. Then the systematic account of a passage of Scripture is provided to make exactly the same point. I cannot state the exact sense of the passage on the heaven and the firmament, G, but from that point, the discourse is pellucid. Q-R should be separated from G-P, since what Levi's statement does is simply augment the primary passage. The unity of theme and conception accounts for the drawing together of the entire lot. To be sure, B-F can serve other purposes. But since Hunia's statement, E-F, introduces his exegesis of Ps. 19, the greater likelihood is that a single hand has produced the entire matter (possibly excluding Q-R) to make a single point. Why has the redactor thought the passage appropriate here? The offering for unwitting sin of Lev. 4, to which K makes reference in the progression through the types of sins, from minor to major, for which David seeks forgiveness, certainly accounts for the inclusion of the whole. Then whoever made up the passage did not find the stimulus in Lev. 4. For the rather general observation of I.A states the framer's message. That message pertains to diverse contexts, as the exposition of Ps. 19 makes clear; nothing would compel someone to make up a passage of this sort to serve Lev. 4 in particular.

vi. Types of Units of Discourse

Let us now turn to the classification of the units of discourse of which the parashah is composed. What we want to know is the structure of the parashah as a whole, where its largest subunits of thought begin and end and how they relate to one another. How shall we recognize a complete unit of thought? It will be marked off by the satisfactory resolution of a tension or problem introduced at the outset. A complete unit of thought may be made up of a number of subdivisions, many of them entirely spelled out on their own. But the composition of a complete unit of thought always will strike us as cogent, the work of a single conception on how a whole thought should be constructed and expressed. While that unitary conception drew upon already available materials, the main point is made by the composition as a whole, and not by any of its (ready-made) parts.

In the first classification we take up the single most striking recurrent literary structure of Leviticus Rabbah. It is what we may call the base-verse/intersecting-verse construction. In such a construction, a base-verse, drawn from the book of Leviticus, is juxtaposed to an intersecting-verse, drawn from any book other than a pentateuchal one. Then this intersecting-verse is subjected to systematic exegesis. On the surface the exegesis is out of all relationship with the base-verse. But in a stunning climax, all of the exegeses of the intersecting-verse are shown to relate to the main point the exegete wishes to make about the base-verse. What that means is that the composition as a whole is so conceived as to impose meaning and order on all of the parts, original or ready-made parts, of which the author of the whole has made use. For the one example in Parashah 5, the base-verse is Lev. 4:3 and the intersecting-verse Job 34:29-30. Here is the outline of the first three subdivisions of the parashah.

V:I.1.C-F	Lev. 4:3, Job 34:29-30 and the generation of the flood
V:I.2.A-C	Lev. 4:3, Job 34:29-30 and the generation of the flood
V:I.2.E-G	Lev. 4:3, Job 34:29-30 and the generation of the flood
V:I.3.A	Lev. 4:3, Job 34:29-30 and the generation of the flood
V:I.3.B-D	Job 21:11
V:I.4	Job 21:11
V:I.5.A-B	Generation of the flood
V:I.5.C-F	Ma^{c}aseh
V:I.6.A-E	Job 34:29-30, Gen. 7:23. Relevance: Reference to God's hiding his face.
V:I.7.A-C	Job 34:29. Refers to Noah.
V:II.1	Job 34:29. Refers to Sodomites. First comes tranquility, then punishment. Job 28:7
V:II.2	Further exegesis of Job 28:7.
V:II.3	God hid his face from Sodomites (Job 34:29) and then punished them (Gen. 19:24).

V:III.1	Job 34:29. Refers to Ten Tribes, first tranquility, then punishment. Amos 6:1.
V:III.2	Further comment on Amos 6:1
V:III.3	Further comment on Amos 6:2
V:III.4	Amos 6:3
V:III.5	Amos 6:4
V:III.6	Amos 6:5
V:III.7	Amos 6:6
V:III.8	Amos 6:6
V:III.9	Amos 6:6, 7. All of the units on Amos simply comment on clauses of verses.
V.III.10	Job 34:29. How God hid his face from the Ten Tribes. Isaiah 36:1.
V:III.11	Isaiah 36:1
V:III.12	Job 34:29. Refers to Sennacherib (Joel 6) and Israel (Ez. 34:31).
V:III.13	Job 34:29 linked to Lev. 4:3-4. God exacts the same penalty from an individual or a community, so Job 34:29 and also Lev. 4:13-14.

As we saw when we followed the text in detail, the composition moves with striking cogency over its chosen examples: the Generation of the Flood, the Ten Tribes, Sennacherib and Israel. So three large-scale illustrations of Job 34:29-30 are laid out, and then the entire composition reverts to Lev. 4:3ff. to make a single point about all that has gone before.

Another form is the <u>intersecting-verse/base-verse</u> construction. Secondary in size and in exegetical complexity to the one just now surveyed, here the intersecting-verse is worked out, then comes the base-verse, given a simple exemplification. Just as in the first type, the exegete may assemble passages on that exemplificatory entry. We have two instances. The first example is V:V. Since Lev. 4:3 refers to the sin of an anointed priest, the exegete wishes to show us how an anointed priest may sin and so he invokes the name of Shebna. The rest follows.

V:V.1	Lev. 4:3. Refers to Shebna.
V:V.2	Shebna (Is. 22:15-19)
V:V.3	Shebna (Is. 22:16-18)
V:V.4	Shebna and Joahaz

The second example is somewhat more subtle. Here we have a play on a word used in the base-verse. Then a whole series of verses will be adduced to make a point based on that play on words. These proof-texts cannot be called intersecting-verses in the way in which, in the earlier classification and in the first example of the present one, the cited verses intersect with, but take over discourse from, the base-verse. Quite to the contrary, the base-verse generates a point, which then is richly expanded by the cited verses. Nonetheless, I should regard the present example as a variation on the foregoing. The reason is that, in a strictly formal sense, the pattern remains what we have seen to this point: a set of illustrative verses that make the main point the exegete wishes to associate with or about the base-verse, given at the end.

  V:VII.1-2 Lev. 4:13-15. Exegesis of the verse, with special attention to a word-play. The upshot is that Israel is distinguished from the nations. Then a long catalogue of such distinctions is appended.

  A third classification derives from the clause-by-clause type of exegesis of the base-verse, with slight interest in intersecting-verses or in illustrative materials deriving from other books of the Scripture. The base-verse in this classification defines the entire frame of discourse, either because of its word-choices or because of its main point. Where verses of other passages are quoted, they serve not as the focus of discourse but only as proof-texts or illustrative-texts. They therefore function in a different way from the verses adduced in discourse in the first two classifications, for, in those former cases, the intersecting-verses form the center of interest. As we see at V:VI, we deal with the subject-matter of Lev. 4:3-4, on the one side, and we also explain the derivation of words used in the cited verse, on the other. These are distinct modes of exegesis -- ideational, philological -- but the difference is slight in determining the classification at hand. It is simply exegesis of verses of Leviticus, item by item. Here are examples of the exegetical type of unit of discourse.

  V:VI.1 Lev. 4:3. Precedence in atonement rite.
  V:VI.2 Lev. 4:3. How can an anointed priest sin?
  V:VI.3 Lev. 4:3. Explanation of a word used in the cited verse.
  V:VI.4 Lev. 4:3 and Shebna. Illustration.
  V:VI.5 Lev. 4:4. Why bring the bell to the tent of meeting as Lev. 4:4 specifies.

  The category of miscellanies and how they are joined now demands attention. By a "miscellany," I mean a construction that does not relate to any base-verse in Leviticus 4 or to the cited intersecting-verses; that does not address any theme or principle pertinent to the base-verse or to its larger context; and that appears to have been formed for purposes entirely distinct from the explanation or amplification of a passage of the book of Leviticus. One such example is at V:IV.1-4, at which, as we see, the general theme of Lev. 4:3 -- the sacrifices of several officials, in order -- triggers the inquiry into which offering comes first. But at issue is the principle that whoever sacrifices proportionately more in terms of his means is the one who gets the more credit. That notion is unrelated to Lev. 4:3. The passage is cogent. Here is the outline, which, as we see, deals with Prov. 18:16 and provides anthology of rather coherent materials for that verse.

  V:IV.1 God recognizes the value of a gift to the cult, e.g., in accord with the donor's sacrifice. Deut. 12:19, 20; M. Hor. 3:6.
  V:IV.2 "A man's gift makes room for him" (Prov. 18:16) and long illustrative story.
  V:IV.3 Prov. 18:16
  V:IV.4 Prov. 18:16

A second example, drawn from Parashah 5, serves Ps. 19:2-3, 13-14, and the reason for its inclusion with reference to Lev. 4 is not entirely clear.

V:VIII.1   Israel knows how to placate God. The point is joined to Ps. 19:23, 13-14. This construction does not belong to Lev. 4.

We therefore discern three categories of units of discourse, illustrated by generally rather sizable subunits. These are, first, the (complex) base-verse/intersecting-verse construction (I); second, the (simple) intersecting-verse/base-verse construction (II); and, third, the clause-by-clause exegetical construction (III). We note, finally, the category of miscellanies (IV), always marked by the simple trait of irrelevance to the concrete context at hand.

Can we discern an order followed by the several types of units of discourse?

1. Base-verse/intersecting-verse construction:

    V:I-III

2. Intersecting-verse/base-verse construction:

    V:V

    V:VII

3. Clause-by-clause exegetical construction:

    V:VI

4. Miscellanies:

    V:IV, V:VIII

The obvious problem is at V:V-VII. Can we account for the insertion of V:VI between V:V and V:VII? We certainly can. V:VI.1-4 form an appendix to V:V -- pure and simple. The organizer of the whole had no choice but to insert his appendix behind the materials supplemented by his appendix. The same sort of reasoning then accounts for the insertion of miscellanies, e.g., V:IV after V:I-III. What V:IV does is simply carry forward the problem of which beast comes first when a number of beasts are awaiting offering for the purposes of atonement for various officials. That issue is very important to the author of V:III. So the first of the two cases in which we have miscellanies turns out to exemplify a rather careful mode of arranging materials. Where a major point carries in its wake exemplificatory materials, these will be inserted before the parashah moves on to new matters. There is no difficulty in explaining why the arranger of the whole has placed V:VIII at the end; what we do not know is why, to begin with, he selected that unit of discourse. But that issue need not detain us.

We emerge with two hypotheses, one firm, the other less so.

The first is the hypothesis that the units of discourse are framed in accord with conventions that define and distinguish three recurrent literary structures: (1) base-verse/intersecting-verse construction; (2) intersecting-verse/base-verse construction; (3) clause-by-clause exegetical construction (invoking a broad range of intersecting-verses only for narrowly-illustrative purposes). We noted, in addition, a category we called "miscellaneous."

The second hypothesis is that the categories of units of discourse also explain the order of arrangement of types of units of discourse. First will come the (I) base-verse/intersecting-verse construction; then will come (II) intersecting-verse/base-verse construction; finally we shall have (III) clause-by-clause exegetical constructions. If we were to assign cardinal numbers to these types of constructions I, II, and III, we should also be able to use ordinal numbers, first, second, third. Why? Because in accord with the stated hypothesis, type I will come first, type II second, and type III third. Type IV encompasses miscellanies.

Let us now survey the whole. I count, in all of Leviticus Rabbah, 304 entries in four catalogues of types of units of discourse:

I.	38	12.5%
II.	84	27.6%
III.	94	30.9%
IV.	88	28.9%

The three defined taxa thus cover 71% of the whole. The two truly distinctive patterns, types I and II, cover a sizable part of the whole -- 40%.

vii. Order of Types of Units of Discourse

Having classified the units of discourse of which our thirty-seven parashiyyot are composed, we now ask whether the types of units of discourse follow a single pattern, or whether a given type will appear in any sequence promiscuously, at the beginning, middle, or end of a given parashah. So from the taxonomy of the units of discourse, we proceed to the structure of the thirty-seven parashiyyot as a whole. We ask whether the editors exhibited preferences for a given type of unit of discourse when they faced the task in particular of beginning a parashah or of ending one. The facts may be stated through the summary that follows:

Type I comes in first position in the following parashiyyot:
    I, II, III, IV, V, VI, VII, VIII, IX, X, XI, XII, XIV, XV, XVI, XVII, XVIII, XIX, XX, XXI, XXII, XXIII, XXIV, XXV, XXVI, XXVII, XXVIII.

Type II comes in first position in the following parashiyyot:
    XII, XXXII, XXXIII, XXXIV, XXXV

Type III comes in first position in the following parashiyyot: --

Type IV comes in first position in the following parashiyyot:
    XXXVI

Type I comes in second position in the following parashiyyot:
    V, VI, IX, X, XI, XV, XVII, XXII, XXIII, XXVI, XXVII, XXVIII, XXXVII

Type II comes in second position in the following parashiyyot:
    III, IV, VII, VIII, XIII, XIV, XVI, XVII, XVIII, XIX, XX, XXI, XXIV, XXV, XXIX, XXX, XXXI, XXXII, XXXIV, XXXV, XXXVI

Type III comes in second position in the following parashiyyot:
    II

Type IV comes in second position in the following parashiyyot:
    XII, XXXIII

Type I comes last in the following parashiyyot: --
Type II comes last in the following parashiyyot: --
Type III comes last in the following parashiyyot:
   II, VIII, XV, XVI, XVII, XVIII, XIX, XX, XXI, XXIV, XXVI, XXVII, XXVIII, XXX, XXXI, XXXV
Type IV comes last in the following parashiyyot:
   I, III, IV, V, VI, VII, IX, X, XI, XII, XIII, XIV, XXII, XXIII, XXV, XXIX, XXXII, XXXIII, XXXIV, XXXVI, XXXVII

We may compare the proportions as follows:

Type I comes in first position in	31/37	83.7%
Type II comes in first position in	5/37	13.5%
Type III comes in first position in	0/37	0.0%
Type IV comes in first position in	1/37	2.7%
Type I comes in second position in	13/37	35.1%
Type II comes in second position in	21/37	56.7%
Type III comes in second position in	1/37	2.7%
Type IV comes in second position in	2/37	5.4%
Type I comes in last position in	0/37	0.0%
Type II comes in last position in	0/37	0.0%
Type III comes in last position in	16/37	43.2%
Type IV comes in last position in	21/37	56.7%

I have probably overstated the instances in which type I comes in second position. Many of the entries of type I involve sustained and unitary compositions, in which a single intersecting-verse is worked out over a series of two or three subdivisions of a parashah. Otherwise the proportions conform to the impressions yielded by the catalogues just now presented.

To state the result very simply: the framer of a passage ordinarily began with a base-verse/intersecting-verse construction. He very commonly proceeded with an intersecting-verse/base-verse construction. Then he would provide such exegeses of pertinent verses of Leviticus as he had in hand. He would conclude either with type III or type IV constructions, somewhat more commonly the latter than the former. So the program of the authors is quite simple. They began with types I and II -- 100% of the first and second position entries, proceeded with type III, and concluded with type III or IV.

So, to conclude, Leviticus Rabbah consists of two main types of units of discourse, first in position, expositions of how verses of the book of Leviticus relate to verses of other books of the Hebrew Bible, second in position, exposition of verses of the book of Leviticus viewed on their own, and, varying in position but in any event very often concluding a construction, miscellaneous materials.

We now therefore know that units of discourse that fall into the classifications of types I, II, or III in their fixed order define that literary structure that imparts to Leviticus Rabbah the formal and stylistic unity exhibited by its principal components. So we may indeed speak of literary patterns -- structures of completed discourse -- that recur in Leviticus Rabbah. The recurrent traits prove to be both in formal character (for types I and II) and in conventional sequence (for all four types). Leviticus Rabbah, viewed whole and in its constitutive components, finds definition in a dominant literary structure and a recurrent mode of literary organization.

viii. Not Unique, Not Important

What proportion of a probe of three parashiyyot (7, 12, 18) is made up of shared materials -- those occurring in another, earlier or contemporary document? For this purpose I count up the number of stichs encompassed by the materials at hand and also the number of stichs shared by Leviticus Rabbah and documents prior to its time or contemporaneous with it. A stich for this rough estimate is constituted by a lettered unit, whether that unit is made up of one sentence or several.

Stichs Particular to Leviticus Rabbah (in 7, 12, 18)			Shared Stichs
Parashah 7	103	96.2%	4
Parashah 12	172	97.7%	4
Parashah 18	152	92.8%	12

The analysis for Parashah 18 omits reference to items that occur also in the Mishnah, on the one side, or the Bavli, on the other. If we add these to the totals, we have another 13 stichs, thus 85.8% are particular to Leviticus Rabbah.

In all, the results are one-sided. While rough, they confirm the impression of the essential autonomy of Leviticus Rabbah. How so? Nearly everything, that is, something like 95% of all stichs, in our probe of the composition, from the viewpoint of the extant canon in hand prior to the redaction of, or contemporary with, Leviticus Rabbah, is unique.

When we ask about the integrity of the document as a whole, we take up the encompassing traits, the definitive literary and redactional characteristics. Accordingly, we ask whether Leviticus Rabbah is an anthology or a sustained composition. On formal grounds we conclude that it constitutes a text with its own integrity, not merely a collection of this and that. When we examine a sample of the smallest components of the document, brief sayings of various kinds, we find two facts. First of all, a probe of three parashiyyot yields an astonishingly small proportion of materials that are not unique. We may conclude that, in the context of the whole document, what is not unique takes up a very minor place and contributes episodic and unsustained supplements.

Second, much of that shared component turns out to be formally diverse. Little indicates that the items shared with other documents fit well into Leviticus Rabbah. Why not? Within Leviticus Rabbah, the shared items do not conform to the formal preferences, as to the construction of large-scale discourse, dominant in the document as a whole.

Accordingly, our probe leaves no doubt that a catalogue of phrases and sentences or even groups of sentences -- from two to ten stichs -- that occur in both Leviticus Rabbah and another document of its own time or earlier would list little more than editorial detritus. Such a catalogue of all of the passages shared with documents other than Scripture and the Mishnah, at the beginning, through to the Yerushalmi and other contemporary writings, at the end, would prove a random collection of this and that. That is to say, all we should turn up is lists of items shared by Leviticus Rabbah and, e.g., Sifra, the two Sifres, the Yerushalmi, and the like. If our now-completed probe is suggestive, such lists by themselves would not tell us anything we wish to know. Leviticus Rabbah does not stand "very close" to any other document so as to present a synoptic problem. It scarcely intersects with any other document of its day. (As to its relationship with Pesiqta deR. Kahana, we take up that matter in a moment.)

ix. Miscellanies or a Source: In Search of "Q" and the Synoptic Problem

We now turn to an analysis of the repertoire of materials shared between Leviticus Rabbah and other documents of its own day or succession. We raise two simple questions, one cursorily, the other at length.

First, do the shared materials exhibit literary traits in common? Second, do the shared materials conform to the literary preferences of Leviticus Rabbah?

The importance of the former of the two questions can be briefly explained. (The latter is the focus of part X.) If the materials that occur in two or more compilations follow a single pattern of literary formulation and construction, then we may postulate that those materials derive from a cogent source and so constitute part of a larger, itself autonomous, document. By such a postulate, that autonomous and distinct source will then have made its contribution here and there, to the Yerushalmi, to Leviticus Rabbah, to Genesis Rabbah, not to mention to Pesiqta deR. Kahana and even to the Bavli. Enjoying its own definition, organized around its own lines, exhibiting its own distinctive formal traits, one must call this otherwise unknown source by the German name for source, that is, Quelle, or merely RQ for rabbinische Quelle.

On the basis of the surveyed population, may such a source indeed be reconstructed? That is, out of a broad range of existing compilations and even compositions of rabbinic writings, are we able to collect and restore those bits and pieces of an antecedent rabbinic source (or set of sources) that have circulated on their own and also exhibit distinctive traits in common? And will these collected pieces then allow us to see part of that original source, the one from which they broke off? At stake in asking whether the materials common to two or more compilations and compositions is a considerable possibility.

A mere glance at the materials catalogued below, Part X, suggests that the quest for the unknown rabbinic source leads nowhere. Why so? Because materials common to two or more documents turn out to be everything and its opposite: long and short;

exegetical statements on verses of Scripture, autonomous statements of individual authorities, protracted stories, brief stories. In short, those shared materials may be anything at all. Among themselves they share no distinctive traits. That is to say, these same shared sources draw upon a broad variety of authorities' names or lack any identified authority. They focus upon a vast range of topics but coalesce around none in particular. They exhibit every sort of literary pattern. Some fit neatly into the literary structures of Leviticus Rabbah, which I have demonstrated to be subject to definition. Others exhibit traits or structures evidently characteristic of Genesis Rabbah (thus: similar to those of Leviticus Rabbah) on the one side, Yerushalmi's episodic sayings, on the second, the Pesiqta's protracted constructions (again: similar to those of Leviticus Rabbah), on the third. But still others share traits with none of the foregoing, on the fourth. And there are yet other sides and aspects too.

To avoid repeating the obvious through each of the appropriate criteria for definition of a single and uniform composition -- whether formal, topical, or even merely logical -- I state one simple fact. The shared sources share only one trait. It is that they appear in more than a single composition. We have therefore to dismiss the notion that sizable compositions, circulating from document to document, in fact originated in a single composition, one marked off by its definitive and distinctive traits.

That judgment pertains not only to sizable compositions, entire units of discourse or more, such as are shared between Leviticus Rabbah and Genesis Rabbah and Pesiqta deR. Kahana. It applies also to brief sayings, such as pop up hither and yon, for example, in the Yerushalmi, Leviticus Rabbah and Genesis Rabbah (not to mention numerous other, still later compositions and compilations). Let me spell out what I mean. We note that there are two types of shared sources, long and brief. The long ones clearly conform to a variety of patterns. In no way do these long sayings suggest that they originate in a single, uniform, and now-lost, document. But what about the _brief_ lemmas? These short sayings may make an appearance in a well-composed and sizable unit of discourse, e.g., a piece of a passage of Leviticus Rabbah, but also in a quite different, and also well-composed and sizable unit of discourse, e.g., a piece of a passage in the Yerushalmi. Clearly, these brief lemmas did circulate broadly. No one can doubt that. But if we draw together all of those lemmas that appear in two or more documents, do they exhibit distinctive traits in common? And if we compare all such sayings to equivalently brief lemmas that appear in only one document, do the latter exhibit traits of formulation and formation into larger compositions different from the former? These two questions govern. For we must establish dual criteria, one group of criteria to exclude, the other group of definitive traits to include. If then we attempt to include all the circulating brief sayings, those that appear in two or more compositions, by reference to shared and distinctive traits, and if we then propose to exclude all one-time brief sayings, the ones appearing in only one document, by reference to the _absence_ of the shared and distinctive traits of the circulating sayings, we come up with nothing.

I lay down that judgment flatly and without proof. Why not? Because we should have to compose long lists of traits _not_ distinctive to one set of sayings as against the other and demonstrate that said traits occur at random among either of the two sets of sayings. But a mere glance at the context of any brief saying shared among two or more documents provides adequate information. That is, brief sayings that occur in Leviticus Rabbah ordinarily share the traits of other sayings of Leviticus Rabbah and unique to that document, among which they occur, fore and aft. These same sayings, however, appear just as randomly and comfortably but episodically in, e.g., Genesis Rabbah or the Yerushalmi. So the simple fact is that brief sayings, consisting of a line or two, rarely conform to those distinctive formal traits that allow us to distinguish, in a given compilation or composition, between one unit of discourse and another unit of discourse.

Only at a larger scale than the brief sayings, viewed one by one, do the processes of literary definition and differentiation begin to make sense in analyzing our documents. (As we shall see below, large-scale constructions prove miscellaneous too and rarely exhibit traits distinctive to Leviticus Rabbah.) Accordingly, brief sayings clearly serve numerous, that is, two or more, contexts. The reason brief sayings prove serviceable hither and yon is simple. By themselves they do not exhibit distinctive traits, so they present no formal problems to the compositors, or authors, of larger discussions. They are neutral, whether viewed formally or construed substantively. Brief sayings constitute available building blocks. Shared or unique, they are bricks all of a single dimension. Only in context, e.g., large examples of a single pattern of syntax or structure, do these brief sayings form discernible compositions.

Since that is the fact, we must wonder not at how many, but at how few, such shared brief sayings have come to our attention. Our original result, showing in a rough way that something in the range of 95% of the stichs of three <u>parashiyyot</u> of Leviticus Rabbah appear to be particular to that composition, now returns to mind. Given the formal consistency and the absence of what seem to me to be highly patterned and distinctive formulary character of brief sayings (so often: X says, plus a standard or entirely commonplace and therefore random syntactic pattern), we should have expected a different result. We ought to have had sound reason to expect a far broader portion than we have found, a pattern in which a given composition is composed of sayings shared with two or more other compositions.

It would carry us far afield to speculate on the reason for the near-uniqueness of the document at hand. But the issue in its proper context demands considerable reflection. A suitable answer cannot be merely that, in a given document, one set of subjects, rather than some other set of subjects, required one set of sayings, rather than some other. Or, to put it simply, no one can imagine that we can explain the near-uniqueness of the bulk of the contents of a given composition, in this case, Leviticus Rabbah, by reference to the near-uniqueness either of the overall topical program or of the concrete sentiments and values to be expressed. Such a thesis would contradict what, to the naked eye, constitutes the definitive trait of <u>all</u> of the documents of the canon of Judaism. That is, that they are <u>canonical</u>. The document's authors therefore wish in many different ways to say some one thing.

x. Differentiating among Shared Sources in the Setting of Leviticus Rabbah in Particular

We now ask whether the materials shared by Leviticus Rabbah with some other composition of the same age conform to the distinctive literary patterns of Leviticus Rabbah, on the one side, and organize materials in the same sequence of types of units of discourse as Leviticus Rabbah, on the other. What we shall see in a catalogue of details is that nearly all units of tradition -- brief and long alike -- shared by Leviticus Rabbah with some other composition of composition or compilation prove miscellaneous. These shared miscellaneous materials both testify against use by these authors of a RQ and also attest to the integrity of Leviticus Rabbah. How so?

First, they point to the distinctiveness of the literary patterns of Leviticus Rabbah as well as to the uniqueness of the organization of types of units of discourse by the compositors of Leviticus Rabbah. So on the face of it the compositors of our document have given us a composition that conforms to a clearcut plan, distinctive to their group, for both organization and expression of ideas.

Second, beyond the miscellaneous character of the shared materials is the simple fact of the slight and inconsequential place taken up by those shared materials in Leviticus Rabbah. What that means is that the compositors have made their document mainly of materials particular to their interests. They expressed their own literary and redactional preferences and only tangentially and randomly included bits and pieces of materials serviceable for purposes other than those of Leviticus Rabbah.

The upshot is simple. Leviticus Rabbah is no scrapbook, no random collection of this and that. It is an orderly, proportioned, well-considered composition. Leviticus Rabbah exhibits integrity. It enjoys autonomy. Why so? It is quite distinct from other collections or compositions of its age, even though it shares with them a small and miscellaneous corpus of brief sayings and even protracted discussions. Let us now catalogue these shared materials in two taxa, first, brief, then, protracted, and, in both cases, among four classifications, namely, the four types of units of discourse I identified in Part Two. We now classify the two varieties of shared materials -- brief, then protracted -- in accord with the four taxa yielded by the several units of discourse of Leviticus Rabbah: I. Base-verse/intersecting verse, II. Intersecting verse/base-verse, III. Exegesis of verse, IV. Miscellany. We deal only with the shared materials occurring in Genesis Rabbah and the Yerushalmi. My sample is now a population, covering the bulk of the document.

1. The classification of brief sayings

I. Base-verse/intersecting verse

(Y. + Gen. R.)

None

Studying Synoptic Texts Synoptically   197

        2. The classification of brief sayings
           II. Intersecting verse/base-verse
              (Y. + Gen. R.)

None

        3. The classification of brief sayings
           III. Exegesis of a verse
              (Y. + Gen. R.)

III:III   Lev. 2:1,8

        4. The classification of brief sayings
           IV. Miscellanies
              (Y. + Gen. R.)

VII:I	2N	Mishnah-citation
VII:V	1D-E	Yerushalmi-Tanna-saying
VII:VI	1D	Said x
XII:I	9C	X said
XII:II	2A	Said x
XII:IV	4A	X said
	3B	Mishnah-citation
XVIII:I	1C-H	Mishnah-citation + exegesis
XVIII:I	10A-B	X said ... he said to him
	12G	X + Y + saying
	12J	Mishnah-citation
III:II	1B	X, Y: + saying

        1. The classification of protracted sayings
           I. Base-verse/intersecting verse
              (Y. + Gen. R.)

V:I	1-7	Gen. 9:18/Job 34:29, Lev. 4:3/Job 34:29
X:I	1	Gen. 18:25/Ps. 45:7-8, Lev. 8:1-3/Ps. 45:7

        2. The classification of protracted sayings
           II. Intersecting verse/base-verse
              (Y. + Gen. R.)

None

3. The classification of protracted sayings

    III. Exegesis of a verse

       (Y. + Gen. R.)

XVIII:I	4A-G	Qoh. 12:3 + phrase by phrase exegesis. N.B. Qoh. 12:3 is part of the intersecting-verse construction here.
XVIII:II	1C-F	Ps. 139:5. Proposition followed by proof-text.
XVIII:III	2H	Ex. 32:16 + read not. Proposition + proof-text.
IX:VI	1	X said, Y said + proof-texts on proposition.
XVI:VIII	2	Exegesis of Deut. 7:15
XIX:V	6	Exegesis of Lev. 15:25
XXXIII:V	1-2	Exegesis of 2 Chr. 13:17, etc.
XXXIV:XIV	1-5	Exegesis of Is. 58:7 + story.
XXXVII:I	1	Exegesis of Qoh. 5:5
X:IX:3	8	Gen. 1:9 + exegetical observation
XXXIV:IX	1-2	Deut. 28:13 + clarifications, + other verses clarified.
XXVI:I	2	Gen. 7:2, 11:4, etc., explained.

4. The classification of protracted sayings

    IV. Miscellanies

       (Y. + Gen. R.)

III:III	1B-C	Said x.
V:IV	2-4	Verse + extended stories.
V:VI	2	Said x + story.
IX:IX	1	Long story.
X:VI	1	Proposition + proof-texts (not exegetical).
X:VIII	1	As above.
XXI:X	1	As above.
XXII:IX	1	As above.
XXV:I	4	As above.
XXXII:VII	1-3	Thematic essay.
XXXVI:VI	1	Propositions + proof-texts.
XXXVII:III	1	Story
IX:IX	3-4	X said + sayings + proof-text.
XVII:V	3	Proposition + proof-text.
XIX:II	6	As above.
XXIII:IX	3	As above.
XXV:VI	1-3	Argument a portion + proof-text + various propositions.

| XXXVI:I | 1 | Proposition + proof-texts. |
| XXXVII:IV | 1-5 | Proper petitionary language + proof-texts. |

xi. Shared Sources and the Literary Structures of Leviticus Rabbah: Genesis Rabbah and the Yerushalmi

To state in a few sentences the results of the preceding classification, we note that the shared sources, whether brief or protracted, fall into two categories, exegesis of a cited verse of Scripture (III) and miscellanies (IV). As to the brief sayings shared between Leviticus Rabbah and the two documents with which it most commonly intersects, Genesis Rabbah and the Yerushalmi, only one falls into category III, 12 into category IV. So when we deal with brief sayings that float from one document to another, in the case of the Yerushalmi and Genesis Rabbah, such sayings, when they occur in Leviticus Rabbah, very rarely will conform to the literary structures of Leviticus Rabbah. That is hardly a surprising result, since the literary structures distinctive to Leviticus Rabbah and its classification of literature -- types I and II -- are by definition protracted and exhaustively worked out.

But when we come to the classification of protracted sayings, we find the same result. That is another matter indeed. Now we have two entries in category I as against 13 in category III and 19 in category IV. So once more we must conclude that what is shared among two or more compilations of materials will not exhibit traits distinctive to Leviticus Rabbah (or any one of those compilations). What this means is very simple. When Leviticus Rabbah shares materials with other documents, those shared materials will not ordinarily take on or exhibit the literary traits definitive of Leviticus Rabbah.

The shared materials prove simply miscellaneous and casual. They are miscellaneous in that they exhibit no traits both uniform and also particular to themselves. As I said at the outset, all that marks shared materials in common is the fact that they occur in more than one compilation. By themselves, the shared materials common to Leviticus Rabbah and Genesis Rabbah or the Yerushalmi exhibit no single formal pattern. They express no distinctive viewpoint. They pursue no uniform program of inquiry. No "Q" here. If we study this allegedly synoptic text, part of a synoptic canon, synoptically, we learn nothing in particular either about the text or about the canon ("the tradition") of which it forms a component. Not only is there no "RQ," there also is no "synoptic problem."

xii. The Five Parashiyyot Shared with Pesiqta deR. Kahana

When we come to materials shared between Leviticus Rabbah and Pesiqta deR. Kahana, we deal with a quite different problem. Now, the shared materials cover a sizable portion of both documents, 5 out of 37 complete Parashiyyot (13.5%) of Leviticus Rabbah, 5 out of 28 pisqaot (17.9%) of Pesiqta deR. Kahana, according to the count of Braude and Kapstein. The correspondences are word for word, with minor exception, in the parashah/pisqa I examined in detail. The question before us is not whether or not the shared parashiyyot "belong" or prove "particular to" Leviticus Rabbah as against their place, primary or secondary, original or borrowed, in Pesiqta deR. Kahana. The sole issue is whether these enormous constructions -- I repeat, entire parashiyyot -- exhibit traits characteristic of Leviticus Rabbah. They certainly do. How do we know it? Because in a survey of the shared parashiyyot/pisqaot, they conform to exactly those literary structures I have shown to characterize Leviticus Rabbah. The order of the types of units of discourse is the same -- I, II, III, with IV interspersed according to rules we can discern -- as the order of types of units of discourse I have shown to characterize the remainder of Leviticus Rabbah.

It follows that where entire parashiyyot of Leviticus Rabbah are shared with some other composition, these parashiyyot prove integral to Leviticus Rabbah. Since they conform to the literary patterns and redactional program of the remainder of Leviticus Rabbah, they give ample evidence that Leviticus Rabbah, as a whole, is a document that exhibits integrity. Its definitive traits of literary composition -- form, pattern, redaction alike -- mark the document as autonomous at the very point at which the document intersects in a truly substantial and extensive way with some other document. As to the integrity or miscellaneous character of Pesiqta deR. Kahana, that is a question not relevant to the present inquiry.

xiii. Miscellanies, Not a Shared Source

The materials shared by Leviticus Rabbah with other compositions of the same period or shortly afterward, Genesis Rabbah, the Yerushalmi, and Pesiqta deR. Kahana, as is now clear, exhibit in common only the trait that they occur in one or more documents of the age. They otherwise follow no uniform pattern or patterns. They reveal no cogent program of topics. They express no single viewpoint. The shared materials prove miscellaneous by every objective criterion of form and order we can devise. In no way can we demonstrate that two or more documents drew upon a single, prior composition. All we know is that two or more documents drew upon miscellaneous materials, circulating hither and yon, coming we know not whence, deriving from whatever circles or schools made up materials of the type at hand. That is to say, about the shared materials, miscellanies, we know nothing of consequence. There was no autonomous source, now represented only by the bits and pieces, uniform and cogent among themselves, scattered among the four documents with which we have dealt. Excluding the five parashiyyot shared by Leviticus Rabbah with Pesiqta deR. Kahana, the shared sources, whether long or short, prove random. Of them we cannot reconstruct a single cogent source, "Q." We may state flatly that the evidence at hand in no way suggests the existence of a rabbinic "Q." So supposedly-synoptic sources, represented by those at hand, cannot ever be read synoptically; only odds and ends compare and intersect. And then there is little basis for comparison, because they are nearly identical. All we get out of the comparison of versions of a shared item is alternative wordings of a single text, raw materials not for the history of ideas (or of religious groups) but only for the apparatus of a critical text.

If, then, we may return to the point at which we began, we may simply declare that shared sources do not derive from a single source, "Q." The shared materials, to be sure, ordinarily ignore the literary patterns of Leviticus Rabbah. But what is common on two or more documents turns out to be itself diverse and to exhibit random formal and formulary traits. On that basis we look in vain for "Q." How so? We search hopelessly for some large-scale and ubiquitous body of floating materials, fully formed, exhibiting characteristic literary traits, and entirely composed, available for use by any authorship for any given purpose. True, we may imagine that such a vast corpus of floating materials did circulate. But, lacking evidence as to its character, contents, viewpoint(s), and purpose(s), we can say nothing about it. Appeal to origin in such a shared an common "tradition" therefore tells us nothing that we did not know without the postulate that such a "tradition" circulated among the various rabbinic authorships. So if such a "Q" was there, we cannot define it or demonstrate what it contained and did not contain, how authors used it or did not use it, why people would have reshaped one of its sayings for one set of purposes rather than for some other set of purposes. We cannot pursue any of those questions that make the postulate of "Q" suggestive and fructifying in other fields of inquiry into anonymous and collective authorships, parallel to the authorships at hand. So apart from the possibility of "Q," there is nothing at stake in the hypothesis of a floating "tradition."

What must follow? It is that if we cannot show there was such a source common to two or more documents but can demonstrate only that random sayings circulated hither and yon, we also cannot invoke the perspective of analysis that demands systematic and synoptic reading of what otherwise constitute discrete documents. That is to say, we cannot link document to document as a common synoptic exercise and present the result as a shared position ("Judaism"). We also cannot show how the authors of document X have used shared materials in a way distinctive from the way in which the authors of document Y have used those same shared materials. Why not? There is no fixed point, no shared source that permits comparison. And without a common point for comparison, information on what is like, and what is unlike, document X in document Y, lacks context, perspective, therefore also meaning. So, as I said, I see nothing at stake in the postulate of a shared source, short of the discovery of "Q," and a rabbinic source behind two or more documents. We cannot show and so do not know that there was a "Q," that is, a single harmonious rabbinic "tradition."

xiv. Leviticus Rabbah in Particular

This discussion has carried us far from our specific purpose, which is to ask whether or not Leviticus Rabbah exhibits the traits of integrity, therefore autonomy. Lest we lose touch with the purpose for the assembly of the facts at hand, we have now carefully to restate our purpose.

Let us begin with the restatement of the facts at hand.

1. Leviticus Rabbah conforms to distinctive literary patterns. There are three readily defined classifications to which we may assign approximately 70% of the units of discourse of which the document is composed. In the exposition of ideas of a complete <u>parashah</u>, moreover, discourse conform to a fixed order, I, II, III. The other 30% of the document fall into the category of miscellany.

2. Leviticus Rabbah includes passages shared with other documents of its day. These are of two types, short and long. They turn out to be miscellaneous by all available criteria.

What we wish to ask, having described the simple literary traits of the document and investigated the passages of the document shared with other compositions or compilations, has to do only with Leviticus Rabbah. It is whether and to what extent Leviticus Rabbah exhibits integrity and so constitutes an autonomous and distinctive composition. It is, further, whether and to what extent Leviticus Rabbah constitutes a scrapbook, a collection of materials in no way formed into a single, formally disciplined, sustained and harmonious statement: a text.

The ultimate purpose of asking whether Leviticus Rabbah constitutes an autonomous composition or a scrapbook, whether it exhibits the trait of integrity or the trait of miscellany, is to deal in a concrete documentary context with the claim framed by Smith and others. They hold that rabbinic documents are "always" to be studied synoptically and not (as I claim) both in isolation from one another as well as in relationship to one another. So the heart of the matters is represented by the conception of "Q."

Let me review the arguments and facts adduced here as these relate to the issue of "Q," that is, the claim that rabbinic documents (here represented by Leviticus Rabbah) constitute components of an essentially synoptic system (or, in Judaic theological language, of a "tradition" or "one whole Torah"). What we have done is to ask whether on the basis of common materials we discover that "parallel of parallelism" to which Smith points. That is to say, do we really find the relationships which exist between the books of one canon (or some of those books) parallel to the relationships which exist between the books of the other canon? Can a theory begun in the study of the Gospels -- e.g., "studying synoptic texts synoptically" -- immediately apply to the study of two or more documents of the rabbinic canon of late antiquity? Specifically, do documents of the latter canon go over the same materials, and do the materials shared among the documents point toward a common source, upon which the several compositions at hand have drawn? Are the documents "very close" to one another? If these points prove to characterize two or more documents of the rabbinic cannon, then Smith's fundamental observation will prove sound and define further research.

The three questions at hand required that we focus, to begin with, on one document, only then to work our way to examine others with which it intersects. Why so?

1. We established the extent to which a given document stands on its own, and the extent to which it shares materials -- phrases, sentences, paragraphs, whole units of discourse -- with some other. For the proportion, not only the character, of the materials shared among the Gospels defines the relationships among them, as Smith alleges at the very outset ("all the four are very close to each other"). We found that the proportion of shared materials in a given composition proved negligible. So, to begin with, any allegation of parallel relationships proves false on a merely quantitative basis.

2. A single document, moreover, supplied a logical place from which to go off in search of parallels in other and related documents. Why so? The canon of Judaism in late

antiquity is sizable. Compiling lists of parallels among a vast variety of compositions thus far has yielded collections merely of variant readings [for example, Melamed, 1943, 1967, 1973]. So it seemed best to work from a well-defined point of reference and collect parallels relevant to that one point. So we required a base-document that intersects in substantial ways with more than a single composition.

3. The one document I chose for an appropriate probe of the results to be expected from studying synoptic texts synoptically is Leviticus Rabbah. The reason is simple. That document intersects with two others of the period in which it came to closure, Genesis Rabbah and the Yerushalmi (the Talmud of the Land of Israel). Conventional dates for the Yerushalmi, Genesis Rabbah, and Leviticus Rabbah, tend to come together around the end of the fourth century and the beginning of the fifth. These documents in time stand far closer to one another than do those in Smith's catalogue of "Tannaitic literature." They share materials of various kinds, all deriving from the same geographical area and (people generally suppose) the same schools. Accordingly, if we are going to uncover relationships to begin with relevant to comparison with the relationships among the Gospels, we do well to begin with that family of writings circumscribed by the same place and time represented by the three documents at hand.

Leviticus Rabbah intersects, moreover, with yet another, somewhat later document, Pesiqta deR. Kahana. Here we found the condition met that the documents be "very close," since Pesiqta deR. Kahana and Leviticus Rabbah share nearly verbatim no fewer than five complete and really protracted compositions or chapters. Accordingly, we were able to frame questions about the character of the source of shared materials ("Q") not at random and on a small scale but in a systematic way and upon a large scale. And, it goes without saying, that curious claim that "synoptic texts must always be studied synoptically" has now come up to the light of day, for we can see precisely what it means to do exactly that. So we may now ask whether the results are such as to require "always" doing so.

4. The answer is that the intersecting materials among the documents (excluding Pesiqta deR. Kahana) took up too slight a portion of Leviticus Rabbah to sustain the allegation that the only way to study the allegedly-synoptic documents, Genesis Rabbah and Leviticus Rabbah, or the Yerushalmi and Leviticus Rabbah, was synoptically. To state the simple truth, if we were to study those documents "always," but also only, synoptically, we should end up ignoring most of the materials in those documents. Why so? Because much that is shared proves episodic and random. Little that is shared plays a significant role in those components of a large-scale composition in Leviticus Rabbah.

So far as the data we have examined indicate, Smith simply is wrong to allege there is any sort of "parallel of parallelism." The opposite is the case. Cohen's contribution, of course, turns out a still more extreme error and makes me wonder whether I have accurately understood what he wishes to claim. In any event, to conclude, for Genesis Rabbah, Leviticus Rabbah, and the Yerushalmi, there is no "Q." As to the shared compositions of Leviticus Rabbah and Pesiqta deR. Kahana, these prove integral to

Leviticus Rabbah (whatever role they play in the other composition). The shared materials only reenforce the claim that the document is autonomous and exhibits a profound integrity of both literary pattern and redactional policy.

REFERENCES

Braude and Kapstein	W.G. Braude and I.J. Kapstein, Pesikta de Rab Kahana (Philadelphia, 1975: Jewish Publication Society of America), pp. xlix-l.
Cohen	Shaye J.D. Cohen, "Jacob Neusner, Mishnah, and Counter-Rabbinics," Conservative Judaism 1983, 37:48-63.
Herr	Moshe David Herr, "Tosefta," Encyclopaedia Judaica (Jerusalem, 1971) 15:1283-5.
Melammed, 1943	E.Z. Melammed, Halachic Midrashim of the Tannain in the Talmud Babli (Jerusalem, 1943). In Hebrew.
Melammed, 1967	E.Z. Melamed [sic], The Relationship between the Halakhic Midrashism [sic] and the Mishna and Tosefta. I. The Use of Mishna and Tosefta in the Halakhic Midrashim. II. Halakhic Midrashim in the Mishna and Tosefta (Jerusalem, 1967). In Hebrew.
Melammed, 1973	E.Z. Melammed, An Introduction to Talmudic Literature (Jerusalem, 1973). In Hebrew.
Neusner, 1974	Jacob Neusner, The Tosefta. Translated from the Hebrew. Sixth Division. Tohorot. The Order of Purities (N.Y., 1974: Ktav), pp. ix-x.
Smith	Morton Smith, Tannaitic Parallels to the Gospels. Philadelphia, 1951: Society of Biblical Literature Journal of Biblical Literature Monograph Series, Volume VI.

PART FOUR

THE BAVLI AS THE ONE WHOLE TORAH

XI
THE BAVLI IN PARTICULAR
DEFINING A DOCUMENT IN THE CANON OF JUDAISM

While within the framework of the theology of Judaism, all documents of the canon contribute equally and without differentiation to that "one whole Torah of Moses, our rabbi," that is called Judaism, the facts of the matter are otherwise. How so? Each composition within the canon is to be viewed on its own terms and not only as an essentially uniform component of an undifferentiated canon. Whether we speak of the Mishnah, ca. A.D. 200, or the Tosefta, ca. A.D. 300, or the Yerushalmi (Talmud of the Land of Israel, Palestinian Talmud), ca. A.D. 400, or Genesis Rabbah or Leviticus Rabbah, of about the same period, or the Bavli (Talmud of Babylonia), ca. A.D. 600, the issue remains constant. We have to define a given document on its own terms, not only asking where and how that document intersects with and so forms part of that encompassing "one whole Torah of Moses, our rabbi."

The route of differentiation and hence definition begins with comparison, for the documents do constitute a set of interrelated statements. That is to say, from the Mishnah through the Bavli, the several documents make use of some materials in common, refer to the same antecedent writings (for the Talmuds, the Mishnah, for the midrash-compilations, Scripture), and in other ways share that common program of thought that validates the theological view of the whole as one. It must follow that when we wish to define a given document, part of the definition derives from the comparison of one composition to others of its species within the genus of the canon as a whole. Seeing the Bavli as autonomous and defining it in its own terms, as we must, paradoxically requires that we compare the Bavli to its antecedent, the Yerushalmi, and define the Bavli through the similarities and differences exhibited by the Bavli and the Yerushalmi when the two documents, both serving to provide an exegesis of the same Mishnah, are brought into juxtaposition. In the present exercise I want to show what makes the Bavli different from the Yerushalmi. The answer summarizes some results of a sustained inquiry, <u>Judaism in Conclusion: The Evidence of the Bavli</u> (Chicago, 1986: University of Chicago Press). The point of differentiation derives from the relationship of the two documents to the Old Testament, so what we have is a somewhat old chapter in the history of Old Testament exegesis in the unfolding of formative Judaism.

i. The Talmuds and the Written Torah

Sizable units of discourse in both Talmuds take up the exegesis of verses of Scripture. The purpose in composing such Scripture-units proves diverse. Some such compositions take shape around problems of law, either to link rules of the Mishnah to proof-texts of the Pentateuch or to explore in a context autonomous of the Mishnah the legal implications of legal passages of Scripture. These units of discourse in general link up to sequential passages of the Mishnah, one way or the other, and prove common in both Talmuds. But there are other Scripture-units, exhibiting no link to the Mishnah or to problems of legal theory. They prove propositions through citing statements of Scripture. They elaborate values or ideals by reference to Scriptural cases. They focus upon the meaning of a verse or a sequence of verses of Scripture. While the intent of the authors of units of discourse such as these cannot be exhaustively described, we can point to at least one reason they did their work. It is clear that, in some cases, their purpose was systematically to expound, in terms of a quite separate set of issues from those explicit in the passage at hand, the sense of a verse or sequence of verses in Scripture. In other such constructions we find a manifest interest in a virtue or a vice, with verses of Scripture supplying ample proof-texts or examples to prove that said virtue brings reward, or vice, punishment. In further instances we have a single verse subjected to close reading and exposition. In still others, there are sequential groups of verses.

The main point is simply that Scripture, as much as the Mishnah, served some authors of sizable units of discourse and editors of conglomerates of units of discourse as the frame, the structure, around which to organize ideas. What we now ask is only how much of the work of those authors of what we may call Scripture-units of discourse found its way into the one Talmud as against the other. Then we inquire about what sort of work each set of compositors -- those for the Yerushalmi, those for the Bavli -- appears to have preferred. The question at hand is whether or not, on the basis of proportions of Scripture-units of discourse in each of the two Talmuds, we are able to differentiate one Talmud from the other. As we shall now see, the evidence is quite decisive.

ii. Scripture in the Talmuds

Our first point of differentiation between Yerushalmi and Bavli asks whether one Talmud devotes a larger proportion of its interest to Scripture-units of discourse than does the other. That matter proves fundamental. While we do not know what choices the framers of the Talmuds faced, the sorts of material they rejected not now being available, we do have in our hands precisely what has survived of what they preferred. The Talmuds tell us. So we ask to begin with their policies of selection and composition: where and how units of discourse devoted to systematic exposition of a verse or verses of Scripture for other than legal-exegetical purposes made their appearance. In surveying three important and diverse tractates which form our sample for both Talmuds -- Sotah, Sukkah, and Sanhedrin -- we simply review the particular items devoted to Scripture and indicate their proportion of the larger composite in which they appear.

Let me state the question simply. How many units of discourse serving a given Mishnah-paragraph focus upon not the Mishnah but Scripture, and what proportion of the total units of discourse serving said paragraph is devoted to Scripture?

The result is consistent and one-sided. While the Yerushalmi contains a negligible proportion of Scripture-units of discourse, 5.9% in Sotah, 0.7% in Sukkah, and 6.5% in Sanhedrin, the Yerushalmi's successors in the Bavli made use of sizable numbers and vastly larger proportions of the same sort of units. In proportion to the whole, these are 32.1% in Sotah, 2.9% in Sukkah, and 35.3% in Sanhedrin, five times the percentage for Sotah, four times for Sukkah, and five times for Sanhedrin. We need not suppose that the work of composing Scripture-units of discourse took place mainly in Babylonia. Nor can we imagine that the work got underway only after the Yerushalmi had come to closure. These hypotheses are not relevant here. The sole evidence at hand hardly permits us to entertain such propositions. All we know, after all, is what the framers on the two Talmuds have given us, not what they decided not to include. Thus far, therefore, all we have done is differentiate the two documents by showing that the compositors of the Bavli have made far more extensive use of Scripture-units of discourse than did those of the Yerushalmi. To point toward the meaning of the facts at hand, we have now to undertake a further exercise of differentiation.

iii. Scripture and the Talmuds

At issue is whether or not a single taxonomy serves both Talmuds. If it does, then the difference in proportion proved just now bears one set of meanings. If it does not, then that same difference requires a different set of interpretations. So the heart of matters lies in the sort of taxonomic structure I am able to propose for sorting out the types of Scripture-units of discourse.

Unlike the Yerushalmi, the Bavli makes proportionate use of Scripture-units of discourse for a purpose other than Mishnah-exegesis, on the one side, or other than the amplification of points established in the context of legal or theological exposition, on the other. Scripture-units of this sort occur out of context; one might say it is "for their own sake." The Bavli's framers therefore were prepared to organize their larger composition around more than the single focus of a context of discourse dictated by the Mishnah or by points of law or theology deemed pertinent to the Mishnah. For Sotah and Sukkah the latter sort of redactional utilization presents lower proportions -- 21% vs. 6%, 1.6% vs. 1.25%. For Sanhedrin, to be sure, the comparison yields nearly equal proportions -- 15% vs. 17.6%. The main point, however, is not what the Bavli's compositors found more useful than the Yerushalmi's. Let me state the contrast with emphasis: <u>It is that they were prepared to build large-scale discourse around a framework deriving from other than that context that commenced with sustained Mishnah-exegesis</u>.

That is to say, the redactors of large-scale and protracted units of discourse in the Yerushalmi rarely organized their ideas around exegetical materials serving the Old Testament. They mainly relied upon the sequence of paragraphs of the Mishnah as the framework and structure for laying out units of discourse or completed thoughts. The redactors of the Bavli, by contrast, turned to the Old Testament as much as to the Mishnah and drew upon sequences of verses as much as upon a succession of Mishnah-sentences or paragraphs. So the Bavli's framers found Scripture (the Written Torah) as much as the Mishnah (the Oral Torah) serviceable as a foundation and organization for laying out protracted sequences of completed thoughts.

So for the Bavli's authors, two distinct principles guided selection and large-scale redactional arrangement of Scripture-units of discourse. One, available from the Yerushalmi, instructed them to use Scripture-units of discourse as these served the larger and established purposes of Mishnah-exegesis and amplification. The other, not generated by the needs of Mishnah-exegesis and amplification, told them to allow Scripture-units of discourse, especially rather substantial ones, to find a place within their composition out of all relationship with the frame of reference and context of discourse defined by the available program of inquiry. In this simple, redactional framework, therefore, we may say that, while the Yerushalmi builds its lines of structure around paragraphs of the Mishnah alone, the Bavli utilizes a second redactional focus. It is redactional construction upon passages of Scripture, which, linked one way or another, serve as suitably as do passages of the Mishnah. So the Yerushalmi rests upon a simple, and the Bavli upon a complex, principle of what both defines redactional logic and also dictates inner cogency between units of discourse. The one speaks to the Mishnah, the other to the Mishnah and also Scripture.

iv. Taxonomy of Types of Scripture-Units of Discourse

If we ignore the compositors' purposes in inserting Scripture-units of discourse and deal only with the diverse principles of conglomeration, may we resort to a single taxonomy for both Talmuds? That is to say, do all, or nearly all, units of discourse concerning Scripture in both Talmuds fall into the same framework? Or do we find that one Talmud contains greater diversity of types of Scripture-units of discourse than the other? These questions define the next exercise.

Let me spell out what I mean by principles of conglomeration, for this second exercise focuses on a fresh criterion of differentiation. What I now ask is how, viewed <u>on its own</u> -- out of redactional context -- as a cogent unit of discourse, a Scripture-unit of discourse hangs together. What makes the parts of such a single composite form a whole?

The simplest answer to this question, based both on formal and on rhetorical traits, derives from the point of origin of the verses cited in a given construction, on the one hand. Then we distinguish Scripture-units of discourse that are organized around a sequence of verses, for instance, half a chapter of Scripture. Some of these sequences of verses will follow the exact order of verses, much as the Talmuds will take up a paragraph of the Mishnah and explain each of its sentences, one by one. Other sequences of verses will take shape around a single biblical figure, e.g., Samson or Ahab or Korah (as in Sanhedrin).

A second principle of conglomeration derives from a theological or moral value or principle, for example, the importance of study of Torah, the danger of strong drink, and the like. Then many verses, from diverse passages of Scripture, will come forth to give testimony. The principle of organization derives from the ideal or value under discussion (normally for purposes of exposition and advocacy). The logic of that principle or value will dictate which verses will make an appearance.

The framer of the former type of Scripture-unit of discourse will have resorted to Scripture, as much as his colleague at the next table will have resorted to the Mishnah, when he wanted to string together various singleton-sayings into a cogent unit of discourse. The author of the latter type of Scripture-unit of discourse, by contrast, will have followed a different theory of utilization of Scripture in the composition of a cogent and sizable statement.

The Yerushalmi contains a negligible proportion of Scripture-units of discourse composed around sequences of verses. The Yerushalmi's compositors clearly neglected units of discourse that find cogency in Scripture, not in the Mishnah, on the one side, or in some well-established value or virtue, on the other. The Bavli's framers by contrast made use of units of discourse of this type, in which Scripture, as much as the Mishnah, defines a principle of redactional cogency and rhetorical coherence. The Bavli finds itself entirely at home in the utilization of such units of discourse, which, we recognize, can as readily have served the purposes of the redactors of exegeses of Scripture ("midrashim"), such as Genesis Rabbah or Lamentations Rabbah. We find no examples in our sample of the Yerushalmi's inclusion of units of discourse built up around the exposition of a single verse of Scripture.

Just as the Yerushalmi's redactors composed large-scale discourse on a principle of law, rather than on a Mishnah-paragraph in particular, so they put together equivalently sizable units of discourse in which a single theme, topic, value or ideal formed the focus, then to be amplified, illustrated, or validated by scriptural verses. The framers of the Yerushalmi in the tractates surveyed however did not resort to Scripture in search of principles of cogency and coherence of discourse. Those of the Bavli did. And that has made all the difference.

v. Alike and Not Alike

What the Bavli's framers accomplished in organizing and composing units of discourse was to form a synthesis of two of the available components of the canon, the Mishnah and Scripture. First, they made far more ample use than did the authors of the Yerushalmi of units of discourse focused upon Scripture, rather than upon the Mishnah. Second, they drew upon the redactional structure supplied by Scripture, as much as upon that provided by the Mishnah, when they went about organizing their units of discourse into large-scale compositions. That is why the Bavli's more sizable stretches of exposition will be made up of two quite distinct types of materials, first, those focused upon the Mishnah-paragraph, second, others centered upon verses of Scripture. While the Yerushalmi's authors built their scripture-units of discourse around one or the other of those two sources of cogency, the Bavli's had yet a third. In selecting as a redactional principle the order of the Mishnah, the framers of the Bavli followed the example of the authors of the Yerushalmi. In asking Scripture to dictate the sequence of discourse, they followed the example of the authors of Genesis Rabbah and Leviticus Rabbah, not to mention Sifra, the two Sifres, and Lamentations Rabbah.

Viewed from a literary angle, as compositors and redactors of large-scale compositions, the authors of the Bavli therefore constructed a vast synthesis of the two principles of composition and redaction employed prior to their time in available and distinct types of literature. These were Mishnah-exegesis in the (already-completed) Yerushalmi and Scripture-exegesis in the (now-available) collections of scriptural-exegeses ("midrashim"). The Bavli differs from the Yerushalmi in the clear and self-evident program of its compositors and redactors. Specifically, these compositors and redactors synthesized the two formerly-distinct principles of, first, redaction of completed units of discourse concerning the Mishnah, and, second, composition or conglomeration of cogent units of discourse using Scripture. Their Talmud is not like the one that had come before specifically because it appealed to two components of the available tripartite canon -- Scripture, Mishnah, Sage -- not only for law and theology, but also for the logic and rhetoric of cogent discourse. So, to state the result in one sentence, Scripture as much as the Mishnah told the Bavli's, but not the Yerushalmi's, authors and compositors how to organize completed thoughts, on the one side, and how to hold together the components of completed thoughts and make of them a cogent statement of size and consequence, on the other. The distinction between the Bavli and the Yerushalmi lies not in the contents of Scripture-exegesis, any more than it lies in the provenance of sage-units of discourse.

The upshot demands emphasis: <u>The distinction lies solely in the redactional character of the Bavli. The difference between the Bavli and the Yerushalmi is the Bavli's far more ample use of Scripture not only for proof, nor even only for truth, but solely the Bavli's resort to Scripture for the redaction and organization of large-scale discourse.</u> In the Bavli the Scripture serves alongside the Mishnah, and in volume not enormously less than it (60% to 40% in our sample). Scripture and the Mishnah in the Bavli together define structure and impart proportion and organization. In the Yerushalmi, by contrast, Scripture forms an important component of the canon. But it does not dictate lines of order and main-beams of structure. So that is the distinction, the only distinction I am able to find fundamental and generative, between the Bavli and the Yerushalmi. What difference did it make?

vi. "<u>And That Has Made All the Difference</u>"

On the basis of the simple fact before us, I may now propose an answer to the simple question of why the Bavli, and not the Yerushalmi, enjoyed the definitive status that it did. I dismiss at the outset the notion that the Bavli presents doctrines or conceptions essentially different from those in the Yerushalmi. While, in some minor detail, differences do exist, overall, they do not. When, as in my <u>Torah: From Scroll to Symbol</u> and <u>Messiah in Context</u> (Philadelphia, 1983, 1984), we examine two central and generative symbols -- Torah, messiah -- we cannot materially distinguish the conceptions on the messiah of the Bavli from those of the Yerushalmi. Nor can we claim that in the matter of the symbol of the Torah the Bavli vastly improves upon what the Yerushalmi lays down. The topical programs of the two Talmuds exhibit a rough but ample correspondence. The Bavli's systematic addition of details to tales and sayings received from the earlier tradents and redactors constitutes marginal improvements at best.

What distinguishes the one document from the other is one thing, which has made all the difference: the Bavli's complete union, in its redactional substrate, of the Mishnah and Scripture. In presenting what was received as the summa of Judaism, the Bavli joined the two streams that, like the Missouri and the Mississippi at St. Louis, had until its time flowed separate and distinct within the same banks. The one stream, coursing from the source of the Mishnah, and the other stream, emanating from the source of Scripture, had mingled only in eddies, at the edges. But the banks of the mighty river had been set from Sinai, and (in the mythic dimension) the two streams had been meant to flow together as one river. In the Yerushalmi Scripture found a place along the sides. The Mishnah formed the main stream. In the collections of scriptural exegesis ("midrashim"), Scripture had flowed all by itself down the center, wholly apart from the Mishnah. In the Bavli, for the first time, the waters not only flowed together but mingled in the middle and in the depths, in common and sustained discourse. So the Bavli for the first time from Sinai (to speak within the Torah-myth) joined together in a whole and complete way, in both literary form and doctrinal substance, the one whole Torah of Moses, our rabbi.

That is why the Bavli became the Torah par excellence, the Torah through which Israel would read both Torahs, Scripture and Mishnah, the Torah all together, the Torah all at once, as God at Sinai had revealed it to "Moses, our rabbi." It was because the Bavli's writers accomplished the nearly-perfect union of Scripture and Mishnah in a single document that the Bavli became Israel's fullest Torah. That is why, when the people of the Torah, Israel, the Jewish people, for the next fifteen hundred years, wished to approach the Mishnah, it was through the reading of the Bavli. It is why when that same people wished to address Scripture, it was through the reading of the Bavli. All the other components of the canon, while authentic and authoritative too, stood in line, from second place backward, behind the primary reading of the Bavli. It is no accident that authentic avatars of the classical literature of Judaism even today learn Scripture through the Bavli's citations of verses of Scripture, just as much as, commonly, they learn the Mishnah and assuredly interpret it exactly as the Bavli presents it.

vii. The Bavli in Context: The Crisis Precipitated by the Mishnah, the Resolution Accomplished by the Bavli

To place these facts into historical context, we recall that the advent of the Mishnah in ca. 200 A.D. demanded that people explain the status and authority of the new document. The lines of structure emanating from the Mishnah led to the formation of a vast and unprecedented literature of Judaism. The explosive force of the return to Zion, in the time of Ezra, had produced the formation of the Torah-book and much else. The extraordinary impact of the person and message of Jesus (among other things) had led to the creation of an unprecedented kind of writing in yet another sector of Israel's life. So too would be the case with the Mishnah, Israel's response to the disaster wrought by Bar Kokhba's calamity.

The reason the Mishnah, a philosophical and arcane essay, rich in theoretical, philosophical initiatives (in the setting of the Second Sophistic), which also serves as a law code, presented a stunning challenge to its age and heirs, is simple. It was because of the Mishnah's sponsorship in Israel's politics. To begin with, the Mishnah enjoyed the sponsorship of the autonomous ruler of the Jewish nation in the Land of Israel, namely, Judah the Patriarch. The result was that the Mishnah served for purposes other than those of simple learning and speculative thought. Whatever had been intended for it, at its very beginnings the Mishnah was turned into an authoritative law code, the constitution, along with Scripture, of Israel in its Land. Accordingly, when completed, the Mishnah emerged from the schoolhouse and forthwith made its move into the politics, courts, and bureaus of the Jewish government of the Land of Israel. Men (never women, until our own day) who mastered the Mishnah thereby qualified themselves as judges and administrators in the government of Judah the Patriarch, as well as in the government of the Jewish community of Babylonia. As we know, over the next three hundred years, the Mishnah served as the foundation for the Talmuds' formation of the system of law and theology we now know as Judaism. Exegesis of the Mishnah in the Judaic framework furthermore defined the taxonomy for hermeneutics of the Old Testament as well.

The vast collection constituted by the Mishnah therefore demanded explanation. What is this book? How does it relate to the (written) Torah revealed to Moses at Mount Sinai? Under whose auspices, and by what authority, does the law of the Mishnah govern the life of Israel? These questions, we realize, bear both political and theological implications. But, to begin with, the answers emerged out of an enterprise of exegesis of biblical literature. The reception of the Mishnah followed several distinct lines, each of them symbolized by a particular sort of book. Each book, in turn, offered its theory of the origin, character, and authority of the Mishnah. For the next three centuries these theories would occupy the attention of the best minds of Israel, the authorities of the two Talmuds and the numerous other works of the age of the seed-time of Judaism.

One line from the Mishnah stretched through the Tosefta, a supplement to the Mishnah, and the two Talmuds, one formed in the Land of Israel, the other in Babylonia, both serving as exegesis and amplification of the Mishnah.

The second line stretched from the Mishnah to compilations of biblical exegesis of three different sorts. First, there were exegetical collections framed partly in relationship to the Mishnah and the Tosefta, in particular Sifra, on Leviticus, Sifre, on Numbers, and Sifre, on Deuteronomy. Second, exegetical collections were organized mainly in relationship to Scripture, with special reference to Genesis Rabbah and Leviticus Rabbah. Third, exegetical collections focused on constructing abstract discourse out of diverse verses of Scripture but on a single theme or problem, represented by Pesiqta de Rab Kahana and Lamentations Rabbati.

This simple catalogue of the types, range, and volume of creative writing over the three or four hundred years from the closure of the Mishnah indicates an obvious fact. The Mishnah stands at the beginning of a new and stunningly original epoch in the formation of Judaism. Like such generative crises as the return to Zion for the nation as a whole and the advent of Jesus for his family and followers, the Mishnah ignited in Israel a great burst of energy. The extraordinary power of the Mishnah, moreover, is seen in its very lonely position in Israelite holy literature of its time and afterward. The subsequent normative literature, for centuries to come, would refer back to the Mishnah or stands in some clearcut hermeneutical relationship to it. But for its part, the Mishnah referred to nothing prior to itself -- except (and then, mostly implicitly and by indirection) to Scripture. So from the Mishnah back to the revelation of God to Moses at Sinai -- in the view of the Mishnah -- lies a vast desert. But from the Mishnah forward stretches a fertile plain.

The crisis precipitated by the Mishnah therefore stimulated wide ranging speculation, inventive experiments of a literary and (in the nature of things) therefore also political, theological, and religious character. As I showed in <u>Midrash in Context</u> (Philadelphia, 1983), for example, the Yerushalmi's work of defining and explaining the Mishnah in relationship to the (written) Torah, interpreting the meaning of the Mishnah, expanding upon and applying its laws, ultimately precipitated the making, also, of compilations of exegeses of Scripture. The taxa serving the Yerushalmi on the Mishnah and Genesis Rabbah on Genesis prove identical. The formation of the Talmuds and scriptural-exegetical collections thus made necessary -- indeed, urgent -- extraordinary and original reflection on the definition of the Torah, through inquiry into the nature of canon and scriptural authority, the range and possibilities of revelation. The results of that work all together would define Judaism from that time to this. So crisis presented opportunity. And Israel's sages took full advantage of the occasion.

What then was this crisis? Let me tell the tale by returning to the Mishnah itself. I have first of all to explain why and how the Mishnah presented such an unprecedented problem to the patriarch's sages who received the Mishnah. It is easy to do so in a way accessible to people to whom all of these events and writings have been, up to now, entirely unknown or, if known, alien and incomprehensible. To phrase the theological question so that anyone in the West may grasp it, I need simply point out one fact. So far as Judaism was concerned, revelation had been contained in the Old Testament, those Hebrew Scriptures later on called the written Torah. True, God may have spoken in diverse ways. The last of the biblical books had been completed -- so far as Jews then knew -- many centuries before. How then could a new book now claim standing as holy and revealed by God? What validated the authority of the people who knew and applied that holy book to Israel's life? These questions would define the critical issue of formative Judaism, from 200 to 600. The successful resolution of the problem in the Bavli defines Judaism today. Accordingly, the crisis precipitated by the Mishnah came about because of the urgent requirement of explaining, first, just what the Mishnah was in relationship to the Torah of Moses; second, why the sages who claimed to interpret and apply the law of the Mishnah to the life of Israel had the authority to do so; and, third, how Israel, in adhering to the rules of the Mishnah, kept the will of God and lived the holy life God wanted them to live.

But why should the Mishnah in particular have presented these critical problems of a social and theological order? After all, it was hardly the first piece of new writing to confront Israel from the closure of Scripture to the end of the second century. Other books had found a capacious place in the canon of the groups of Israelites that received them and deemed them holy. The canon of some groups, after all, had made room for those writings of apocryphal and pseudepigraphic provenance so framed as to be deemed holy. The Essene library at Qumran encompassed a diverse group of writings, surely received as authoritative and holy, that other Jews did not know within their canon. So, as is clear, we have to stand back and ask why, to the sages who received and realized the Mishnah, that book should have presented special, particularly stimulating, problems. Why should the issue of the relationship of the Mishnah to Scripture have proved so pressing in the third, fourth, fifth, and sixth centuries' circles of Talmudic rabbis? After all, we have no evidence that the relationship to the canon of Scripture of the Manual of Discipline, the Hymns, the War Scroll, or the Damascus Covenant perplexed the teacher of righteousness and the other holy priests of the Essene community. To the contrary, those documents at Qumran appear side by side with the ones we now know as canonical Scripture. The high probability is that, to the Essenes, the sectarian books were no less holy and authoritative than Leviticus, Deuteronomy, Nahum, Habakkuk, Isaiah, and the other books of the biblical canon they, among all Israelites, revered.

The issue had to be raised because of the peculiar traits of the Mishnah itself. But the dilemma proved acute, not merely chronic, because of the particular purpose the Mishnah was meant to serve and because of the political sponsorship behind the document. As I said above, it was to provide Israel's constitution. It was promulgated by the patriarch -- the ethnic ruler -- of the Jewish nation in the Land of Israel, Judah the Patriarch, who governed with Roman support as the fully recognized Jewish authority in the Holy Land. So the Mishnah was public, not sectarian, nor merely idle speculation of a handful of Galilean rabbinical philosophers, though, in structure and content, that is precisely what it was.

The Mishnah thus emerged as a political document. It demanded assent and conformity to its rules, where they were relevant to the government and court system of the Jewish people in its land. So the Mishnah could not be ignored. It therefore had to be explained in universally accessible terms. Furthermore, the Mishnah demanded explanation not merely in relationship to the established canon of Scripture and apology as the constitution of the Jews' government, the patriarchate of second-century Land of Israel. The nature of Israelite life, lacking all capacity to distinguish as secular any detail of the common culture, made it natural to wonder about a deeper issue. Israel understood its collective life and the fate of each individual under the aspect of God's loving concern, as expressed in the Torah. Accordingly, laws issued to define what people were supposed to do could not stand by themselves. They had to receive the imprimatur of Heaven, that is, they had to be given the status of revelation. Accordingly, to make its way in Israelite life, the Mishnah as a constitution and code demanded for itself a theory of beginnings at (or in relationship to) Sinai, with Moses, from God. As was pointed out above, other new writings for a long time had proved able to win credence as part of the Torah, hence as revealed by God and so enjoying legitimacy. But they did so in ways not taken by the Mishnah's framers. How did the Mishnah differ?

It was in the medium of writing that, in the view of all of Israel until about A.D. 200, God had been understood to reveal the divine word and will. How so? The Torah was a written book. People who in intertestamental times claimed to receive further messages from God usually wrote them down. They had three choices in securing acceptance of their account. All three involved linking the new to the old. In claiming to hand on revelation, they could, first, sign their books with the names of biblical heroes. Second, they would imitate the style of biblical Hebrew. Third, they could present an exegesis of existing written verses, validating their ideas by supplying proof-texts for them. From the closure of the Torah literature in the time of Ezra, ca. 450 B.C. to the time of the Mishnah, nearly seven hundred years later, we do not have a single book alleged to be holy and at the same time standing wholly out of relationship to the Holy Scriptures of ancient Israel. The pseudepigraphic writings fall into the first category, the Essene writings at Qumran into the second and third. We may point also to the Gospels, written down within a generation of Jesus' life, which take as a principal problem demonstrating how Jesus had fulfilled the prophetic promises of the Old Testament and in other ways carried forward and even embodied Israel's Scripture.

Insofar as a piece of Jewish writing did not find a place in relationship to Scripture, its author laid no claim to present a holy book. The contrast between Jubilees and the Testaments of the Patriarchs, with their constant and close harping on biblical matters, and the several books of Maccabees, shows the differences. The former claim to present God's revealed truth, the latter, history. So a book was holy because in style, in authorship, or in (alleged) origin, it continued Scripture, finding a place therefore (at least in the author's mind) within the canon, or because it provided an exposition on Scripture's meaning.

But the Mishnah made no such claim. It entirely ignored the style of biblical Hebrew, speaking in a quite different kind of Hebrew altogether. It is silent on its authorship through sixty-two of the sixty-three tractates (the claims of Abot, a generation later than the rest, pose a special problem). In any event, nowhere does the Mishnah contain the claim that God had inspired the authors of the document. These are not given biblical names and certainly are not alleged to have been biblical saints. Most of the book's named authorities flourished within the same century as its anonymous arrangers and redactors, not in remote antiquity. Above all, the Mishnah contains scarcely a handful of exegeses of Scripture. These, where they occur, commonly play a trivial and tangential role. So here is the problem of the Mishnah: different from Scripture in language and style, indifferent to the claim of authorship by a biblical hero or divine inspiration, stunningly aloof from incessant allusion to verses of Scripture for nearly the whole of its discourse -- yet politically authoritative for Israel.

So the Mishnah was not a statement of theory alone, telling only how things will be in the eschaton. Nor was it a wholly sectarian document, reporting the view of a group without standing or influence in the larger life of Israel. True, in some measure it bears both of these traits of eschatology and sectarian provenance. But the Mishnah was (and is) law for Israel, the Jewish nation. It entered the government and courts of the Jewish people, both in the motherland and also overseas, as the authoritative constitution of the courts of Judaism. The advent of the Mishnah therefore marked a turning in the life of the nation-religion. The document demanded explanation and apology.

The one thing one could not do, as a Jew in third-century Tiberias, Sepphoris, Caesarea, or Beth Shearim, in Galilee, was ignore the thing. True, one might refer solely to ancient Scripture and tradition and live life out within the inherited patterns of the familiar Israelite religion-culture. But as soon as someone dealt with the Jewish government in charge of everyday life -- went to court over the damages done to a crop by a neighbor's ox, for instance -- he came up against a law in addition to the law of Scripture, a document the principles of which governed and settled all matters. So the Mishnah rapidly came to confront the life of Israel. The people who knew the Mishnah, the rabbis or sages, came to dominate that life. And their claim, in accord with the Mishnah, to exercise authority and the right to impose heavenly sanction came to perplex. Now the crisis is fully exposed.

The Mishnah therefore made necessary the formation of the Talmuds, its exegetical companions. Within the processes of exegesis of the Mishnah came the labor of collecting and arranging these exegeses, in correlation with the Mishnah, read line by line and paragraph by paragraph. The sorts of things the sages who framed the Talmuds did to the Mishnah, they then went and did to Scripture. Within the work of exegesis of Scripture was the correlative labor of organizing what had been said verse by verse, following the structure of a book of the Hebrew Bible. The type of discourse and the mode of organizing the literary result of discourse which were suitable for the one document served the other too. The same people did both for the same reasons. So to the Tosefta, Sifra, and the Yerushalmi alike, the paramount issue was Scripture, not merely its authority, but especially, its sheer mass of information. The decisive importance of the advent of the Mishnah in precipitating the vast exegetical enterprise represented by the books at hand emerges from a simple fact. The documents all focus attention on the Mishnah in particular. Two of them, the Tosefta and the Yerushalmi organize everything at hand around the redactional structure supplied by the Mishnah itself.

The importance of the Bavli's distinctive contribution, the mode of redaction, now becomes entirely clear. The Bavli carried forward a long-established enterprise, namely, the forging of links between the Mishnah and Scripture. But the organizers and redactors of the materials compiled in the Bavli did something unprecedented. It was to allow sustained passages of Scripture to serve, as much as sustained and not merely episodic passages of the Mishnah served, as main beams in the composition of structure, proportion, and order. In a single document, in the Bavli, the Mishnah and Scripture functioned not only together but for the first time in much the same way. The original thesis, that the Mishnah depended upon the written Torah, so that all of its statements were to be linked to proof-texts of Scripture, now gave way to its natural and complete fulfillment. Once sets of verses of Scripture could be isolated and made, in all of their continuity, to provide a focus of discourse just as sequences of sentences of the Mishnah did, Scripture would join the Mishnah in a single statement. It was one cut-down and reshaped to conform to the model of the Mishnah. So Scripture now joined the Mishnah in a new union, in mythic language, "one whole Torah," or in my language, the Bavli at the end. In so revising Scripture as to recast it into that same discursive and rhetorical framework that defined how and where the Mishnah would serve, the authors -- framers of larger-scale units of discourse, ultimate redactors alike -- made their unique contribution. Imposing a literary and redactional unity upon documents so remarkably disparate in every respect as the Mishnah and Scripture, the Bavli's authors created something both entirely their own and in no way original to them: Judaism in its final and complete statement, Judaism in conclusion.

So to conclude, it was for good reason that the Bavli has formed the definitive statement of Judaism from the time of its closure to the present day. The excellence of its composition, the mastery and authority of those who everywhere studied it and advocated its law, the sharpness of its exegesis and discussion, the harmonious and proportionate presentation of all details, these virtues of taste and intellect may well have secured for the document its paramount position. The Babylonian Talmud, moreover, incorporated a far broader selection of antecedent materials than any other document that reaches us out of Judaism in late antiquity, far more, for instance, than the Yerushalmi. This vast selection, moreover, was so organized and put together that systematic accounts of numerous important problems of biblical exegesis, law and theology alike emerged. Consequently, the Bavli would serve from its closure as both an encyclopedia of knowledge and a summa of the theology and law of Judaism. But what to begin with gained for the Bavli the priority it would enjoy was the comprehensive character, in form as much as in substance, of its statement, based as it was on both the Scripture's and the Mishnah's redactional framework. No one had done that before. No one had to do it again.

INDEX

Academy
  32, 33, 76, 84
Alexander Jannaeus
  61-63, 66, 67
Alexandra
  61-63, 66
Alexandra Salome
  63, 66
Aqiba
  32, 46, 48, 49, 51, 74, 75, 96, 98, 99, 101, 177
Babylonia
  4, 7, 13, 28, 31, 32, 35-37, 70, 72, 82-84, 165, 207, 209, 214
Babylonian Talmud
  31, 56, 84, 106, 219
Bavli
  4, 8, 52, 53, 102, 103, 167, 169, 170, 192, 193, 205, 207-213, 215, 218, 219
Bible
  37, 87, 113, 114, 191, 218
Christian
  2, 5, 16, 17, 36, 58, 108, 111, 114-16
Christianity
  5, 15, 37, 56, 60, 106, 110, 115, 116
Church Fathers
  16, 115
Deuteronomy
  37, 87, 214, 216
Development of a Legend
  45, 46, 51, 95, 96, 101
Eleazar b. Arakh
  41, 43, 79, 91, 93
Eliezer b. Hyrcanus
  68, 79
Essenes
  62, 63, 66, 114, 216, 217
Exilarch
  32-34, 36, 82-84
Exilarchate
  32, 34, 35, 83
Exodus
  37, 46, 57, 87, 96, 107
Frankel
  55, 56, 105, 106
Gamaliel
  19, 63-65, 67, 68, 73, 80-84, 151, 152
Genesis
  37, 52, 87, 102, 167, 193-96, 199, 200, 203, 207, 211, 214, 215
Genesis Rabbah
  52, 102, 167, 193-96, 199, 200, 203, 207, 211, 214, 215
Gnostic
  15-18
Gospels
  5, 37, 87, 163-65, 202-204, 217

Halperin, David J.
  41-43, 45, 91-93, 95
Herod
  62, 63, 66, 67, 70
Hillel
  19, 61, 64-67, 70-77, 79, 81, 83-85
Hyrcanus
  46, 61, 66-70, 79, 80, 96, 125
Ishmael
  32, 46, 47, 49, 51, 96, 97, 99, 101, 179
Israel
  2, 4-7, 9, 13, 16, 17, 20, 21, 23, 25-31, 35, 40, 47, 48, 57, 63, 83, 90, 97, 98, 107, 135-37, 139, 140, 142, 156, 158, 160, 161, 165, 173, 175, 176, 179, 182, 183, 187-89, 203, 207, 213-218
Israeli
  38, 55, 88, 105, 111, 137
Jeremiah
  2, 155
Jerusalem
  16, 24, 55-57, 60, 62, 64, 68, 73, 82, 85, 86, 105-107, 110, 111, 136, 156, 157, 159, 160, 179, 180, 204
Jerusalem Talmud
  136
Jesus
  37, 70, 87, 113, 114, 213, 214, 217
Jews
  3, 5, 16, 24, 31-38, 51, 57, 63, 64, 70, 82, 88, 101, 107, 215, 216, 218
Josephus
  58, 61-64, 66-70, 108
Judah
  33, 63, 65, 67, 68, 70-72, 75, 76, 79, 81-83, 154, 157, 158, 173, 175, 179, 180, 214, 216
Judah the Patriarch
  33, 68, 76, 79, 214, 216
Judaism
  1-11, 13-16, 20, 21, 24, 26, 28, 30-32, 35, 38, 44, 51-53, 55-57, 59, 60, 63, 72, 79, 84, 88, 94, 101-103, 105-107, 109, 110, 113-17, 135, 137, 161, 166, 167, 169, 195, 201, 202, 204, 207, 213-215, 218, 219
Leviticus
  4, 8, 19, 52, 102, 163, 166-70, 176, 180, 181, 186, 188, 190-96, 199-204, 207, 211, 214, 216
Leviticus Rabbah
  4, 8, 52, 102, 163, 166-70, 186, 190-96, 199-204, 207, 211, 214
Maccabean
  63

Maccabees
    217
Magus
    37
Mani
    37
Manichaean
    32
Mazdean
    32
Mekhilta
    46-48, 51, 53, 84, 96-98, 101, 103, 164
<u>Merkavah</u>
    41-43, 45, 79, 80, 85, 91-93, 95
Mishnah
    4, 7-9, 13-31, 33, 39, 40, 42, 52, 53, 58, 59, 64, 69, 75, 79, 82-84, 89, 90, 92, 102, 103, 108, 109, 119, 135-49, 152-56, 160, 161, 163, 164, 167, 169, 170, 177, 178, 182, 192, 193, 197, 204, 207-219
Mishnaic
    16-20, 23, 28, 42, 43, 92, 93, 137
Moses
    4, 5, 13, 16, 52, 75, 76, 80, 81, 102, 158, 169, 207, 213-216
Nag Hammadi
    17
Nahman
    33, 180
New Testament
    5, 113-16
Nisibis
    32
Numbers
    19, 34, 37, 72, 87, 143, 145, 163, 190, 208, 214
Old Testament
    207, 209, 214, 215, 217
Oral Torah
    7, 8, 75, 209
Palestine
    32, 33, 35, 63, 64, 66, 71, 84
Pesiqta
    193, 194, 199, 200, 203, 214
Pharisaism
    66, 76, 77
Pharisees
    14, 20, 46, 61-70, 71, 73, 75, 76, 80, 96
Philo
    58, 63, 108
Prayer
    177
Pumbedita
    71, 83, 84
Qumran
    69, 216, 217
Rabbi
    4, 5, 13, 27, 32, 34-37, 40, 52, 53, 56, 69, 70, 84, 90, 102, 103, 106, 113, 151, 152, 155, 158, 167, 169, 179, 180, 207, 213

Rabbis
    14, 27, 28, 31-37, 64, 66, 68-70, 75, 77, 82, 84, 86, 115, 135, 151, 153, 161, 171, 174, 175, 216, 218
Rav
    33, 37
Roman
    18, 35, 62, 63, 66, 83, 143, 149, 216
Rome
    17, 20, 62, 66, 67
Sadducees
    61-63, 66, 68, 69, 70, 72
Sasanians
    31, 32, 34
Scripture
    7-9, 13, 16, 18, 19, 22, 31, 48, 52, 56, 74, 85, 98, 102, 106, 113-15, 135, 145, 157, 159, 171-75, 178-80, 185, 188, 193, 194, 199, 207-219
Scripture-exegesis
    8, 212
Second Temple
    14, 58, 108
Shammai
    19, 61, 64-67, 71-74, 76, 77
Sifre
    84, 163, 214
Simeon b. Gamaliel
    19, 64, 65, 67, 68, 73, 81, 151
Simeon the Just
    65, 68
Simon
    47, 97, 163
Smith, Morton
    63, 64, 163, 164, 202-204
Synoptic
    4, 53, 66, 76, 103, 163-65, 167, 193, 199-203
Talmud
    4, 7, 13, 31, 32, 37, 39, 56, 84, 89, 106, 135-40, 142-50, 152-54, 156, 160, 161, 203, 204, 207, 208, 210, 212, 219
Targum
    73, 113, 114
Temple
    14-27, 30, 40, 47, 58, 60, 61, 66-69, 72, 73, 75, 76, 79, 80, 82, 83, 85, 86, 90, 97, 108, 110, 156, 158-60
Torah
    2, 4-8, 10, 13, 15-18, 33, 35-37, 40, 47-49, 52, 75, 76, 80, 81, 84, 85, 90, 97-99, 102, 127, 157, 161, 169, 202, 205, 207, 209, 210, 212-219
Tosefta
    41, 42, 52, 53, 59, 82, 84, 86, 91, 92, 102, 103, 109, 119, 139, 142-45, 148, 149, 152, 153, 163, 164, 167, 170, 204, 207, 214, 218
Usha
    75-77, 81, 85, 125

Weiss, I.H.
  55, 56, 105, 106
<u>Wissenschaft des Judentums</u>
  56, 60, 106, 110
Written Torah
  7, 207, 209, 215, 218
Yavneh
  49, 50, 64, 72-77, 79-81, 83, 85, 99, 100, 125

Yerushalmi
  4, 8, 53, 103, 136, 137, 139, 140, 142, 143, 145, 161, 167, 169, 170, 193-97, 199, 200, 203, 207-213, 215, 218, 219
Yohanan ben Zakkai
  4, 39, 40, 45, 46, 48, 50, 51, 79, 80, 82-86, 89, 90, 95, 96, 98, 100, 101
Zealots
  63

BROWN JUDAIC STUDIES SERIES

Continued from back cover

140040	Israeli Childhood Stories of the Sixties: Yizhar, Aloni, Shahar, Kahana-Carmon	Gideon Telpaz
140041	Formative Judaism II: Religious, Historical, and Literary Studies	Jacob Neusner
140042	Judaism in the American Humanities II: Jewish Learning and the New Humanities	Jacob Neusner
140043	Support for the Poor in the Mishnaic Law of Agriculture: Tractate Peah	Roger Brooks
140044	The Sanctity of the Seventh Year: A Study of Mishnah Tractate Shebiit	Louis E. Newman
140045	Character and Context: Studies in the Fiction of Abramovitsh, Brenner, and Agnon	Jeffrey Fleck
140046	Formative Judaism III: Religious, Historical, and Literary Studies	Jacob Neusner
140047	Pharaoh's Counsellors: Job, Jethro, and Balaam in Rabbinic and Patristic Tradition	Judith Baskin
140048	The Scrolls and Christian Origins: Studies in the Jewish Background of the New Testament	Matthew Black
140049	Approaches to Modern Judaism	Marc Lee Raphael
140050	Mysterious Encounters at Mamre and Jabbok	William T. Miller
140051	The Empire and the Subject Nations: The Middle Eastern Policy of Imperial Rome	Eliezer Paltiel
140052	Sparda by the Bitter Sea: Imperial Interaction in Western Anatolia	Jack Martin Balcer
140053	Hermann Cohen: The Challenge of a Religion of Reason	William Kluback
140054	Approaches to Judaism in Medieval Times I	David R. Blumenthal
140055	In the Margins of the Yerushalmi: Glosses on the English Translation	Jacob Neusner
140056	Approaches to Modern Judaism II	Marc Lee Raphael
140057	Approaches to Judaism in Medieval Times II	David R. Blumenthal
140058	Approaches to Ancient Judaism VI	William Scott Green
140059	The Commerce of the Sacred: Mediation of the Divine Among Jews in the Graeco-Roman Diaspora	Jack N. Lightstone
140060	Major Trends in Formative Judaism I: Society and Symbol in Political Crisis	Jacob Neusner
140061	Major Trends in Formative Judaism II: Texts, Contents, and Contexts	Jacob Neusner
140062	A History of the Jews in Babylonia. I: The Parthian Period	Jacob Neusner
140063	The Talmud of Babylonia: An American Translation. XXXII: Tractate Arakhin	Jacob Neusner
140064	Ancient Judaism: Debates and Disputes	Jacob Neusner
140065	Prayers Alleged to Be Jewish: An Examination of the Constitutiones Apostolorum	David Fiensy
140066	The Legal Methodology of Hai Gaon	Tsvi Groner
140067	From Mishnah to Scripture: The Problem of the Unattributed Saying	Jacob Neusner
140068	Halakhah in a Theological Dimension	David Novak